Knitting Patterns FOR DUMMIES®

by Kristi Porter

BICENTENNIAL
1807
WILEY
2007
BICENTENNIAL

Wiley Publishing, Inc.

**Knitting Patterns For Dummies®**

Published by
**Wiley Publishing, Inc.**
111 River St.
Hoboken, NJ 07030-5774
www.wiley.com

WILEY

# About the Author

**Kristi Porter** is an author, designer, technical editor, and teacher. In addition to authoring *Knitting for Dogs,* her work has been featured in the *Knitgrrl* series, the *Big Girl Knits* series, *No Sheep For You,* and *Knit Wit.* She is a frequent contributor to *Knitty.com* and has been a part of that online magazine since its start in 2002.

Kristi doesn't remember learning to knit as a child, but she captured the basics and an enthusiasm for the craft from her mother, her aunt, and her grandmother. She began her first projects as a designer *and* a knitter, realizing only later that not everyone designed their own patterns. Though her first attempts were boxy and oversized (thank goodness it was the '80s!), once she grasped the importance of gauge, she was on her way to creating wearable designs. She began approaching the craft in a serious way in the late '90s and learned how to read and write patterns in order to share her designs with others.

As a knitting instructor, Kristi teaches students at all levels and ages. Getting feedback about what knitters want to knit, what they enjoy, and what they find difficult has given her a strong sense of what knitters need to know. She delights in helping her students create their own patterns to suit their own needs and senses of fashion.

Kristi makes her home with her husband and two daughters in La Jolla, California.

# Author's Acknowledgments

Creating a book is inevitably the work of many hands, and I am truly grateful to those who helped bring *Knitting Patterns For Dummies* into being. I am struck, in writing these acknowledgments, by how lucky I am to be doing a job that I love and to be surrounded by others who clearly love what they do.

I am grateful to my husband, Leo Bleicher, and my daughters, Zoe and Ella, for their support and encouragement.

Thanks to the helpful folks at Wiley: Lindsay Lefevere for getting the project started, Georgette Beatty for keeping things going, copy editor Jessica Smith, technical editor Mandy Moore, and everyone in Composition Services who helped bring this book to print. Thanks also to the great people at Kreber for the photos of all the projects.

Special thanks to Cameron Taylor-Brown and the kind people at Schaefer Yarns, Cascade Yarns, Rowan, Westminster Fibers, Crystal Palace, Colinette, Unique Kolors, Curious Creek Fibers, and Berroco for providing yarn for these projects, as well as Moving Mud for the closures used in the photographs. Their support of this project is much appreciated.

To my wonderful group of knitters who made undertaking this book conceivable . . . and possible. It's a delight to be able to thank them here, not only for their nimble fingers, but for their feedback on the patterns at all phases: Lacy Province, Donna Warnell, Joan Kass, Wannietta Prescod, Lisa McAllister, Laurie Weiss, Beth Wood, Irene Wetsman, Dawn Talbot, Linda Sellers, and Mary-Kay Tilden.

And to Suzanne Pineau of Knitting in La Jolla, who has been unfailingly generous with her time, her counsel, her yarn, her knowledge, and, most of all, her unflagging enthusiasm.

## Publisher's Acknowledgments

We're proud of this book; please send us your comments through our Dummies online registration form located at www.dummies.com/register/.

Some of the people who helped bring this book to market include the following:

### Acquisitions, Editorial, and Media Development

**Project Editor:** Georgette Beatty

**Acquisitions Editor:** Lindsay Sandman Lefevere

**Copy Editor:** Jessica Smith

**Technical Editor:** Mandy Moore

**Editorial Manager:** Michelle Hacker

**Editorial Assistants:** Erin Calligan Mooney, Joe Niesen, Leeann Harney

**Cover Photo:** Photographs, Kreber/Mark Madden; Art Direction, Kreber/LeeAnn Kolka; Set Stylist, Kreber/Suzanne King

**Cartoons:** Rich Tennant (www.the5thwave.com)

### Composition Services

**Project Coordinator:** Patrick Redmond

**Layout and Graphics:** Karl Brandt, Laura Campbell, Carrie A. Foster, Brooke Graczyk, Denny Hager, Stephanie D. Jumper, Julie Trippetti, Christine Williams

**Special Art:** Photographs, Kreber/Mark Madden; Art Direction, Kreber/LeeAnn Kolka; Set Stylist, Kreber/Suzanne King

**Anniversary Logo Design:** Richard Pacifico

**Proofreaders:** Broccoli Information Management, Susan Moritz, Dwight Ramsey

**Indexer:** Slivoskey Indexing Services

---

### Publishing and Editorial for Consumer Dummies

**Diane Graves Steele,** Vice President and Publisher, Consumer Dummies

**Joyce Pepple,** Acquisitions Director, Consumer Dummies

**Kristin A. Cocks,** Product Development Director, Consumer Dummies

**Michael Spring,** Vice President and Publisher, Travel

**Kelly Regan,** Editorial Director, Travel

### Publishing for Technology Dummies

**Andy Cummings,** Vice President and Publisher, Dummies Technology/General User

### Composition Services

**Gerry Fahey,** Vice President of Production Services

**Debbie Stailey,** Director of Composition Services

# Contents at a Glance

# Table of Contents

## Part IV: Patterns with Circles, Triangles, and More .....................161

# Introduction

*I* have great enthusiasm for knitting and for sharing the craft with others. Because you've picked up this book, it's clear that you share at least some of my enthusiasm. It's hard to put a finger on what it is about knitting that pulls us in. Maybe it's the simple, repetitive motions, and the feel and look of the fibers and fabrics that we create; or maybe it's the chance to share in a long tradition that cuts across boundaries of age and background. It's also pretty cool to be able to point to a garment and say "I made that beautiful, warm thing with some string and a couple of sticks!" Whatever it is that attracts us, knitting is something that you can return to your whole life, making all kinds of projects — and friends — along the way.

I love teaching people how to knit. And, even more, I love teaching them to knit the things that *they* want to knit. Putting this book together challenged me to come up with straight-forward patterns with broad appeal and lots of room for improvisation. I charged myself with two goals: to make designs that would flatter lots of different people, and to think carefully about keeping the shapes simple, relying on basic shapes like rectangles, cylinders, and triangles to create patterns that are knittable and easy to understand.

I hope that you take the patterns in this book and make them your own. Even if you're new to knitting, you can still make design decisions, whether it's the color combination you choose or the yarn and stitch pattern you decide to knit. I firmly believe that every knitter can be her own designer. So, I try to provide opportunities for you to master not only knitting skills but also skills that you need to understand why things are the way they are in a pattern — and how to change them if you want to.

Whether you're a brand new knitter, a seasoned stitcher, or someone returning to the needles after a long absence, this book gives you lots of great patterns to choose from and plenty of help along the way. *Knitting Patterns For Dummies* is filled with classic knits that won't go out of style — and they're all presented in an easy-to-follow format.

## About This Book

*Knitting Patterns For Dummies* is chock full of knitting patterns. In fact, the book contains nearly 40 basic designs. And with the variations offered at the end of many of the patterns, you have lots of projects to choose from! You'll find that the patterns are flexible, which means that you can knit from the same pattern more than once using different yarns or details. So, each time you knit from the pattern you can come up with something new and fresh.

The offerings in this book have a broad range of appeal. You can find things for women and men, babies and kids, and things for your home — there's something for everyone. But more important, perhaps, is the fact that there's something for every *body*. While many knitting patterns top out at rather diminutive sizes, *Knitting Patterns For Dummies* offers patterns in sizes up to 3X.

You may have noticed that this is a big book — a big book with lots of writing. Because of all this writing, it may not be as pretty as some of the other knitting books on the shelf. But *Knitting Patterns For Dummies* has room for lots of patterns, with plenty of space left over for me to explain everything I think you need to know to work your way through them.

For instance, Part II offers a mini stitch dictionary with practice opportunities for trying different stitches; it's helpful to consult if you want to substitute a different stitch pattern, figure out how to work successfully with more than one color, or turn your first cable. In addition, if you come across a technique that's unusual or a skill that you may not have picked up yet, you can find it right there in the pattern in the "New skill" section. You won't have to run to your reference shelf, consult other sources, or wait until Friday morning for knitting class; things like picking up and knitting are explained right where you need them (with accompanying diagrams even!). Hopefully you'll feel like you have an expert knitter right there with you.

Don't worry; you don't have to read more than 300 pages to get started on knitting the great projects in this book! If you're familiar with knitting basics, you can dive right in and start knitting. Look through the Table of Contents or browse through the photographs in the color insert to decide what you want to make. Pick and choose the information you need at any time.

# Conventions Used in This Book

I include a few standard conventions to help you navigate this book:

- *Italics* point out defined terms and emphasize certain words.
- **Boldface** text indicates the key words in bulleted and numbered lists.
- `Monofont` highlights Web addresses.

Each pattern in this book begins with a photograph of the finished project. And if you have to use any techniques that may be new to you, they're explained in the "New skill" section of the pattern. I also give you the materials and vital statistics needed for the project right up front; look there to find information regarding the size of the finished project, the materials you need to complete it, the gauge you need to knit at, and any diagrams that may help you complete the project. After the directions for the basic pattern, you'll often find one or more variations. These variations provide instructions and inspiration for altering the pattern, which allows you to knit the same pattern in lots of different ways. I suggest that you read the variations before you start the pattern to see if you want to knit one of the variations instead. In some cases, the supplies you need are different from those listed in the basic pattern.

Like most books of knitting patterns, this book uses conventional pattern formatting and some standard knitting abbreviations. You can familiarize yourself with the abbreviations and find out how to read patterns in Chapter 4.

# Foolish Assumptions

This book isn't a "learn to knit" book, though I do think it's a "learn to knit better" book. I assume that you're either a beginning knitter who's looking for an easy introduction to patterns or an experienced knitter who wants some new patterns to try and to experiment with. If you've never knit a single stitch, you may want to flip through *Knitting For Dummies* by Pam Allen (Wiley), take a lesson, or have a friend guide you through the steps of casting on, knitting, purling, and binding off. Once you have the hang of the absolute basics, you'll be ready to jump into the patterns presented in this book.

And despite the title of the book, I'm assuming that you're no dummy and that you're absolutely capable of doing what you set your mind to. I have little tolerance for those people who claim they can't do basic math or can't follow a set of instructions. The directions in this book are broken down step by step and are written without unnecessary jargon or knitterese. Over half the projects are suitable first projects and all of them are within the grasp of the adventurous novice. Sure, you'll sometimes run into frustration along the way, but I firmly believe that doing something a little bit challenging is good for you. Challenges are good for your brain and good for your self-esteem. In fact, science has shown that having the right amount of challenge is what makes a hobby engaging. So go ahead and be ambitious.

# How This Book Is Organized

The first two parts of this book contain information that you may want to know before you start knitting, particularly if you're a new knitter. The bulk of the book, Parts III and IV, are the pattern chapters. The patterns in these parts are organized by their basic geometry, starting with the rectangle and moving up in complexity to fully shaped sweaters for the whole family. Similarly, each chapter is organized by level of difficulty, so choose patterns at the beginning of a chapter if you're looking for a simpler project and choose ones at the end of a chapter if you want a more ambitious project.

## Part 1: The Nuts and Bolts (or Sticks and String) of Knitting

Part I is packed with useful information. Chapter 1, for instance, introduces you to the basic tools of the trade: yarn, needles, and the other gadgets that you want to have at hand. Chapter 2 gives you the lowdown on gauge. Understanding what gauge is and how to knit at the gauge specified in a pattern is vital to knitting pieces that fit well and turn out right. If you're a new knitter, or if the garments you knit never seem to fit right, read Chapter 2 and take it to heart! If you take the opportunity to practice gauge and get it right, you'll be richly rewarded. Chapter 3 deals with taking body measurements and knowing what size garments to knit. Because you can't try your sweater on before you knit it, it's imperative to know what size is right for you. Finally, in Chapter 4, I give you guidance on reading knitting patterns. Knitting can seem like a foreign language at times, but after you master the lingo, you'll be ready to read.

## Part 11: A Primer on Stitches and Color

Part II provides step-by-step instructions for the stitch patterns used in this book and some others you might like to try. If, for example, you need a refresher on how to knit seed stitch in the round or want to try your hand at half linen stitch, Chapter 5 is the place to turn. This chapter is where I cover the simplest stitches. Chapter 6 introduces you to a variety of textures that can be used all over a piece or as accents. Study this chapter to master the basics of ribbing, cabling, and knitting lace. If you want to learn about stripes, Fair Isle, or mosaic patterns, check out Chapter 7, which introduces color work. There, I also show you how to add a bit of color with duplicate stitch or surface crochet after your handknit is complete.

# Part III: Patterns with Rectangles and Related Shapes

The easiest shape to knit is a rectangle, but the simplicity of the knitting doesn't mean that these patterns are boring — they're anything but! Start off with rectangles to wear in Chapter 8. You'll find scarves here, of course, but you also can choose from stoles, hats, slippers, and even a top — all of which are rectangles. Really. But wait, there's more! Chapter 9 gives you rectangular projects for the home: pillows, potholders, a lovely and smart looking baby blanket, and a journal cover perfect for your knitting notebook. Chapter 10 introduces just a hint of shaping. By binding off and casting on in the right places, you can make a wonderful messenger bag, a baby sweater, a couple of fantastic coats, or a great shell that you'll love to wear. To look at these pieces, you'd never guess that the knitting was so straightforward. These projects are well within the grasp of any knitter who's whetted her needles on her first scarf or dishcloth and who's ready for something a bit more ambitious.

# Part IV: Patterns with Circles, Triangles, and More

After you've gotten the hang of all things rectilinear, try your hand at the patterns presented in Part IV. This part begins with circles in Chapter 11. Working in the round is no more complex than knitting a rectangle. In fact, it's easier in some cases! So why not choose a storybook-inspired stocking cap, stylish wrist warmers, or a ruffled cowl to warm your neck? If you're feeling ambitious, cast on for the mosaic-patterned felted purse. Chapter 12 familiarizes you with triangles. Easy kerchiefs and shawls help you understand the ins and outs of shaping, and you can practice short rows by making the surprisingly simple short row scarf or harlequin blanket.

The next two chapters — Chapters 13 and 14 — put all the shapes together as you move on to more involved projects: classic sweaters for the whole family. These projects combine the skills used in earlier chapters, but in their basic forms they're fine choices for a knitter who's ready to make her first sweater.

In Chapter 13, you find an all-purpose pattern for a kid's top. Make it with short or long sleeves, cabled or not, wool or cotton — the choice is yours. I also include patterns for a women's T-shirt and two men's sweaters. One of the men's sweaters is more casual with rolled edges and a bit of color, and the other is a fine-gauged sweater with traditional finishing.

Chapter 14 includes two top-down cardigans. One is bulky and zipped — ready for weekends outdoors — and the other is half-ribbed with a wide collar and clean lines. Finally, you can also choose from two women's pullovers. These feminine pullovers have shaping at the waist, and you can knit either a scooped neck or a wide V-neck. The scoop neck is shown with Fair Isle borders and the V-neck is cropped and accented with lace. However, the details on these sweaters are interchangeable, which allows you to create a top that's just what you want.

## Part V: The Part of Tens

This part of the book is a mixed bag of little chapters that are full of tips and whimsy. They're great to read when you need a break from your knitting. Discover what to do with your swatches, how to knit with some unusual things, and how to care for your knits after they're complete.

## Appendix

If you find yourself stuck at some point, look to the appendix, featuring basic knitting skills. The appendix can refresh your memory on knitting basics, such as casting on, knitting, purling, binding off, and more. Remember too that the index can point you to pages where skills are described in greater depth.

# Icons Used in This Book

See those little pictures in the margins of this book? Those pictures are icons, and they indicate the following information:

When you see this icon, know that it's pointing out something that you shouldn't forget. It marks information that you can apply to your knitting whenever a similar situation arises.

This icon highlights the tricks of the trade that experienced knitters have discovered and shared with one another along the way. Following these tips will make your knitting easier.

This icon marks points where things can get confusing. When you see text highlighted by this icon, be sure you're reading carefully. This information may save you from making frustrating mistakes.

# Where to Go from Here

Remember, unless you want to, you don't need to read this book from front to back like a novel. Instead, you can jump around to the parts that you need to read for a specific project. Here are some suggestions as to how to get started:

- If you haven't already, take a few minutes to look through the photographs in the color insert. Checking out the photos will give you a quick introduction to the many patterns presented in the book.

- If you've just started knitting or want to improve your knitting skills, I strongly suggest that you read through Part I before you start a project. I know it's no fun to get a bit of meat and potatoes before the dessert, but the time that you spend getting to know how to choose yarn, read patterns, and accurately measure yourself and your knitting will be returned to you with interest when you get satisfying results (with less aggravation!).

✔ If you're comfortable knitting and reading patterns, flip right to the project that you want to make and dive in. Each pattern stands on its own, so you can start anywhere you want. Remember that the patterns in Part III are easier than the ones in Part IV. If you find that you're having trouble with one of the later patterns, refresh yourself with something easier and then go back to the more ambitious project.

✔ If you're looking for a certain kind of pattern or want to gain experience with a certain skill, look to the Table of Contents. All projects, as well as their variations and the new skills, are listed there.

And don't forget: If you want even more knitting information, be sure to check out *Knitting For Dummies* by Pam Allen (Wiley).

# Part I
# The Nuts and Bolts (or Sticks and String) of Knitting

The 5th Wave                    By Rich Tennant

"I honestly think that yarn is going to be strong enough."

# In this part . . .

A lot of knitting focuses on your fingers; this part of the book, however, focuses on your brain. It's packed with all sorts of stuff you really should know if you want to knit successfully. Whether you've just completed your first scarf or you're returning to the needles after a long separation, there are a few things that you ought to understand to make your knitting projects turn out the way you want them to — and more important, make your knitting experience more pleasurable.

In this part, you find out about all the tools of the trade: the yarn, the needles, and the various other doodads that you may want to buy. I also lay gauge on the line. Knitting the right number of stitches in an inch is what determines the size of your finished piece. Understanding how to measure your gauge accurately (and correct it if it's off) is one of the most important steps to knitting success. Once you have a solid grasp on gauge, read about measuring yourself and choosing your size. Finally, I do a bit of decoding to reveal the secret language of knitting. Reading patterns and charts can seem like a foreign tongue, but after you master those few key phrases, you'll be knitting like a seasoned traveler. Reading and understanding the chapters in this part puts you in good stead, not just for the patterns presented in this book, but for wherever you go with your knitting.

# Chapter 1

# The Right Stuff: Knitting Supplies

· · · · · · · · · · · · · · · · · · · · · · · · · · · · · · · · · · · · · · · · · · · · · · · · · · ·

· · · · · · · · · · · · · · · · · · · · · · · · · · · · · · · · · · · · · · · · · · · · · · · · · · ·

*B*efore you start knitting, you need a few supplies. Unlike many hobbies, though, knitting doesn't require a lot of fancy equipment. In fact, one of the great allures of knitting, I think, is that the technology is about as basic as you can get: a couple of pointy sticks and some string. With these simple tools you can create even the most intricate projects, just as others have done for centuries. This chapter guides you through choosing the right yarns, needles, and other little gadgets that make your knitting easier.

## Unraveling the Basics of Yarn

The first thing you need for knitting is yarn. You can find yarn in lots of places — in drug stores, at craft emporiums, and on the Internet — but the best place to go is your local knitting shop. Hanging out at a yarn store can make you feel like the proverbial kid in a candy shop; there are so many beautiful colors, textures, and fibers to look at and touch. A yarn store will likely have most of the yarns called for in the patterns in this book. Plus yarn stores have knowledgeable and helpful staff members that can guide you in selecting yarns and projects that are just right for you.

In the following sections, I explain some yarn basics, including the different ways yarn is put up, the important information found on a yarn label, selecting the right yarn for a project (if you want to use something different from the pattern's suggested yarn), and knowing how much yarn to buy.

### Checking out different types of packaging

Yarns come *put up*, or packaged, in a variety of ways. They can be wound into balls or skeins, or they may come in hanks, which you wind into balls yourself. It doesn't matter which way your yarn comes put up, so don't worry if you have yarn in skeins and the pattern asks for balls.

If the yarn you're using comes in a hank, you must wind it into a ball before you can knit it. To do so, take off the label and follow these steps:

1. **Untwist the hank so that it opens into a circle.**

   Place this circle onto the back of a chair, someone's outstretched hands, or a *swift* (a tool that looks like a wooden umbrella, which is specially designed for this task). Untie the short loops of yarn that hold the hank together.

2. **Take one of the ends and begin winding the yarn into a ball.**

   Begin winding around two or three fingers, and then, as the ball is established, wind around the ball. Don't wrap tightly or pull the yarn; it's best to keep the yarn relaxed as you wind. As long as the circle of the hank is uncompromised, you shouldn't get any tangles as you wind. However, mess with the circle and you'll end up with a Girl Scout Badge in knots. Go slowly, and be patient if you have to do some untangling.

## Reading a yarn label

Every yarn you buy comes with a label. The label is filled with really important information, so don't just throw it away. Take a look at the label in Figure 1-1 (or at the ones in your yarn basket) to find the information described in this list:

✔ **Name and manufacturer:** Each label gives you the name of the manufacturer and the name of the yarn. Yarn names can be descriptive, evocative, or just silly. If you're looking for a certain yarn, ask for it by its name and manufacturer.

✔ **Fiber content:** The fiber content tells you what the yarn is made of. Yarns can be made of wool, cotton, synthetics, exotic animal and plant fibers, or blends of different fibers. If you're looking for a substitute for a given project, consider the fiber content as well as the suggested gauge, because different fibers behave in different ways. I discuss fiber content and weight in more detail later in this chapter.

✔ **Gauge and suggested needle size:** Remember that the label's gauge and needle suggestions are just that: suggestions. So, no matter what the label says, you should swatch with the yarn to make sure that you're getting the right gauge for your project before you begin knitting. See Chapter 2 for more on gauge and swatching.

   The gauge may be written out like this: "4 stitches/inch on US 10 needles." Or there may be a funny little grid with some numbers. If there's a grid, here are some tips on how to read it:

   • The grid always represents 4 inches (10 cm).

   • The number along the bottom is the number of stitches per 4 inches. In Figure 1-1, this number is 16.

   • The number along the side is the suggested number of rows per 4 inches. In Figure 1-1, this number is 20.

   The grid in Figure 1-1 tells you that the manufacturer thinks the yarn will look best if you knit 16 stitches and 20 rows per 4 inches, likely on size 10 needles. So, if you wanted to, you could substitute this yarn in patterns that call for a gauge of "16 stitches/20 rows per 4 inches." You can probably use it for something that calls for 15 or 17 stitches per 4 inches, but probably not for 12 or 20 stitches per 4 inches.

✔ **Care instructions:** Most yarn labels contain information on caring for your finished projects (which is one reason to save the label in a notebook or file!). A year from now when you decide to wash your hat, you'll likely need to reread this information. (Chapter 18 offers lots of tips for caring for your handknits.)

✔ **Color name and dye lot number:** The color name may be a specific color, such as Fuchsia, or it may be just a color number, such as #322 (or it may be both). Many yarns also offer a dye lot number. Some yarns vary significantly depending on when they were dyed, particularly hand-dyed yarns. Whenever possible, stick to one dye lot when you're selecting your yarns so that your project will have a uniform color. Sometimes the differences between dye lots are subtle enough that you won't notice them while you're knitting, and they'll become apparent only when you wear your finished garment in the sunlight the first time!

✔ **Length and weight:** Yarns are usually packaged in standard weights. A weight of 50 grams (1¾ ounces) is typical, but some skeins weigh 100 grams or more. The yarn label tells you how many yards or meters are in the skein. Use the yardage numbers rather than weight to figure out how much yarn to buy. Check out the section "Determining how much yarn you need" later in this chapter for more on this task.

## Choosing the right yarn for the job

Deciding which yarn to use for a project can be a challenge because there's much more to choosing the right yarn than deciding what your favorite color is! Each project in this book calls for a specific yarn, but that doesn't mean that you need to use that exact yarn. Part of what makes knitting fun is that by choosing yarns and colors that appeal to you, you make something that's truly your own.

Consider the fabric that the yarn will make based on its fiber content and decide whether that fabric is appropriate for the pattern you've chosen. A pattern designed for a whisper-light mohair won't look the same if you knit it in cotton chenille! You'll also need to consider the weight of the yarn; read more about weight and matching gauge later in this chapter.

Find out a bit about the different sorts of yarn in the following sections so that you can choose your yarns with confidence.

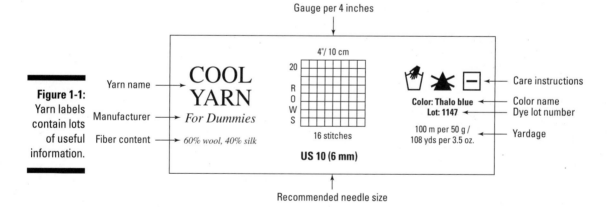

**Figure 1-1:** Yarn labels contain lots of useful information.

### Fibers

Talking about the fibers used to make yarn starts like a game of Twenty Questions. Is it animal, vegetable, or mineral? Each of these categories has certain characteristics that influence how the yarn behaves and knits up. Here are the categories:

▎ ✔ **Animal Fibers:** When you think of yarn, you may first think of wool. And there's good reason for that. Sheep's wool has been spun into yarn for a long time. It's warm but breathable, is somewhat elastic, wears well, and is probably the easiest to knit with. Other animal fibers include alpaca, llama, mohair, angora, and cashmere. Silk is sort of a special case, because though it comes from bugs, it behaves more like a vegetable fiber than an animal fiber.

Unless they're specially treated or blended with other fibers, animal fibers can turn to felt if you wash them in a machine. Buy superwash wool if you're looking for easy-care yarn. (See Chapter 18 for more tips on caring for knits.)

✔ **Vegetable Fibers:** Many yarns are made from plant fibers. These yarns are most commonly made of cotton, but you'll also find ones made from linen, bamboo, and hemp. Vegetable fibers don't have any natural elasticity and are generally heavier (though cooler!) than their wool counterparts. Still, cotton, linen, and the other vegetable fibers can be wonderful to knit with, and they make great knits to wear year-round.

✔ **Synthetics:** Not so long ago, synthetic yarns meant that you were stuck with acrylic. If acrylic yarn still makes you think of those indestructible afghans that were knit in the mid-century, look around at what technology has done for yarn! There are many synthetics with exotic textures that knitters call *novelty yarns*. Whether they're shiny, hairy, fuzzy, or bumpy, these yarns can add great texture and zing to your projects.

What's really great about new synthetics is that there are now many blends that mix natural and man-made fibers to create wonderful, knittable yarns. For instance, adding a bit of microfiber acrylic to cotton makes a stretchier yarn; and adding rayon to wool creates a wonderful sheen and minimizes the itch of wool. Synthetic blends can make yarns that are sturdier and easier to care for. They also make luxury fibers easier on the pocketbook.

### Weights

Regardless of their fiber content, yarns are classed by weight. This classification can throw knitters off because it really doesn't have much to do with what the yarn actually weighs. The term "yarn weight" is a holdover from the days when most knitting was done with pure wool and there wasn't such a rich cornucopia of yarns to choose from. In those days, you could count on 50 grams of worsted wool measuring just about 100 meters. But with the addition of so many new fibers to the marketplace and new ways to make yarn, you shouldn't assume that 50 grams of one yarn is equivalent to 50 grams of another yarn. Yarn weight classes, such as "worsted" or "fingering," are used to describe how thick the yarn is. So, look at the gauge listed on the label, not the weight of the skein, to determine which weight class your yarn fits into.

The Craft Yarn Council of America has created a standardized set of six weight classes, which are shown in Table 1-1. You can see, for instance, that bulky yarns knit at a gauge of between 12 and 15 stitches per 4 inches. However, don't be fooled into thinking that yarns within one category are all the same and therefore interchangeable. Instead, these standards simply allow you to have a general sense of whether a yarn is, say, medium or bulky.

| Table 1-1 | Yarn Classes | | | |
|---|---|---|---|---|
| *Yarn Weight Category Name* | *Types of Yarn in Category* | *Knit Gauge Range in Stockinette Stitch per 4 inches* | *Recommended US Needle Sizes* | *Recommended Metric Needle Sizes* |
| 1 Superfine | sock, fingering, baby | 27 to 32 sts | 1 to 3 | 2.25 to 3.25 mm |
| 2 Fine | sport, baby | 23 to 26 sts | 3 to 5 | 3.25 to 3.75 mm |
| 3 Light | DK, light worsted | 21 to 24 sts | 5 to 7 | 3.75 to 4.5 mm |
| 4 Medium | worsted, aran | 16 to 20 sts | 7 to 9 | 4.5 to 5.5 mm |

| Yarn Weight Category Name | Types of Yarn in Category | Knit Gauge Range in Stockinette Stitch per 4 inches | Recommended US Needle Sizes | Recommended Metric Needle Sizes |
|---|---|---|---|---|
| 5 Bulky | chunky, craft, rug | 12 to 15 sts | 9 to 11 | 5.5 to 8 mm |
| 6 Super bulky | bulky, roving | 6 to 11 sts | 11 and larger | 8 mm and larger |

Generally, you use small needles with the thinnest yarns and very large needles with the thickest yarns. Table 1-1 suggests a range of needle sizes that are commonly used with yarns of different weights. But remember that the size of needle that *you* need depends also on what you're making and what your knitting style is. I discuss needle sizes later in this chapter.

## Determining how much yarn you need

Whenever you start a new project, you have to know how much yarn you need. In the following sections, you find out the calculations to make, whether you're substituting one yarn for another in a pattern or whether you just have a general sense of what you'd like to knit, say, a hat or a scarf.

Patterns usually call for a little more yarn than you'll actually use, but because you want to swatch and account for the unknown (you actually hate three-quarter sleeves, you want to make a larger collar, or there's been some terrible yarn accident), buy a little extra yarn, particularly if it's being discontinued. Buying extra yarn also is a good idea because a ribbed or cabled pattern takes more yarn than stockinette stitch, and your knitting may vary. One extra ball is plenty for a small project; buy a couple of extra balls for a very large project. If you don't use the extra yarn, most yarn shops allow you to return unused balls in good condition for store credit; be sure to ask about the store's return policy before you buy. And remember that there are great uses for odd balls, too.

### Calculating yardage when you're substituting yarns

When you buy yarn, you obviously need enough to finish your project. But how much do you need? If you're using the yarn called for in a pattern, the pattern usually tells you how many balls to buy for each size. However, if you choose to use a yarn different from the pattern's suggestion, you may need to do a little calculating.

For instance, imagine that you want to knit a vest from a pattern that calls for eight skeins that each have 75 yards of yarn. But the yarn you want to use (that knits to the same gauge, of course!) has 109 yards per ball. How many balls should you buy?

This sounds like a story problem from my daughter's math homework. And you can solve it just the way she would — by simply plugging in numbers. Use this general formula to determine how much yarn you need:

Number of skeins called for in the pattern × yards per skein = total yards needed for the pattern

Total yards needed for the pattern ÷ yards per skein of your chosen yarn = number of skeins you need (round up to the nearest whole number, if necessary)

Using my vest example, the math works out like this:

8 skeins × 75 yards per skein = 600 yards

600 yards ÷ 109 yards per ball = 5½ balls of yarn

So, because you can't buy five and a half balls of yarn, you need to buy six balls to make your vest.

### Estimating your yarn needs when you're knitting on the fly

In the previous scenario, it's easy to decide how much yarn to buy, but many times you don't have all the variables decided. For example, if you aren't working directly from a pattern or are working at a different gauge than a pattern recommends, you don't have a tidy way to determine how much yarn to buy. Or say you happen by a really big yarn sale. There's some wonderful wool on sale, but how much should you buy if you know you want to knit a sweater but haven't chosen a pattern yet? One approach is to just buy it all and sort it out later. A more cautioned approach is to decide on the garment you want to make and guesstimate how much you need. Table 1-2 gives yardage approximations for various projects in a variety of gauges.

| Table 1-2 | | Estimates of Yards of Yarn Needed for Projects | | |
|---|---|---|---|---|
| Yarn Weight Category | Stitches per Inch | Yards Needed for a Hat | Yards Needed for a Scarf | Yards Needed for an Adult Sweater |
| 1  Superfine | 7 to 8 | 300 to 375 | 350 | 1,500 to 3,200 |
| 2  Fine | 6 to 7 | 250 to 350 | 300 | 1,200 to 2,500 |
| 3  Light | 5 to 6 | 200 to 300 | 250 | 1,000 to 2,000 |
| 4  Medium | 4 to 5 | 150 to 250 | 200 | 800 to 1,500 |
| 5  Bulky | 3 to 4 | 125 to 200 | 150 | 600 to 1,200 |
| 6  Super bulky | 1.5 to 3 | 75 to 125 | 125 | 400 to 800 |

If you like more precision, take a look at Table 1-3, which tells you how many inches of yarn you need to knit one square inch at a variety of gauges.

| Table 1-3 | Yarn Needed to Knit One Square Inch | | |
|---|---|---|---|
| Yarn Weight Category | Stitches per Inch | Rows per Inch | Inches of Yarn Needed |
| 1  Superfine | 7 to 8 | 10 | 28 |
| 2  Fine | 6 to 7 | 8½ | 26 |
| 3  Light (DK) | 5½ to 6 | 7½ | 24 |
| 3  Light (light worsted) | 5 to 5½ | 7 | 22 |
| 4  Medium (worsted) | 5 | 6½ | 20 |
| 4  Medium (aran) | 4 to 4½ | 6 | 18 |
| 5  Bulky | 3 to 4 | 5 | 14 |
| 6  Super bulky | 1½ to 3 | 4 | 12 |

Using Table 1-3 is pretty easy if you're making a scarf, but it's a bit more involved for something like a sweater. Still, it all comes down to geometry. For each piece of your project, multiply the length of the piece by the width, and then multiply this result by the length of yarn used per knitted inch. Here's how it works:

Length × width × the length of yarn per knitted inch = inches of yarn needed

Inches of yarn needed ÷ 36 inches per yard = number of yards of yarn

Suppose you're making a scarf that's 60 inches long and 6 inches wide. You're using a medium weight yarn that knits to a gauge of 5 stitches per inch. With this gauge, Table 1-3 shows that you need 20 inches of yarn to knit a square inch. Multiply 60 by 6 by 20, and you need 7,200 inches of yarn. Divide that number by 36 inches in a yard and you get 200 yards.

# Getting to the Point of Needles

The other must-have for knitting (besides yarn, of course!) is needles. While there aren't as many kinds of needles as there are kinds of yarn, you still have a lot to choose from and the decision of what to buy (or use) can be a bit bewildering. Read through the following sections to get a handle on your needle options.

## Looking at different kinds of needles

It won't surprise you that knitters have preferences when it comes to yarn, but it may surprise you that sometimes their preferences for needles are even stronger. I like to knit on metal circular needles and find it faintly annoying to knit on anything else. Then again, I know tremendously skilled knitters who love straight, wooden needles. There's no right or wrong here. Take the opportunity to try out different needles to see what you like best.

Needles generally fit into a few basic categories, including straight needles, circular needles, double-pointed needles, and cable needles. You can see what they look like in Figure 1-2. Here are the characteristics of each:

✔ **Straight needles:** The most classic knitting needles are straight needles, which are about 14 inches long and made of metal or wood. They have a point on one end and a stopper of some sort on the opposite end to keep the stitches from falling off. You can knit almost anything on these, except for those projects that were designed to be knit in the round (see Chapter 11) or something extremely wide, such as a blanket. You can get shorter 10-inch length needles also, which are a bit more manageable for something like a scarf. These shorter needles are also easier to tuck into your bag.

✔ **Circular needles:** These needles have two pointy ends connected by a cable. They come in different lengths as well as different gauges. The length of a circular needle is measured from tip to tip. A pattern will specify which length you need for your project. For instance, to knit a hat you need a short length, such as 16 inches. A sweater, on the other hand, knits up on a needle that's 24 or 36 inches long. If you're knitting something with a huge number of stitches (like a blanket or the shawl collar on the coats in Chapter 10), you may need an even longer needle.

Note that you can use circular needles even if you aren't knitting in the round. Just like you do with straight needles, turn the work around at the end of the row and switch the needle tips to the opposite hands. Think of your circular needle as two straight needles that happen to be stuck together. Some knitters prefer circular needles for all their projects because it's more difficult to lose a needle and because it keeps the weight of the knitting more centered in your lap. If you have trouble with repetitive stress injuries, circular needles may lessen the strain on your wrists.

✔ **Double-pointed needles:** Double-pointed needles are used less often than straight and circular needles, unless you make a lot of socks. Double-pointed needles look like large toothpicks and come in sets of four or five. These needles are used to knit in the round to create tubes that are smaller than you can make on a single circular needle, mainly socks and the tops of hats.

✔ **Cable needles:** Cable needles come in a few different varieties. Some are shaped like U's or J's; others are like short double-pointed needles with a narrow or bent spot in the center. One sort doesn't work better than another, so if you're having trouble with the one you've got, experiment a little with a different type. Read more about cables in Chapter 6.

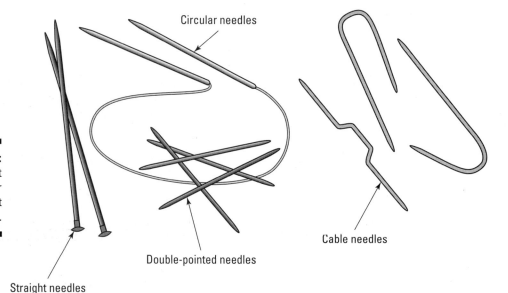

**Figure 1-2:** Different needles for different jobs.

Circular needles

Cable needles

Double-pointed needles

Straight needles

Needles, whether circular or straight, can be made out of a variety of things: aluminum, steel, bamboo, exotic hardwoods, plastic, and even glass. The weight, price, slipperiness, and even the noise that the needles make can influence which needle is right for you. As a very general rule of thumb, use a slippery needle like metal for yarns that are sticky or catchy, such as mohair or chenille. Conversely, with slippery yarns, such as some ribbons and novelty yarns, try needles that are a little less smooth, like bamboo. As you take on new projects, you're likely to need different-sized needles every now and then. Why not try a needle made from something new the next time you buy?

## Understanding needle sizes

Needles come in a range of sizes based on the diameter of the needle. In the United States, needles are numbered according to a somewhat logical but obscure system. It starts out okay with 0, 1, 2, and so on, but then it gets weird later with 9, 10, 10½, 11, 13, 15, and so on. Most of the rest of the world relies on the metric system to size knitting needles, so you'll also see needle sizes like 5 mm and 8 mm. You can compare metric and US needle sizes by looking at Figure 1-3.

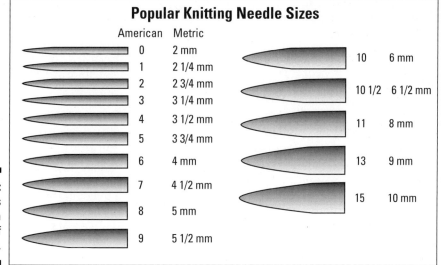

**Popular Knitting Needle Sizes**

| American | Metric |
|----------|--------|
| 0 | 2 mm |
| 1 | 2 1/4 mm |
| 2 | 2 3/4 mm |
| 3 | 3 1/4 mm |
| 4 | 3 1/2 mm |
| 5 | 3 3/4 mm |
| 6 | 4 mm |
| 7 | 4 1/2 mm |
| 8 | 5 mm |
| 9 | 5 1/2 mm |
| 10 | 6 mm |
| 10 1/2 | 6 1/2 mm |
| 11 | 8 mm |
| 13 | 9 mm |
| 15 | 10 mm |

**Figure 1-3:** Needles come in a variety of sizes.

If you're reading a pattern that was written in Europe or you're reading the suggested needle size from a yarn label printed outside the United States, take note of whether the needle sizes are given in metric or US form. That way, you'll be sure to use the right size.

If you're having trouble deciding which size needle is right for the yarn you've chosen, check out Table 1-1 to help guide you to the right needles.

# Filling Your Knitting Bag with Other Gadgets

Some people have absolutely every accessory for their craft. Others wander around with their stuff tossed into a grocery sack. And while I adore looking at someone's beautifully styled knitting bag with matching needle holder and cellphone cozy, I also admire the less-is-more approach; you can knit happily for years with a simple bag, a couple pairs of needles, and whatever yarn comes your way. And for the most part, you don't need specialized tools (see Chapter 17 for ways to MacGyver your knitting with everyday items).

Think for a moment about what you knit and where you knit it. If you mainly knit socks during your commute on the bus, you'll need a small bag to hold your project — likely something that tucks into your purse (or *is* your purse). If you're knitting a bulky Fair Isle sweater at home in front of the fire, however, you don't have to worry about carrying things around, in which case you might use a large basket to hold your work-in-progress and extra yarns. Realistically, if you fall for knitting in a big way, you'll have a sock in your purse, the basket by the fire, a simple scarf waiting by the TV, and maybe something stashed in the car for some sort of knitting emergency. Wherever you knit, the following sections list some tools that come in handy.

## Measuring tools

If you want a garment to fit properly, you have to measure it properly. And it never hurts to measure yourself either (see Chapter 3 for more on measuring yourself). Here are a few tools that can help you master measurements and numbers when knitting:

✔ **Tape measure:** A small cloth tape measure that retracts is handy. A plastic tape measure is okay too, though it may stretch out over time. Metal tape measures are great for carpenters but not so good for knitters because they aren't flexible enough.

✔ **Gauge measurement tool:** When searching for your own gauge measurement tool, you have a couple of different models to choose from. Some are metal and some are plastic. They all have a window that allows you to count the number of stitches and rows per two inches, which helps you to see whether you're knitting to the gauge specified. These tools also feature holes with different diameters to check the size of your needles. You can measure gauge just fine with a tape measure, but a gauge measurement tool is pretty handy to have. (Find out more about gauge and see a gauge measurement tool in Chapter 2.)

✔ **Calculator:** I find it useful to have a calculator with my knitting paraphernalia because there are times when calculations come up. I applaud both the scrap-of-paper and the in-the-head techniques, but most knitters prefer to use a calculator.

## Markers and holders

Knitters use a variety of tools to mark particular spots in their knitting and to hold *live* stitches. (Live stitches are stitches that you aren't working with at the moment, but that you'll do more with later.) Shoulder stitches that will later be bound off with the three-needle bind-off or the stitches for half the neckline after you've divided the left and right neck are common examples of stitches that you may want to put on a holder. Check out these marking and holding tools, which are shown in Figure 1-4:

✔ **Markers:** Knitters sometimes need to leave a mark to note a stopping or starting place. There are several different sorts of markers for this purpose. If you want an easy way to spot where you started your armhole decreases, for instance, you place a marker on a stitch in that row and leave it there so you can measure from it later. Markers used for this purpose are often called *split ring markers* or *locking markers*. More often, though, you'll use markers on your needle. Markers used in this way are sometimes called *ring markers*. These are placed on the needle between stitches and slipped from needle to needle whenever you encounter them.

✔ **Safety pins:** You can use safety pins to remind yourself which is the right side of your work by pinning them through the fabric on that side (this is particularly helpful when your stitch pattern looks the same on both sides). This way, when the instructions read "Decrease at each end every right-side row" you know that if you can see the safety pin, it's a decrease row.

Safety pins are also helpful when you notice a dropped stitch way down in your work. If you can't fix it (or you can't fix it at the moment), put the dropped stitch onto the safety pin and pin it to its neighbor. The stitch will be safe until help arrives. Coilless pins are particularly nice because the yarn doesn't catch on them and they can hold more stitches.

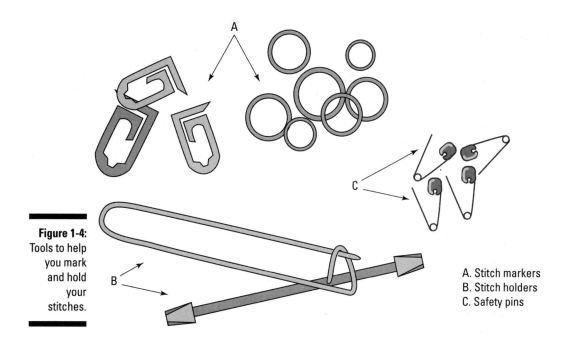

A

C

**Figure 1-4:**
Tools to help
you mark
and hold
your
stitches.

B

A. Stitch markers
B. Stitch holders
C. Safety pins

✔ **Holders:** A safety pin is a great stitch holder for a few stitches, but if you have more than you can fit on your pin, you need to resort to something else. In this case, that something else is a *stitch holder.* The old-school models look like kilt pins. Newer varieties look a bit like hair curlers and have the advantage of opening on each end so you can access the stitches from either side. A spare needle or length of smooth scrap yarn can also hold your stitches for you.

Whatever kind of holder you use, slip the specified stitches to the holder purlwise. When it's time to address these stitches again, slip them back to the working needle, again slipping purlwise so the stitches aren't twisted.

## *Tools for keeping track of your knitting*

When knitting, you'll find that there are inevitably little bits of information that you want to write down. Whether you need to remind yourself that you're on Row 27 or you need to remember the title of a recommended book or the name of the yarn the person next to you in class was using for her shawl, something to write on often comes in handy. The grocery-bag-toting knitter will make do with a receipt or another piece of scrap paper, but it's smart to carry a notebook for your knitting ideas. And don't forget to throw in something to write with.

Many knitters also like to make photocopies of the patterns that they're working on. While you're at it, feel free to enlarge any charts so they're easy for you to read. With the copy, you're free to make your notes right on the pattern.

Sticky notes can come in handy too. You can use them to mark your place in this book, or you can make tally marks on them as you finish your rows. If you're using a chart, it's handy to place the sticky note right under the row that you're working on so you don't get lost every time you look from your book to the knitting and back again.

## Finishing tools

Most patterns have a section called "Finishing." Usually this means sewing up and blocking (see the appendix for details on these tasks). Parts of finishing are simply more knitting, but here are a couple of other tools that you want to have that help get the job done (see Figure 1-5):

✔ **Yarn needles:** Sometimes called tapestry needles, yarn needles look like big, fat sewing needles with a blunt tip. Some are straight and some have a bit of a curve at the tip, which helps you scoop up stitches. But be sure to choose a needle meant for yarn! Upholstery needles are nice and big, but anything with a sharp tip will lead you to frustration because you'll tend to sew into the yarn instead of going between stitches. Even a kid's plastic needle will work better than a sharp one.

✔ **Crochet hooks:** Even though you're knitting, a crochet hook or two can come in handy. Generally, you want one about the diameter of the needles that you're working with, or a size or two smaller. Aside from basic crochet used for edging and such, a crochet hook can help you pick up stitches, fix errors, or weave in your ends.

✔ **Scissors:** Though you can break most yarns with your hands, scissors do come in handy. Choose blunt-tipped or folding scissors to prevent nasty pokes if you carry them around with you.

If you're traveling by air and want to take your knitting on board, consider buying a yarn cutter like the one shown in Figure 1-5, since most scissors aren't allowed on planes.

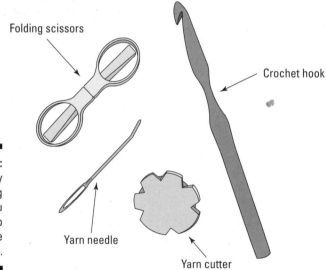

Folding scissors

Crochet hook

**Figure 1-5:**
Handy
finishing
tools you
want to
have
around.

Yarn needle

Yarn cutter

# Chapter 2

# Gauge Your Success

• • • • • • • • • • • • • • • • • • • • • • • • • • • • • • • • • • • • • • • • • • • • • • • • • • • • • • • •

## In This Chapter

▶ Understanding the math behind gauge

▶ Getting your gauge on with some easy tips

▶ Taking steps for successful swatching

▶ Discovering drape and changing a pattern's gauge

• • • • • • • • • • • • • • • • • • • • • • • • • • • • • • • • • • • • • • • • • • • • • • • • • • • • • • • •

Gauge, or tension, is at the heart of following a knitting pattern successfully. Even if you do everything else right, if you aren't matching the gauge given, your project won't turn out properly. If you want to knit something that actually fits anyone (or any part of anyone), take time to read and understand this chapter. I give you the knowledge you need for calculating gauge, tips for knitting to the correct gauge, and steps for making a swatch for any project.

Neither gauge nor tension sound quite like what they really are. Because of this confusion, some knitters fall into the "I don't quite understand it, so I'm just going to ignore it" camp. And even though there are knitting directions that you can ignore without the universe collapsing (say, purl through the back loop), you can't ignore gauge, unless you're content with knitting wide floppy scarves and skinny pinheaded hats for the rest of your life.

## Calculating Gauge for Any Project

*Gauge* refers to how many stitches and how many rows there are in 1 inch. It's a precise way of measuring and describing how loosely or tightly something is knit. Often, gauge is described as the number of stitches and rows per 4 inches in a pattern or on a yarn's label.

To figure out the number of stitches and rows you need in 1 inch, simply divide the listed gauge by four. For instance, a yarn with a gauge of 18 stitches and 24 rows per 4 inches is the same as 4.5 stitches per inch and 6 rows per inch. With these math skills, you're sure to impress most third graders you know, but it's okay to use a calculator if you need to.

The reason that gauge is so important is simple: Your gauge determines the size of whatever you're knitting. *Stitch gauge* (the number of stitches per inch) is more critical than *row gauge* (the number of rows per inch) because the number of stitches determines the width of the piece. Once you cast on, your width is determined, and you can't change it without starting over. Row gauge, on the other hand, determines the length of the piece. Matching row gauge precisely is less crucial because you can usually knit a couple more (or a couple less) rows to compensate and get the length you need.

To figure out how many stitches you need to cast on in order to make a piece that's a certain width, use this formula:

Stitches per inch (stitch gauge) × width (in inches) = number of stitches

To figure out how wide something will be, use this formula (which is based on the previously formula):

Number of stitches ÷ stitches per inch (stitch gauge) = width (in inches)

To understand this math concretely, think of it in terms of a scarf. If you're working with a yarn that knits to a gauge of 2.5 stitches per inch, and you want to make a scarf that's 6 inches wide, simply multiply 2.5 by 6 for a total of 15 stitches. Voila! You now know how many stitches to cast on.

This scarf example is very simple, but the basic equation to calculate stitch gauge is at the root of every increase and decrease and every cast-on and bind-off in knitting. If you can plug numbers into this equation and solve it, you're well on your way to your own basic design work. Even if you stick to knitting things designed by other people, this equation can help you understand what's going on behind the scenes and can help you become better at deciphering patterns.

You can fill in Table 2-1 to practice this math and help you understand the difference that gauge makes. Note the range between the number of stitches you need to cast on with a super bulky yarn at a gauge of 2 stitches per inch and the number of stitches you need to cast on with a fine yarn at a gauge of 6 stitches per inch. You need three times as many stitches to knit the "same" scarf with a thinner yarn! (Flip to Chapter 1 to find out more about these and other types of yarn.) If you think for a moment about what this difference would mean over the width of a whole sweater, you can see why understanding gauge and being able to take the steps needed to match the gauge called for in a pattern is vital to your knitting happiness.

| Table 2-1 | Cast-On Numbers for Scarves in Different Gauges | |
|---|---|---|
| *Stitches per Inch* | *× Width in Inches* | *= Number of Stitches* |
| 2 | 6 | |
| 2.5 | 6 | |
| 3 | 6 | |
| 3.5 | 6 | |
| 4 | 6 | |
| 4.5 | 6 | |
| 5 | 6 | |
| 5.5 | 6 | |
| 6 | 6 | |

# How Tense Are You? Tips for Knitting to the Right Gauge

You know what gauge is and why matching a pattern's recommended gauge is important. But what are you supposed to do about it? Read on to come to grips with getting the correct gauge.

## *Relaxing with your knitting*

Knitters all vary in the way that they hold needles and move yarn. This variation means that with the same yarn and needles, different knitters will knit to different gauges. One may create a fabric that's loose and see-through while another may make something that's practically bulletproof. It's important to recognize that matching the suggested gauge with the suggested needle size isn't a sign of a good knitter; it's only a sign of a knitter who happens to have similar tension to the person who made the pattern or packaged the yarn!

New knitters often ask whether they should change the way they hold the yarn or wrap it around their fingers or whether they should do something to snug up the yarn after each stitch. I always say no. Hold the yarn and needles so that you're comfortable. As long as you're making the stitches correctly, don't try to correct your tension. Correcting your tension generally leads to overcorrection — and only part of the time! So, anything you do to make your stitches tighter or looser will likely change when you relax and get going. The end result will likely be worse, not better, because some spots will be looser and some spots tighter.

Knitting skills, just like all others, are improved with practice. So put in the time. Plan to spend 15 minutes a day with your knitting. Some days you may finish only a couple of rows, but other days you may find that once you pick up your knitting, you can't put it down. By the time you come to the end of your first project, you'll be able to see that your gauge has become much more even and consistent. And you're probably enjoying it more too!

## *Switching needles if your gauge is off*

Okay, so maybe you're comfortable with your needles, and your gauge is more consistent, but it's consistently off. Your stitches are too big and you're getting 4 stitches per inch instead of 4.5. Big deal, you say. It's close enough, right? Wrong! Unlike horseshoes and slow dancing, close doesn't count in knitting. Here's why: Imagine a sweater front that's supposed to be knit at 4.5 stitches per inch. The directions say to cast on 90 stitches. The number of stitches on the needle, divided by the number of stitches per inch (or gauge) gives you the width of your knitting (for more about this formula, see the earlier section "Calculating Gauge for Any Project"). Here's the filled-in equation:

90 stitches ÷ 4.5 stitches per inch = 20 inches

From this equation, you determine that the sweater is 20 inches across. A quick study of the accompanying schematic confirms that this is how wide the sweater should be in the size that you want.

But at a gauge of 4 stitches per inch, what happens? Put the new gauge into the equation as follows to find out:

90 stitches ÷ 4 stitches per inch = 22.5 inches

This math shows that the front of the sweater is 2.5 inches wider at the new gauge. That means the whole sweater will be 5 inches bigger around. That's more than a whole size bigger!

With the following equation, you can see that you have equally ugly problems if your knitting is tighter than the suggested tension. If your gauge is 5 stitches to the inch rather than 4.5 stitches, here's what happens:

90 stitches ÷ 5 stitches per inch = 18 inches

The front of this sweater is 2 inches narrower than your intended size; the whole sweater will be 4 inches smaller around. Depending on the intended fit of the sweater, you may not even be able to get it on! Everything, including the ribbing around the neck, will be too tight.

I've heard many knitters say, "I'll just follow the directions for the next smallest size." This compensation for a loose gauge can work if you're careful (very, very careful) in how you deal with the lengths of each piece, but you haven't really fixed the problem with your stitches that are too big. The fabric you're creating may simply not look right if your gauge isn't correct.

The real way to change the number of stitches that you knit in an inch is to change the needles that you're using. A needle with a smaller diameter means that you make smaller loops when you wrap the yarn, and therefore you get smaller stitches. Likewise, bigger needles make bigger stitches. Check out the differences in Figure 2-1; the same yarn, stitch, and number of stiches are used, but the needle sizes and stitch sizes are different.

**Figure 2-1:**
Different
needles
yield differ-
ent stitch
sizes.

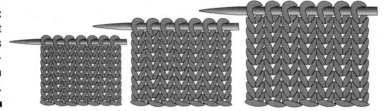

If your gauge is too tight, use bigger needles to correct the problem. If your gauge is too loose, use smaller needles to correct the problem. A lot of knitters get turned around on this point: If you have too many stitches per 4 inches, your gauge is too tight. If you have too few stitches, your gauge is too loose. You can see the difference that your needles make in gauge in the later section "Practicing different gauges in a single swatch." (See Chapter 1 for details about all the types of needles available.)

# Swatching Before You Begin a New Project

So how do you figure out what your gauge is for a particular project? You need to knit a little sample (called a *swatch*) and measure it. This process is called *swatching*. Sure, this takes a bit of time, but the results are absolutely worthwhile. "Take time to save time," the old adage goes. By making a swatch, you'll know that you've worked out the kinks in your gauge and that you're armed with the right needles to knit a project that fits. (See Chapter 16 for some things you can do with your swatches.)

For most projects, you'll likely need to try only a couple of needle sizes when you swatch. Plus, as you get to know yourself better as a knitter, you'll be better able to predict your own gauge. Still, good knitters always swatch.

## Making your swatch

Here's how to make your swatch:

1. **Begin by reading the gauge section at the beginning of your knitting pattern.**

   This section tells you how many stitches and rows you need to knit in 4 inches.

Here's an example: "16 stitches and 20 rows per 4 inches over stockinette stitch on US 9 (5.5 mm) needles."

2. **With the needles listed and the yarn that you want to use, cast on at least 4 inches worth of stitches (see the appendix if you need a refresher on casting on).**

The bigger your swatch, the more accurate your results, so it's best to cast on about 6 inches worth of stitches. For the example in the previous step, that's 24 stitches. (Why 24? 16 stitches divided by 4 inches equals 4 stitches per inch. Multiply 4 stitches per inch by 6 inches, and you wind up with 24 stitches.)

3. **Begin knitting in the stitch pattern specified.**

My example calls for stockinette stitch (see Chapter 5 for more about this stitch), but if the directions specify 2 x 2 rib or garter stitch, you must knit your swatch in that stitch pattern instead.

Whenever you make a swatch in stockinette stitch or some other stitch pattern that tends to roll, always knit the first and last 3 stitches of every row (even the purl rows) to create a garter stitch border. This makes measuring your swatch easier. Make sure you cast on a few extra stitches to accommodate this border, and measure the gauge between the borders.

4. **Knit until the swatch measures 6 inches long and then bind off (see the appendix for more about binding off).**

If you can tell after a couple of inches of knitting that your gauge is off (see the next section for the scoop on measuring your swatch), knit 1 wrong-side row to create a division between sections, change needle sizes, and continue knitting. You still need to knit a full-size swatch with the new needles, but you won't have to cast on again and start over.

5. **If you want your swatch to be as accurate as possible, take the added step of washing your swatch (or at least getting it damp) and allowing it to dry.**

This step helps you figure out what your knit will look like after it's washed. Some yarns don't change much, but others can grow or shrink enough to make a difference. You wouldn't want your sweater to fit only until you wash it and then find that it's grown to an unflattering size! Check the ball band for information about how you should wash your swatch.

## Measuring your swatch

After you've made a swatch, it's time to measure it. To do so, you need a ruler or gauge measurement tool (like the one shown in Figure 2-2) and a couple of straight pins. It's important to make your swatch large enough (as I explain in the previous section) and to take it off the needles before you measure; the cast-on, the bind-off, or having the stitches still on the needle can skew your measurements and give you inaccurate results.

To measure your gauge from your swatch, follow these instructions:

1. **Lay your swatch flat on the table.**

Measuring on your knee or haphazardly in midair will throw off your numbers.

2. **Place one straight pin vertically between two columns of stitches as shown in Figure 2-3.**

Don't work too close to any of the edges, where the stitches may be more uneven.

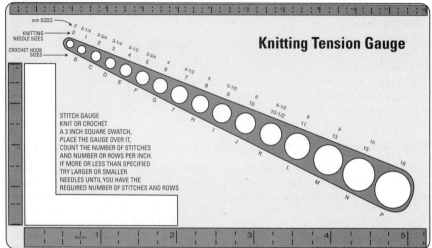

**Figure 2-2:** A handy device for checking gauge and needle size.

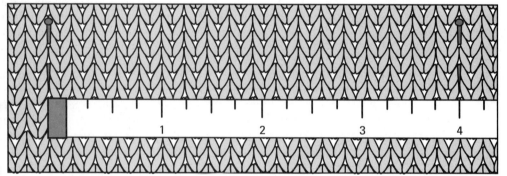

**Figure 2-3:** Measuring your gauge.

3. **Placing your ruler or gauge measurement tool parallel to a single row of stitches (at the bottom of the Vs), measure over 4 inches and place a second pin.**

Pick up the ruler and put it down again to see if you still have 4 inches in between your pins. Many times, simply pushing the ruler down bends the fabric out of shape. You want to avoid this.

4. **Count each stitch or V between the pins and write down the number.**

Include any fractions of a stitch, and count again to make sure you have it right. Sometimes it's helpful to use a pointer, like a spare double-pointed needle, to place on each stitch as you count.

5. **When you're satisfied that you've measured accurately, place your pins 4 inches apart at a different spot on your swatch and count again.**

Are the numbers the same? If not, try a third spot and see what the results are. If the numbers vary a little, use the average of your measurements as your stitch gauge per 4 inches.

6. **Repeat Steps 1 through 5 to measure your row gauge, this time placing your pins 4 inches apart horizontally and counting the number of rows in a single column of stitches.**

When you're finished measuring, compare the numbers you've written down to the gauge listed in the pattern. What counts as "matching" when it comes to gauge? When is "close" close enough? In the earlier section "Switching needles if your gauge is off," I explain how the difference between 4 stitches per inch and 5 stitches per inch was equivalent to 9 inches or *two whole sizes* in a sweater, so, obviously, fractions count!

Gauge is normally given as a whole number per 4 inches. Gauge is reckoned to the nearest stitch per 4 inches, which translates to a quarter stitch per inch. So 4.4 stitches per inch is close enough to be considered correct for a gauge of 18 stitches per 4 inches (which boils down to 4.5 stitches per inch), but 4.2 stitches is not. If your swatch tells you that you're off by more than a quarter of a stitch per inch, you haven't found the right needles yet! Change your needles and start the swatching process over again until you get the right numbers.

## Practicing different gauges in a single swatch

In this section, I show you a good way to practice getting your gauge on target. This gauge practice won't really create any sort of useful or decorative object, but you can either keep the swatch as a reminder or rip it out and reuse the yarn when you're done. If you don't like those two options, make two or three of these swatches into a weird scarf. Or collect them from all your friends and make them into an artful quilt. Whatever you come up with, the process of making this swatch will be well worth your while.

The following statement is something that's said only when you have to rip out half a sweater or reknit the sleeve (or something equally dreadful), but it's still true and worth remembering: "Knitting is as much about the process as it is about the product." Even something boring or goofy can be a pleasure to knit, simply because knitting is pleasant.

Okay, enough talk; it's time to get started on the practice activity! Grab some yarn and needles in several sizes. You can do this with any yarn you have handy, but the numbers I use are based on worsted weight yarn (see Chapter 1 for more about this type of yarn). The manufacturer's yarn label suggests knitting on US 7 (4.5 mm) needles to get a gauge of 20 stitches and 28 rows per 4 inches in stockinette stitch.

Follow these steps to practice assessing your gauge:

1. **Cast on 30 stitches with US 4 (3.5 mm) needles, and then knit 6 rows in garter stitch to prevent the edge from rolling.**

   Remember, always knit the first and last 3 stitches of every row (even the purl rows) if you're working in stockinette stitch or some other stitch pattern that tends to roll at the edges. This creates a narrow garter stitch border and makes measuring easier.

2. **Work 4 inches in stockinette stitch (or the stitch pattern that your pattern calls for).**

3. **Knit 1 wrong-side row to create a division between sections.**

4. **Switch to needles one size larger — US 5 (3.75 mm) needles — and then work 4 more inches in your stitch pattern.**

5. **Make another dividing line and switch to US 6 (4 mm) needles, and then work 4 more inches.**

6. **Continue making 4-inch sections, moving up one needle size each time, going up all the way to US 13 (or larger, if you can stand it).**

7. **Finish your sampler by working 6 rows in garter stitch and then binding off.**

As you work this piece, the one thing you'll notice right away is that one end of your swatch is much wider than the other. What you're seeing is the difference that gauge can make. Measure your stitch gauge for each section (I explain how to do so earlier in this chapter). Chances are a couple of your sections will be good contenders for matching the suggested stitch gauge for the yarn that you're working with. To decide between these needle sizes, measure your row gauge in these sections and choose the one that most closely matches the specified row gauge.

# Checking Your Gauge throughout a Project

The previous section walks you through the elements of making and measuring a gauge swatch. In truth, however, you need to be mindful of your gauge throughout the entire knitting process (at least on projects that are supposed to fit a certain way). In the following sections, I show you when and how to check your gauge throughout a project.

For something that doesn't need to fit exactly, like a scarf or a wrap, you don't need to be nearly as fastidious. If it looks good to you, you don't need to fret about the numbers.

## When to check your gauge

After you've cast on and knit a couple of inches of your project, measure your gauge again to see how it's going (see the next section for the how-to). If you made and measured your swatch a month ago or even a week ago, things may have changed. Your mood, level of alertness, or the fact that you've been knitting more or less often can all affect your knitting tension. Or maybe you swatched on straight wooden needles and now you're knitting with metal circular needles. The material a needle is made of can make a big difference to your gauge.

Check your gauge from time to time as you work on your project, particularly if you have put it aside for a while and have just recently come back to it. If you get in the habit of checking your gauge when you have a tape measure out to determine the length of your knitting, it won't seem like any extra work.

After you verify that you're on the right track with your gauge, you can continue knitting with confidence. It's much easier to rip out a few inches than it is to rip out the whole back when you discover that your gauge is off. And knitters, like everyone else, are often loath to admit their mistakes. If you have a gnawing sense that something isn't quite right, force yourself to do the necessary reality check and measure things. The sooner you correct an error, the better.

## How to check your gauge

To check gauge during a project, many knitters like to use a *gauge measurement tool*. This tool has holes to size up needles and a small window that's 2 inches wide and 2 inches tall (refer to Figure 2-2). To use the gauge measurement tool, lay your knitting flat and, without pressing it down so vigorously that you distort the stitches, lay your gauge meter on top and count how many stitches there are across the window. Don't forget that you have to double the number of stitches to determine the number of stitches per 4 inches.

You can also use a tape measure or ruler to help you count the number of stitches per 4 inches. I have a lightweight clear plastic ruler that works nicely.

Whatever tool you're using, be sure that your knitting is flat on a table and that your measuring device is lying parallel to your rows of stitches.

You might grab a current project or a few knits from the closet (whether they're hand-knit or store-bought) and take a few minutes to practice measuring gauge. Try measuring in different places, over different stitch patterns (like stockinette stitch or ribbing), or even with different tools to get comfortable with taking these measurements.

# Examining the Drapes of Different Gauges

The patterns in this book (and knitting patterns in general) specify a certain yarn and a certain gauge. When you use the yarn suggested by the designer, you're pretty much set because she or he has done most of the behind-the-scenes work for you. But sometimes you won't be able to easily find the yarn called for. And other times you may want to knit with another fiber or use up some yarn that you already have. You can and should experiment — this is how you create things that are unique and exactly what you want.

The gauge on the yarn label is a typical gauge for that yarn. But remember, that number is just someone's opinion, not the gospel truth! So, if you find that you prefer the fabric that the yarn makes when it's knit looser or tighter, that's okay. You should also remember that the listed gauge is also based on certain assumptions about what you'll be knitting. The manufacturer doesn't know whether you're knitting a sock or a stole. A mitten that's meant to keep out snow will require a denser fabric and a tighter gauge than a lacy scarf. So, it's worth exploring gauge not just in absolute numbers, but in terms of the "hand" or "drape" of the fabric that you're making (how the fabric feels or where it falls on a continuum from stiff to floppy). This way you can choose the right yarn and the right gauge for what *you* want to make.

To get a handle on gauge and drape, get out the gauge sampler that you made in the earlier section "Practicing different gauges in a single swatch." Or, at the very least, grab an armful of knitted objects and have a close look at them while keeping the following considerations about drape and gauge in mind:

- ✓ **You'll notice that on the smallest needles, the fabric is very dense.** Maybe you've knit 23 stitches and 32 rows per 4 inches with worsted weight yarn. Hold the fabric in your hand and notice that it's quite stiff. You can't see through it at all, and it doesn't follow the shape of your hand. For almost any purpose, this gauge is just too tight. I call this a bulletproof fabric. It may be okay for a mitten or a purse that's meant to hold its shape, but I bet you also noticed that it wasn't much fun to knit. Just because it's possible to knit this tight doesn't mean that you should. If you want something this dense, try felting instead. (Find out how to felt in the appendix; or try out the potholders in Chapter 9 for a quick introduction to this fun technique.)

  If you're trying to substitute yarns and the fabric that you make ends up in the bulletproof category when knit at the gauge called for in the pattern, it isn't the right yarn for the job. In this case, you need to find a thinner yarn for the project.

- ✓ **When moving up in gauge to somewhere between 21 and 22 stitches per 4 inches, your fabric is still pretty dense, but it moves a little more readily.** With this sort of fabric, you probably would knit something like a mitten, or maybe a structured hat or a cushion cover. The piece won't be floppy at all and will insist on keeping its own shape rather than following the lines of the body. Most projects will be more pleasing if they're knit at a looser gauge than this. A sweater won't look its best if it's knit too tightly.

- ✓ **When you get to the gauge recommended for the yarn (20 stitches per 4 inches in the gauge sampler), you've hit your happy medium.** You'll notice that you can see a bit of light through it when you hold it up. And when you put it on your hand, it moves to follow the shape of your hand, but it isn't see-through. This fabric is perfect for things like sweaters because even though you want the fabric to drape on your body, you also don't want your skin to show through.

- ✓ **At a gauge somewhere between 16 and 18 stitches per 4 inches, you'll definitely be able to see light through the swatch and maybe even some skin.** The fabric drapes easily. Many accessories that are meant to be less structured and show some movement, such as a scarf, poncho, or wrap, are great when knit at this gauge.

✔ **With larger needles still, the stitches are very large.** In this case, the knitted fabric is as much about the light and air between the stitches as it is about the yarn that surrounds these holes. This very open gauge is what you want for something like the multiyarn stole in Chapter 8 or the lacy shawl in Chapter 12.

Whatever type of garment you're making, think a bit about what sort of drape and fabric suits it best when determining whether your gauge is right on target. Any yarn can be knit at a variety of gauges, as the gauge sampler demonstrates. But getting gauge right also means making a more subjective judgment about whether you like the fabric you've knit and whether you think that it's right for the project that you want to make. Chapter 1 has full details on selecting the right yarn for any project at any gauge.

# Chapter 3

# Do You Measure Up? Size Matters

- - - - - - - - - - - - - - - - - - - - - - - - - - - - - - - - - - - - - - - - - - - - - - - - - - - - - - -

## In This Chapter

▶ Understanding pattern sizing

▶ Measuring yourself properly

▶ Picking the right fit

- - - - - - - - - - - - - - - - - - - - - - - - - - - - - - - - - - - - - - - - - - - - - - - - - - - - - - -

*I*f you've ever bought clothes based on the size marked on the label alone only to find out that they didn't fit properly, you know that one designer's medium isn't the same as another's. With off-the-rack clothing, you can always run back to the mall and exchange your purchase for a different size. But if you've spent $100 on yarn and two months' worth of free time on a sweater, it's heartbreaking to discover that you've knit the wrong size. So take the time to figure out which size to knit on every project you make. I confess that pattern designers don't always make sizing easy, so do read through this chapter and take it to heart. In this chapter, I explain the sizing information that you might find in a given pattern and show you the way to measure yourself properly. To wrap up, I explain how to put together your measurements and consider factors such as ease so you can select the best size.

Some knitters don't want to be bothered with the extra steps in this chapter; they just want to knit, and who can blame them? But take heed: Figure out what size you are and what size you need. Even if this figuring takes you all night (and really it'll take about five minutes), you'll still be way ahead of the game because your sweater will fit you when it's done. And after you know your measurements, it'll be that much easier the next time. The phrase "Take time to save time" may sound cliché, but just like doing a proper gauge swatch (see Chapter 2 for more information on this topic), a little prep work on sizing before you grab the needles can save you a lot of heartache.

## Deciphering a Pattern's Size Information

Knitting patterns are famously bad for inconsistent sizing. Patterns from different designers, countries, or eras can vary significantly in what measurements are considered a small. A woman with a 36-inch chest may be considered a small by some designers, a medium by others, and even sometimes a large! Believe it or not, even patterns within one book or magazine may not have standardized sizes.

So, you absolutely must read the fine print on the pattern to know what size to knit. For instance, at the beginning of a pattern, you can almost always find some note about sizes. The least helpful note is "One size fits all." If it's a scarf, that's fine. If it's a garment, however, take time to figure out what its final dimensions will be. If you're petite and the one size is 60 inches around, it can't possibly fit you!

In the following sections, I explain the types of sizing information that you can expect to find in a pattern, and I go over the standard sizes from the Craft Yarn Council of America that I use in this book.

## The kinds of size information in a pattern

Most garment patterns have some sort of small/medium/large sizing. In addition to that method of sizing, most patterns also give you the garment's finished chest circumference. Note that this measurement is the finished size of the garment though, not your actual chest measurement; there's usually a difference between these two numbers, as you find out in the later section about ease.

Some patterns also helpfully tell you that a medium fits a 38- to 40-inch chest. If this is the case, you don't have to do much work because if you know your chest measurement, you know exactly what size to make for the garment to fit as the designer intended.

If you can't find sizing information up front in the pattern, go to the schematic. *Schematics* are illustrations that give you detailed information on the measurements of the garment for each size. By looking at these illustrations, you can figure out, among other things, the garment's chest size and arm length. The numbers given for each measurement in a schematic correspond to the sizes covered by the pattern, with the smallest size first and the largest size last, just as they are in the pattern directions. Remember that unless it's indicated otherwise, schematics give flat measurements, so you need to multiply the width of the front by two to get the garment's chest circumference.

You may want to flip through this book, choose a pattern that appeals to you at this point, and have a look at the schematic. The first number to look at is the total chest circumference in the size that you think is right for you. Grab a tape measure and a sweater you like and compare the chest circumference in the schematic to the chest circumference of the sweater. While you're at it, compare the lengths of things like the sleeve or the distance from the hem to the beginning of the underarm shaping. This exercise shows you how to use a schematic to assess the fit of a garment in a pattern and choose the correct size.

If you have only the finished chest circumference of a garment, you must take ease into account. *Ease* is the amount of room between you and your clothes. In other words, unless the garment is meant to be very close-fitting, you don't want to knit it exactly to your bust size. Take a couple of minutes to read about ease later in this chapter before you start knitting.

## The sizing conventions in this book

The patterns in this book are based on sizing standards set up by the Craft Yarn Council of America to help minimize the confusion of pattern sizing. I use the same size standards throughout this book, so a large size, for instance, is always designed to fit someone with a 40- to 42-inch chest circumference. This book features patterns sized for everyone from XS to 3X. Not every pattern has every size, but knitters of all body types will find patterns to suit them. And while it's always smart to double-check that the size you're knitting is right for you, for the most part, you'll find that a small is a small across the board.

Table 3-1 shows the standardized women's sizes (in inches) from the Craft Yarn Council of America. The elements sized are the following (see the next section for more details on these areas):

✔ **Bust:** The measurement around the fullest part of your chest

✔ **Cross back:** The measurement between your shoulders

✔ **Back waist length:** The measurement from the base of the neck to your waist

✔ **Sleeve length to underarm:** The measurement from your wrist to your underarm

| Table 3-1 | Standardized Women's Sizes | | | | | | |
|---|---|---|---|---|---|---|---|
| | **XS** | **S** | **M** | **L** | **1X** | **2X** | **3x** |
| Bust | 28–30 | 32–34 | 36–38 | 40–42 | 44–46 | 48–50 | 52–54 |
| Cross back | 14 | 15 | 16.5 | 17.5 | 17.5 | 18 | 18.5 |
| Back waist length | 16.5 | 17 | 17.25 | 17.5 | 17.75 | 18 | 18.5 |
| Sleeve length to underarm | 16.5 | 17 | 17 | 17.5 | 17.5 | 18 | 18.5 |

The Craft Yarn Council of America also has standardized sizes for men, children, and babies. For tables and additional information, head to www.yarnstandards.com.

# Measuring Yourself

Figure 3-1 shows the parts of the body that you need to measure before you start knitting a new garment. When you measure, follow these guidelines:

- Use a cloth or plastic tape measure; if yours looks worn and stretched out, spring for a new one. A stretched-out tape measure won't give you an accurate measurement.

- Strip down to your skivvies, or at least wear something close fitting. Measurements taken over a winter parka won't be accurate!

- For all horizontal measurements, try to keep the tape measure untwisted and parallel to the ground. Hold the tape measure snug to the body, but don't cinch it in.

- For all vertical measurements, keep the tape measure perpendicular to the ground. Hold the tape measure close to your body and let it follow your curves, just as the finished garment will.

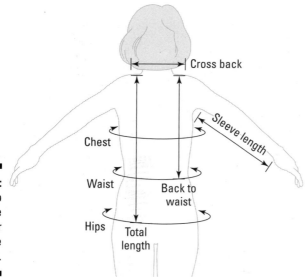

**Figure 3-1:** How to measure yourself (or someone else).

How do you measure yourself accurately? You can't! You really need a friend to help you do this right. You can do pretty well with your bust, waist, and hip measurements, but just try measuring yourself from armpit to wrist or shoulder to shoulder! Find someone to help you measure honestly and accurately.

Here are some specific guidelines for measuring each area in Figure 3-1:

- ✔ **Chest:** Measure around the fullest part of the chest. Remember, this measurement isn't the same number as your bra size!

- ✔ **Waist:** Measure around the tummy at the narrowest point, which usually is even with the belly button. Don't hold your breath or suck in your gut (as much as you may want to!).

- ✔ **Hips:** Measure around the hips at the widest point.

- ✔ **Cross back:** This is the measurement from shoulder to shoulder. Often the cross back measurement is taken incorrectly across the full breadth of the shoulders including the arms. Instead, you want to measure from the shoulder joint where your arm bends (not from the edge of your arm).

- ✔ **Sleeve length to underarm:** In knitting, the critical length of the sleeve is from the wrist to the underarm. The cap of the sleeve can be shaped in a variety of ways, so measure from the underarm to the wrist.

- ✔ **Back waist length:** Measure from the nape of the neck to the waist. It's helpful to measure your front waist length, too. If you have a curvaceous figure, there can be a big difference between the distance from the neck to the waist in the front and in the back.

- ✔ **Total length:** Measure from the top of the shoulder to where you want the garment to end, perhaps at the hip. It may be easier to take this measurement from a finished garment. See the section "Trying the 'favorite sweater' technique if you're still unsure about size" later in this chapter for more information.

Two other helpful measurements include foot length and head circumference:

- ✔ **Foot length:** Put a ruler on the floor and stand on it with your heel at the zero end of the ruler. Note the number even with your longest toe. Make this measurement without shoes on, of course.

- ✔ **Head circumference:** Hold a tape measure snug around the head just above the ears.

Fill in your measurements in the table on the Cheat Sheet so that you always have them ready. I include a couple of extra columns in case you knit items for your loved ones; this way, you always have their measurements handy. And remember to update the numbers from time to time, particularly if your weight has changed.

# Knowing What Size You Should Knit

Compare the numbers you've written down in Table 3-2 to the numbers given for the Craft Yarn Council of America standard sizes in Table 3-1. Do you fit exactly into one of the standard size categories? Probably not. No worries, though; in the following sections, I give you guidelines for determining the size you should knit.

## Focusing on essential fit considerations

In knitting, the chest measurement is the most critical measurement, so that's the number you should focus on. However, if your hips are wider than your chest, take that number into consideration when choosing your size. For a garment that ends at the waist, stick with the chest measurement. For a garment that falls below the hips, such as a coat, you might consider knitting a larger size. If you can't decide what size is right, try out the "favorite sweater" technique that I describe later in this chapter.

If your arms are longer or your waist is shorter than the measurements given in the table, lengthen your sleeves or make the body of your sweater a bit shorter before you begin the armhole shaping to get a perfect fit.

## Factoring in ease

Even though patterns are written for a person with a certain chest size, you'll notice that there's a lot of variability in the size of the actual finished garment — even for things that are the "same size." At first, this may seem confusing, and it can lead people to knit their garments in the wrong sizes. But the variability has to do with what designers call *ease,* or the amount of space between you and your garment. Consider these ease facts:

- ✔ Standard ease is 2 to 4 inches. This means that if your chest measures 40 inches, your garment would measure 42 to 44 inches (that's the chest circumference) for a standard fit.
- ✔ A loose fit can measure 6 inches or more over the body measurement.
- ✔ Something that's meant to fit tightly may be the same as your body measurement or even smaller, which is called *negative ease.* Something with negative ease has to stretch to fit you and will be very form fitting.

Generally, thinner yarns need less ease than bulky yarns — think of the fit of a fitted T-shirt versus a big, bulky sweater. Here's a tip if you're unsure of how much ease to incorporate: Look at the photograph of the finished garment that you want to knit and see how it fits the model. Is it tight? Loose? Close to the body? Billowing? By looking at the finished garment, you should be able to decide how much ease you need. Add that ease number to your chest measurement from Table 3-2, and then choose the finished size that most closely matches that total chest circumference.

## Trying the "favorite sweater" technique if you're still unsure about size

If you still aren't sure what size to knit, try measuring a favorite sweater. You can skip measuring yourself entirely (if you really insist), or you can use this technique in combination with your body measurements to get a good idea of what size fits you best.

Choose something from your closet that fits you well and is of a similar weight and style to what you're planning to knit. It doesn't have to be a handknit — even a sweatshirt can give you useful information. If you're knitting a cardigan, choose a cardigan; if you're knitting a bulky turtleneck, choose a bulky turtleneck. The more of your favorite items you measure, the more complete and accurate your sense of fit will be.

Take an hour some day to sketch and measure all of your favorite sweaters, and then keep these schematics handy in your knitting notebook. This way, when you're ready to choose a new project, you'll have a clear idea of what range of measurements will fit you. In addition to helping you understand your size, measuring all your favorite sweaters can also tell you something about what styles suit you. If your pile of sweaters trends toward V-necks, raglan sleeves, and lightweight yarns, there's probably a reason. In other words, before you knit a bulky, drop-shouldered turtleneck, go try one on!

To measure your favorite sweater, lay it out flat and follow these guidelines (check out Figure 3-2 to see the proper places to measure):

- **Width at chest (A):** Measure across the sweater, just below the underarm. If the sweater is a cardigan, close it before you measure.

- **Width at waist and hip (B and C):** You should note these measurements if the sweater has any shaping.

- **Sleeve length (D):** Measure from the cuff to the underarm.

- **Armhole depth (E):** Holding your tape measure perpendicular to the line of the chest, measure from the bottom of the armhole to the shoulder.

- **Total length (F):** Measure from the shoulder to the bottom of the sweater. Note that most clothing has shoulder shaping, so the outside of the shoulder is lower than the neck. Measure to the shoulder (rather than all the way to the top) and compare this number to the length of the knitted sweater before you begin the shoulder shaping. The difference usually is subtle, but some people are particular about such things.

Make sure you write down the measurements from your favorite sweater. Jot them in on Figure 3-2 (or make a photocopy of Figure 3-2 and write on it). If you prefer, make a quick stick-figure sketch or scale drawing on graph paper to keep in your knitting bag.

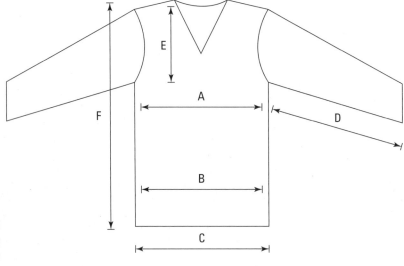

**Figure 3-2:**
What to measure on your favorite sweater.

A. Width at chest    D. Sleeve length
B. Width at waist    E. Armhole depth
C. Width at hip      F. Total length

When you know the measurements of the clothes that you like to wear, you can compare them to the garment specifics given in a pattern's schematics. This comparison, coupled with a more accurate picture of what size you are (based on this book's sizing standards) will help you create with confidence garments that fit.

# Chapter 4

# Break the Code: Reading Patterns

As you know, knitting is made up of stitches, rows, decreases, and increases. You can make it all up as you go along, of course, but if you want to repeat someone else's work, you either have to be by her side the whole time (which might be okay if that knitter is your mom) or you have to come up with a way of translating the knitting onto paper. Just as a composer must write notes on a staff so that someone else can play his music, a designer must describe her work in a way that others can understand and imitate.

So, over the centuries, knitters have developed their own system of writing down knitting instructions in patterns. Most knitting patterns follow a certain set of conventions regarding how things are organized. They also share a unique vocabulary, a set of abbreviations, and even a specialized notation system called *symbolcraft*.

The ability to read knitting patterns fluently won't happen overnight. But knowing what to expect definitely helps. In this chapter, I explain the various abbreviations and symbols that you'll encounter in knitting, and I also describe all the parts of a knitting pattern and how to assess them before you start knitting.

## Deciphering Knitroglyphics

Knitting patterns can be written out in complete sentences, they can be written very concisely with lots of abbreviations, or they can be represented in a chart. You'll encounter all of these styles as you move from knitting pattern to knitting pattern. Read through the following sections so that you know what to expect from knitting patterns written in these various styles.

### Understanding common terms and abbreviations

Especially for new knitters, knitting patterns can seem like they're written in a foreign language. They're made up of lots of abbreviations, strange grammar, and words you may have never heard before. In the end, however, you'll probably only encounter a handful (or a couple of handfuls) of abbreviations regularly. Knitting language really has a small vocabulary (and no future imperfect tense to grasp!), so if you get a handle on the following common terms and abbreviations and what they mean, you can always look up the rest. Most places that you find knitting patterns, such as knitting magazines, books, and Web sites, you also find a glossary. Look for it if you're stuck! Also remember that the way that patterns are written differs among different resources. Some patterns use all the abbreviations in Table 4-1; others use only a few abbreviations and more everyday language.

| Table 4-1 | Common Knitting Abbreviations | | |
|---|---|---|---|
| *Abbreviation* | *Translation* | *Abbreviation* | *Translation* |
| alt | alternate | as set | continue knitting, following any regularly repeating pattern you've begun |
| beg | begin(ning) | BO | bind off (cast off) |
| cab | cable | CC | contrasting color |
| cm | centimeters | cn | cable needle |
| CO | cast on | cont | continue(ing) |
| dec | decrease(ing) | dpn(s) | double-pointed needle(s) |
| EOR | every other row | foll | following |
| g | grams | inc | increase(ing) |
| k | knit | k tbl | knit through back of loop |
| k2tog | knit two together (a decrease) | kfb | knit into front and back of stitch (an increase) |
| knitwise | as if to knit | LT | left twist |
| m | meter(s) | m1 | make 1 stitch (an increase) |
| MC | main color | meas | measures |
| mm | millimeters | mult | multiple |
| oz | ounces | p | purl |
| p2tog | purl two together (a decrease) | patt(s) | pattern(s) |
| pfb | purl into front and back of stitch (an increase) | pm | place marker |
| psso | pass slipped stitch(es) over | purlwise | as if to purl |
| rem | remaining | rep | repeat |
| rev St st | reverse stockinette stitch | rnd(s) | round(s) |
| RS | right (public) side(s) | RT | right twist |
| sc | single crochet | skp | slip 1, knit 1, pass the slipped stitch over (a decrease) |
| s2kp | slip 2 stitches together knitwise, knit 1, pass the 2 slipped stitches over (a double decrease) | sk2p | slip 1 stitch knitwise, knit 2 stitches together, pass the slipped stitch over (a double decrease) |
| sl | slip | sl st | slip stitch |

| Abbreviation | Translation | Abbreviation | Translation |
|---|---|---|---|
| ssk | slip 2 stitches, one at a time, as if to knit, then knit those 2 stitches together (a decrease) | st(s) | stitch(es) |
| St st | stockinette stitch | tbl | through back loop(s) |
| tog | together | w&t | wrap and turn (used for short rows; see Chapter 12) |
| work even | work without increasing or decreasing | WS | wrong (non-public) side(s) |
| wyib | with yarn in back | wyif | with yarn in front |
| x | times (for example, "12 x" means "12 times") | yd(s) | yard(s) |
| yo | yarn over (an increase) | * * | repeat directions between * * as many times as indicated |
| [ ] | repeat directions in brackets the number of times specified | | |

So how do you interpret a pattern that uses abbreviations? Here's an example. A bit of a knitting pattern might read like this:

> CO 21 (31, 41) sts. Work in garter st for 6 rows. Switch to St st and inc 1 st at each end EOR 6 (7, 8) x. Work even until piece meas 6". BO rem sts.

Before you continue reading, you might take a minute or two to translate this sample using the terms and abbreviations in Table 4-1, and then you can read through my translation. In plain English, this bit of pattern text says:

> Cast on 21 stitches for the smallest size, (31 stitches for medium size, 41 stitches for the largest size). Work in garter stitch (knit all rows) for 6 rows. Switch to stockinette stitch (knit right-side rows, purl wrong-side rows) and increase 1 stitch at each end of every other row 6 times for small (7 times for medium, 8 times for large). Work without increasing or decreasing until the piece measures 6 inches. Bind off remaining stitches.

In knitting patterns, numbers for the various sizes covered in the pattern are given with the smallest size first and the other sizes following in parentheses and separated by commas like this: 21 (31, 41) stitches. If you're knitting the second size, you may want to circle the second number in each set to help you stay on track.

You may be wondering why knitting patterns use so many abbreviations. In short, the person writing the pattern is trying to economize on space because printing is expensive, and knitters would rather have more patterns, even if they have to practice deciphering the code a bit to get used to it.

If you struggle to read knitting patterns, before you pick up the needles, write the instructions out on paper in words that *you* understand.

## Following a repeating pattern

Many knitting patterns have a stitch pattern that's repeated. So, in addition to directions like "Cast on 24 stitches" or "Work until your piece measures 12 inches," you may have directions that repeat over a set number of stitches in a row (using asterisks to show you what to repeat) and over a set number of rows (the pattern will tell you which rows to repeat, such as "Repeat Rows 1–6 until the piece measures 12 inches.").

To use such directions, work Row 1 as described, repeating whatever comes between the two asterisks until you get to the end of the row. For instance, if Row 1 says "*K2, p4, k2, repeat from * to end," you knit 2 stitches, purl 4 stitches, and knit 2 stitches, and then repeat the whole sequence (because the asterisk is before the first k2) until you reach the end of the row. From there, you move on from Row 1 and work Row 2 as described. When you get though all the rows of the pattern, you simply go back to Row 1 and work through all the rows again.

Note that, often, the knitting in different rows is the same. So the directions may say "Rows 1, 3, and 5: *K2, p4, k2, repeat from * to end." Just remember what row you're on and find its row number in the directions.

If you have trouble remembering your row, or if you're knitting somewhere with lots of distractions, it helps to use a tool to remind you of what row you're on. You can either make a tally mark on a scrap of paper at the end of each row or you can make a small investment in a row counter. A couple of different styles of row counters are available; some you can attach to your knitting needles and some you just keep at your side. In any case, remember to advance the counter at the end of each row. When you get to the end of the pattern repeat, reset the counter and start again.

## Reading charts and symbolcraft

While many patterns are written out in what is, more or less, English, another approach to conveying the necessary information for all or part of a pattern is to represent it as a chart where each box is equal to one stitch. With this approach, you can map out an entire sweater graphically and not have to use any words at all. For complex color patterns you may show the whole sweater in a chart, but more often only significant parts of a pattern are mapped out on the chart. In this case, the chart is used alongside the written directions. Charts are most often used for things like lace or ornate color work, which are much more difficult to understand when presented only as text.

The funny little slashes, Vs, and circles used in these charts are known as *symbolcraft*. You can see some typical symbols and what they mean in Figure 4-1. But do remember that designers use different fonts, so the symbols aren't always exactly the same (but they should be similar enough that you can recognize them). Every chart you work with, however, should provide a key that explains the symbols used in the chart.

Sometimes there's a darkened box in a knitting chart. This box stands for "no stitch" and means that you should simply pretend that the box isn't there at all and move on to the next one. The "no stitch" boxes are there as placeholders to account for stitches that are increased or decreased elsewhere in the pattern.

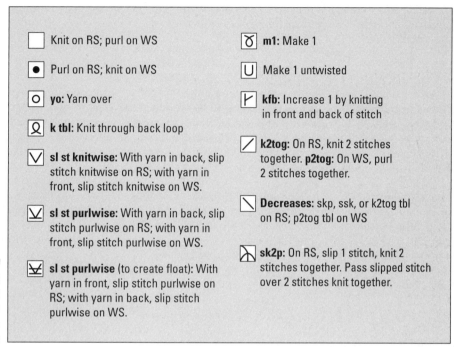

| | | | |
|---|---|---|---|
| ☐ Knit on RS; purl on WS | | ⌀ **m1:** Make 1 | |
| ● Purl on RS; knit on WS | | U Make 1 untwisted | |
| O **yo:** Yarn over | | | **kfb:** Increase 1 by knitting in front and back of stitch |
| Ω **k tbl:** Knit through back loop | | / | **k2tog:** On RS, knit 2 stitches together. **p2tog:** On WS, purl 2 stitches together. |
| V **sl st knitwise:** With yarn in back, slip stitch knitwise on RS; with yarn in front, slip stitch knitwise on WS. | | \ | **Decreases:** skp, ssk, or k2tog tbl on RS; p2tog tbl on WS |
| Ⅴ **sl st purlwise:** With yarn in back, slip stitch purlwise on RS; with yarn in front, slip stitch purlwise on WS. | | ⋉ | **sk2p:** On RS, slip 1 stitch, knit 2 stitches together. Pass slipped stitch over 2 stitches knit together. |
| Ⅴ **sl st purlwise** (to create float): With yarn in front, slip stitch purlwise on RS; with yarn in back, slip stitch purlwise on WS. | | | |

**Figure 4-1:** Symbolcraft — knitting's secret code.

When you read a knitting chart, know that the chart will always show the public side of the work, so the same symbol is read differently on right-side and wrong-side rows. For instance, the symbol that stands for "knit" on right-side rows stands for "purl" on wrong-side rows (since a purl worked on the wrong-side is the same as a knit from the right-side). Follow these general steps to make your way through a chart:

1. **When working a right-side row, start reading the row at the bottom right corner and work your way across to the left, exactly as you knit.**

   The first box is the first stitch that you work; the second box is the next stitch you work; and so on down the line. When you finish your first row, you turn your knitting around so that you're looking at the wrong side.

2. **On the next row (assuming that you're knitting back and forth rather than knitting in the round, which I cover in Chapter 11), you need to read the chart the opposite way (left to right).**

   The chart shows the right side, but because you're on the wrong side, you do the opposite. For instance, if you see a knit symbol, you should actually purl. The good news is that wrong-side rows tend to be the easier ones. So, you won't have to flip much around in your head.

   Some charts don't show the wrong-side rows. If your chart only shows Rows 1, 3, 5, 7, and so on, look carefully at the written directions to find out how to work the wrong-side rows. In many lace patterns, for instance, the wrong-side rows are just purled, so it's unnecessary to show them on the chart.

3. **Follow the chart for as many rows as needed until you finish your piece.**

   Refer to the written directions in the pattern to find out when to start and stop following the chart. You may need to repeat the charted pattern more than once.

In the following sections, I walk you through the process of reading three specific types of knitting charts: cable, lace, and color.

## Cable charts

Cable patterns are usually represented in chart form. Common cables include four-stitch left and right cables and six-stitch left and right cables; other types of cables, such as horseshoe cables, build on these basics (see Chapter 6 for cable details).

Typical cable charts show the background stitches for the cable, how many stitches are involved in the cable, how frequently you turn the cables, and in which direction to turn them. Looking at Figure 4-2, you can see that there are 8 stitches involved in the horseshoe cable in the center of the chart flanked by columns of purl stitches on either side. The horseshoe cable is made up of a left-twisting four-stitch cable directly next to a right-twisting four-stitch cable.

The first 2 rows in Figure 4-2 are simply knits (the empty boxes) and purls (the boxes with black dots). The third row is the turning row (and it's a right-side row). To work this third row, follow these steps, as shown in the chart:

1. **Purl 3 stitches (represented by the three black dots).**

2. **Work a four-stitch left cable.**

   A charted left cable is always drawn as a slanted line from the bottom right corner to the top left corner. To work a left cable, hold the cable needle in the front.

3. **The next 4 stitches in Row 3 make a four-stitch right cable.**

   A charted right cable is always drawn as a slanted line from the top right corner to the bottom left corner. To work a right cable, hold the cable needle in the back.

4. **Finish up your cable row by purling the last 3 stitches, as shown in Figure 4-2.**

The next 3 rows are again just knits and purls, and then you repeat the turning row in Row 7. The pattern concludes in Row 8 with more knits and purls.

**Figure 4-2:**
A cable pattern presented in chart form.

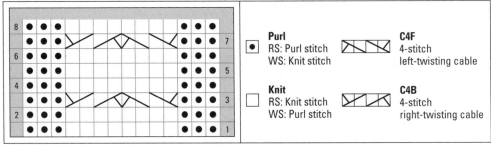

## Lace charts

Lace patterns are often easier to read as charts. Even though they don't look exactly like the knitted piece, if you squint hard enough, you should be able to see the basic structure of the lace in the chart. A written description of what to do in terms of knits, yarn overs, and ssk's doesn't readily give you the same picture in your head (though, of course, following the written directions will give you the same result). After you're comfortable reading lace charts, you'll likely find it quicker and easier to knit lace from a chart than from written instructions.

As you find out in Chapter 6, lace is made up of yarn overs (abbreviated *yo*), which simultaneously form holes and increases, and decreases (typically k2tog and ssk) to make up for all those increases. The lace patterns in this book all feature "plain" wrong-side rows — that is, rows without any decreases or yarn overs.

If you look at Figure 4-3, you'll notice right away that every other row is empty. This means that every wrong-side row is purled — definitely something to look for if you're a beginning lace knitter! On Row 2, you begin with a knit, and then work a right-leaning decrease (k2tog) followed by a yarn over. This increase/decrease unit keeps your stitch count constant. The next stitch is a knit, followed by another lace unit, this one slanting the opposite way (yo, ssk). Most lace is made up of these increase/decrease units, though the yarn overs and their corresponding decreases aren't always right next to each other. Sometimes, as you can see in Rows 4 and 8, you have two increases and a double decrease as a unit. In this case, yo, sk2p, yo. Again, the increases and decreases balance each other out so that your piece maintains its shape.

In lace knitting, it's very important to remember what row you're on. Some lace patterns have stitch counts that vary from row to row, but none of the patterns in this book do this, so your stitch count should always be the same at the end of each row. If it isn't, go back and see if you can spot your mistake. If you have too many stitches, you may have missed a decrease. If you have too few stitches, you likely skipped a yarn over somewhere. If you can't find and fix your mistake, simply unknit the row to one of those plain purl rows and knit the row over.

### Color charts

This book uses two sorts of color charts: Fair Isles and mosaics. Fair Isle, or stranded, knitting patterns use two colors for each row and often use several colors to create a pattern. Mosaics use two colors, but only one at a time and they tend to create very geometric patterns. Check out Chapter 7 for general information about color work.

A color chart will use one symbol to stand for each color. Refer to the key to find out which symbol stands for which color. Typically, color work is done over stockinette stitch, though there are exceptions. In this book, you'll always knit the right-side rows and purl the wrong-side rows as you follow the color chart. Always read through the written directions for the pattern before you dive into the chart; that way you know what comes next.

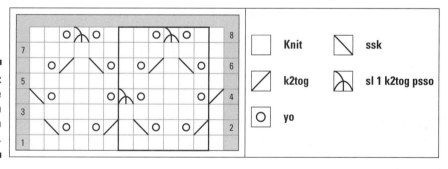

**Figure 4-3:**
A lace pattern presented in chart form.

Figure 4-4 shows a charted color pattern. The outlined box is the pattern repeat (the motif that's worked over and over); the stitches outside the box are worked only at the beginning and end of the row as *selvedge stitches*. These extra stitches help center the pattern on your knitting. This pattern, which is ten rows long, is a four-stitch repeat with 3 extra stitches. As text, the first row would read, "K1 MC, *k1 CC1, k3 MC, repeat from * to the last 2 sts, k1 CC1, k1 MC." Note that on the chart, the even-numbered rows are labeled on the left side to remind you where to start reading them. To work Row 2, you read from left to right and you purl all the stitches because it's a wrong-side row. As text, this row reads, "P2 CC1, *p1 CC1, p1 MC, p2 CC1, repeat from * to last st, p1, CC1."

Continue working through all 10 rows shown on the chart. If the pattern is meant to be repeated, you start again on Row 1. If it's a border or something that's worked only once, carry on with your main color.

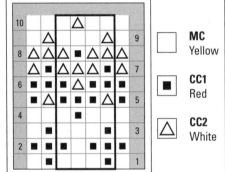

**Figure 4-4:**
A color pattern chart.

MC
Yellow

CC1
Red

CC2
White

# Try Before You Buy! Spot-Checking Patterns

As someone who reads knitting patterns all the time and helps other knitters choose patterns to knit, I can say that not all knitting patterns are perfect. And whether you find a pattern in a book, in a magazine, on the Internet, or scrawled in your grandmother's handwriting, look it over before you start knitting. You should choose a pattern that suits you; and make sure it's one that you feel confident knitting. Particularly if you're new to knitting, consider asking around your knitting group or the yarn shop to see if others have knit the pattern before. If you come across a direction that seems to be a mistake, check the publisher's (or yarn company's) Web site — these companies often publish errata.

Even if a pattern is 100 percent correct, remember that it may not be the right pattern for you. Take a minute to look over the pattern (and not just at the pretty pictures!) before you buy the pattern and the yarn. The following sections provide some easy steps to take to decide if a pattern is right for you.

## Are all the parts there?

Every knitting pattern should have the following parts:

✔ **Materials:** This list tells you what you need in order to knit the project, including needles, yarn (the kind and the amount), and other materials, such as stitch markers or a crochet hook. See Chapter 1 for details about knitting supplies.

✔ **Gauge information:** This information, which is sometimes labeled "tension," tells you the gauge that you need to knit at. If you're substituting yarn, compare the pattern's gauge in stockinette stitch to the gauge listed on the yarn's label. Sometimes a pattern will list a gauge measured over a pattern stitch instead of stockinette stitch, so be sure to read carefully! (Check out Chapter 2 for the scoop on gauge.)

✔ **Size:** The finished dimensions of the project should be written out or given in a diagram. Flip to Chapter 3 for general information about sizing.

✔ **Directions:** The pattern directions should have subheadings for all the parts of the finished piece, such as back, right front, left front, sleeves, and so on. It's also customary to find finishing information that tells you how to sew the pieces together and make and attach any details, such as buttonbands or tassels. Make sure that none of these parts is missing. For instance, if the picture of the garment shows a hood, there should be directions for making the hood.

If everything seems to be accounted for, move on to the next step. If any of the parts are missing, I suggest that you find another pattern or see if the missing parts are available as errata.

## Do you understand the directions?

Pick a part of the pattern and begin reading it. Does it make sense? Can you follow all the steps without getting lost? If there are a couple of new things that you feel ready to try, go ahead and go for it; a pattern that excites you is the perfect way to improve your skills. But if you really can't make heads or tails of it, you're probably wise to choose something else to knit.

## Does the pattern come in your size and style?

Before you choose a pattern and a size to knit, you must know what size you are! Check out Chapter 3 to find out more about how and why you should take your measurements. Don't simply assume that you're a medium or a large. Look at the range of sizes offered and see if the pattern comes in a size that will fit your specific measurements. If the sweater won't fit, it isn't the pattern for you — no matter how much you may like it. Think about what it is that you like in the design and look for another pattern with some of the same elements that comes in your size. And remember that if it's the cable up the front or the stitch pattern used at the sleeves, you may be able to add these to a pattern that suits your body better.

Now a few words about style. A beautiful picture accompanying the pattern of a hand-knit garment can do funny things to your brain. By looking at a picture of the finished product, you may think that knitting a specific sweater could make your chest larger, make your hair curlier, or put you that much closer to the sun-drenched beach in the picture. Unfortunately, that isn't the case. And, because you can't try on handknits before you make them, sometimes it's difficult to know whether you're going to like what you get. So, when choosing a pattern, be aware of the styles that suit you and the ones that don't. The fact that you've knit it yourself probably won't change your feelings about bulky turtlenecks or sleeveless tops; if you never wear them, don't knit them.

# Part II
# A Primer on Stitches and Color

"I learned so many new skills making this one. How to knit and to purl, how to ignore the phone when it's ringing, how to pretend I'm listening to people when they're talking to me, how to get the dog to make its own meals..."

## In this part . . .

The first part of this book focuses on the things that you need to know in order to knit patterns successfully. But now that all the prep work is done, it's finally time to settle down to some knitting! This part of the book is like a stitch dictionary. It's a reference that you can come back to anytime to refresh your memory. Or it can serve as a source of inspiration when you're plotting out a new project. There are knit and purl patterns, including some fun rib variations; an assortment of cables and laces to try; and a variety of ways to add color to your work, including stripes, Fair Isle, and mosaics.

# Chapter 5

# The Simplest Stitches

*In This Chapter*
▶ Reading stitch patterns
▶ Deciphering the lingo
▶ Knitting classic stitch patterns

*I*n Chapter 2, you find out about the importance of making a swatch (a small knit sample of a stitch used in a pattern). Now you finally get to put theory into action and pick up your needles! This chapter covers just a few of the almost infinite number of stitch patterns you can use. The patterns here are everyday classics that you'll see time and again, so they're well worth getting comfortable with.

To practice the six stitch patterns in this chapter, you can make a 4-inch square swatch for each pattern and then sew them into a soft block to give to a baby or to decorate your desk. I give you specific directions for knitting each stitch swatch throughout the chapter. You find other inventive uses for swatches in Chapter 16.

By making several swatches, you'll discover that different stitch patterns knit to different gauges even with the same yarn and needles. For instance, if you cast on 20 (or 21) stitches for each swatch with worsted weight yarn, the widths of your swatches will vary. They'll be close enough in size, however, that you can still make them into your block when you're done. After you've knit your swatches, take time to measure your stitch and row gauge for each swatch. (See Chapter 2 for information on measuring your gauge.) Doing so gives you a chance to get better at measuring your gauge accurately and gives you concrete evidence of how various stitch patterns are more or less similar to one another.

## Starting with Garter Stitch

*Garter stitch* is where all knitters start. This is because all the stitches are knits — as long as you're knitting flat. And, because garter stitch looks the same on both sides, it's completely reversible. It has a bumpy texture, a bit like the purl (or reverse) side of stockinette stitch (see the next section for more about this stitch), but it's much thicker and denser. For this reason, some knitters see it as somewhat humble; though in finer-gauged yarns, garter stitch can be quite refined. Check out a close-up of garter stitch in Figure 5-1.

Because it's easy to knit, garter stitch is usually the best choice if you're using novelty yarns, particularly the hairy or fuzzy varieties that make stitches difficult to see.

Garter stitch is obedient. Like a good dog, garter stitch lies down where you want it to. If you want your edges to stay flat and the piece to keep its shape, garter stitch is the ticket. Garter stitch is an obvious choice for baby blankets or scarves, but it's also great for hems that you don't want to roll (like stockinette stitch) or pull in (like ribbing, which I discuss in Chapter 6). It doesn't need extra finishing around its edges, so garter stitch is a great "quick knit" stitch choice. The baby sweater in Chapter 10 is a great example.

**Figure 5-1:**
Garter
stitch.

Garter stitch has a lot of stretch, particularly vertically. Sometimes this stretch is desirable, but it can also be a disadvantage, particularly if you're knitting a large piece in heavy yarn, as it tends to grow in length.

To knit garter stitch working flat:

>**For all rows:** Knit.

To knit garter stitch in the round (see Chapter 11 for details on knitting in the round):

>**Round 1:** Knit.

>**Round 2:** Purl.

>Repeat these 2 rounds for the pattern.

To make a garter stitch swatch for your block, cast on 20 stitches and knit 40 rows or until your block is square. Bind off (see the appendix if you need a refresher).

# Knitting and Purling Stockinette Stitch

*Stockinette stitch,* or stocking stitch as the Brits call it, is really the ultimate knitting stitch. Chances are that if you summon up an image of knitting in your head, it will be stockinette, with those little rows of V's all lined up so obediently (check out Figure 5-2 to see what I mean).

Stockinette stitch, which alternates rows of knits and rows of purls, makes an even, smooth fabric that drapes pleasantly and can be knit at a wide range of gauges to create different effects. Because it's the smoothest of the knitting stitches, stockinette is usually the best one for many sorts of color work (which I cover in Chapter 7). It also makes a great backdrop for more complex details, such as a lace panel, ruffled cuffs, or contrasting trims.

The one issue with stockinette stitch is that its edges will roll. This is truer with some yarns than with others, but that's just its nature. So, unless you want to use the rolled edge as a feature, as you would with a rolled brim hat, use a different stitch pattern along the exposed edges of your piece.

To knit stockinette stitch when you're working flat:

>**On right-side rows (RS):** Knit.

>**On wrong-side rows (WS):** Purl.

**Figure 5-2:**
Stockinette
stitch.

To knit stockinette stitch in the round (see Chapter 11 for details on knitting in the round):

**For all rounds:** Knit.

When you're knitting in the round, you never turn the work to the wrong side, which means that all rows or rounds are right-side rows.

To make a stockinette stitch swatch for your block, cast on 20 stitches. Alternate between knit and purl rows as I've described. Bind off when the block measures 4 inches.

# Mixing It Up with Reverse Stockinette Stitch

*Reverse stockinette stitch* is simply stockinette stitch viewed from the wrong side, or the purl side (see Figure 5-3). You can use reverse stockinette stitch any time you would use stockinette stitch to get a different look from the "same" piece. In fact, for the most part, you don't really have to decide which side will show until you're almost finished. Just remember that if reverse stockinette stitch is what you want to use, you should do the finishing with the purl side as the right side.

Reverse stockinette stitch is particularly effective as a backdrop for cables, because when knit and purl stitches are worked in columns (think ribbing), the purls recede and the knits come forward. So, a reverse stockinette background for your cables really makes them stand out. (Head to Chapter 6 for more information on cables.)

To knit reverse stockinette stitch when you're working flat:

**On right-side rows (RS):** Purl.

**On wrong-side rows (WS):** Knit.

To knit reverse stockinette stitch when you're working in the round (see Chapter 11):

**For all rounds:** Purl.

To make a reverse stockinette stitch swatch for your block, cast on 20 stitches. Alternate between purl and knit rows as I've described. Bind off when your block measures 4 inches.

**Figure 5-3:**
Reverse
stockinette
stitch.

# Staying Simple with Seed Stitch

*Seed stitch,* shown in Figure 5-4, is both beautiful and simple. It has a regular texture of little bumps that look a bit like seeds (albeit highly organized ones!). Like garter stitch (which I describe earlier in this chapter), seed stitch lies flat and looks the same on both sides, so it's great for edgings and is a beautiful choice for scarves or blankets. Seed stitch makes a wonderful background for cables (see Chapter 6) or other more intricate patterns, but you also can use it on its own for something more understated. And I think it's universally true that people will swoon over any baby garments that are knit in seed stitch.

Seed stitch involves a bit more work than stockinette or garter stitch because you must move the yarn from front to back between each stitch. But remember that the results are well worth it.

To knit seed stitch working flat on an odd number of stitches:

**For all rows:** *K1, p1, repeat from * to last st, k1.

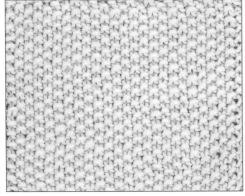

**Figure 5-4:**
Seed stitch.

To knit seed stitch in the round on an even number of stitches:

**Round 1:** *K1, p1, repeat from * to end of round.

**Round 2:** *P1, k1, repeat from * to end of round.

Repeat these 2 rounds for the pattern.

After the knit-purl-knit-purl is established in the first row, all you have to remember to make seed stitch is that you must always knit the purls and purl the knits.

To make a seed stitch swatch for your block, cast on 21 stitches. Follow the directions for knitting seed stitch flat until your swatch measures 4 inches. Bind off.

# Creating Box Stitch

_Box stitch_ is a close cousin of seed stitch in the previous section; they certainly have a lot in common! Box stitch, shown in Figure 5-5, has virtually the same personality as seed stitch, but on a larger scale. Like its cousin, box stitch is a great choice for blankets and scarves, but it can also give a great allover texture to a piece like a jacket. Box stitch also makes a great edging. For instance, if you don't like the bottom of your sweater to pull in at the hips, box stitch makes a fine substitute for 2 x 2 rib (see Chapter 6 for more on this rib).

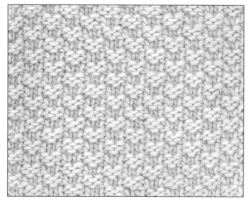

**Figure 5-5:** Box stitch.

To knit box stitch when knitting flat, you need a number of stitches that's equal to a multiple of 4 plus 2:

> **Rows 1 and 4:** *K2, p2, repeat from * to last 2 sts, k2.
>
> **Rows 2 and 3:** *P2, k2, repeat from * to last 2 sts, p2.
>
> Repeat these 4 rows for the pattern.

To knit box stitch in the round (see Chapter 11), you need a multiple of 4 stitches:

> **Rounds 1 and 2:** *K2, p2, repeat from * to end of round.
>
> **Rounds 3 and 4:** *P2, k2, repeat from * to end of round.
>
> Repeat these 4 rounds for the pattern.

To make a box stitch swatch for your block, cast on 18 stitches. Follow the directions for working box stitch flat. Bind off when your swatch measures 4 inches.

# Working Half Linen Stitch

_Half linen stitch_ is one of my favorite stitches! You can see it in Figure 5-6. It isn't difficult to work and it creates an interesting fabric that looks almost woven — it behaves a little more like woven fabric, too. Half linen stitch resists vertical stretching, so it's a great choice for projects like bags or belts or larger garments like a coat. The edges of half linen stitch do roll. But a three- or five-stitch border in seed stitch, which I describe earlier in this chapter, is the perfect fix.

**Figure 5-6:**
Half linen
stitch.

Half linen stitch looks great in a solid color, but if you try it with a variegated yarn or alternate between two colors, switching at the beginning of every right-side row, you can get some great effects.

To work half linen stitch knitting flat on an odd number of stitches:

Cast on and purl 1 row.

**Row 1 (RS):** *K1, bring yarn to front and sl 1 st purlwise, bring yarn to back, repeat from * to last st, k1. (Chapter 9 has details on bringing yarn to the front.)

To slip a stitch purlwise, insert the needle into the stitch as if to purl, and then slide it over to the right-hand needle. But remember that you don't purl the stitch. Instead, you simply move it from one needle to the other, carrying the yarn along the front of the stitch as you do.

**Row 2:** Purl.

**Row 3:** K2, *bring yarn to front, sl 1 st, bring yarn to back, k1, repeat from * to last st, k1.

**Row 4:** Purl.

Repeat these 4 rows for the pattern.

To work half linen stitch in the round on an even number of stitches:

Cast on and knit 1 round.

**Round 1:** *K1, bring yarn to front, sl 1, bring yarn to back, repeat from * to end of round.

**Round 2:** Knit.

Because you don't have edges to worry about, you can start right in with the slip stitches when you work in the round.

**Round 3:** *Bring yarn to front, sl 1, bring yarn to back, k1, repeat from * to end of round.

**Round 4:** Knit.

To make a half linen stitch swatch for your block, cast on 21 stitches and follow the directions for working half linen stitch when knitting flat. Bind off when your swatch measures 4 inches.

# Chapter 6

# Stitches that Look Tricky but Aren't

. . . . . . . . . . . . . . . . . . . . . . . . . . . . . . . . . . . . . . . . . . . . . . . . . . . . . . . . . . .

## In This Chapter

▶ Exploring different kinds of ribs

▶ Understanding and creating cables

▶ Getting to know lace patterns

. . . . . . . . . . . . . . . . . . . . . . . . . . . . . . . . . . . . . . . . . . . . . . . . . . . . . . . . . . .

**M**ost of what you knit is made up predominantly of basic background stitches, such as stockinette or garter stitch (which I discuss in Chapter 5). Ribbing, cables, and lace are the icing on the cake, so to speak. Even if these stitches are used only as details, such as a couple of inches of ribbing or lace at the hem and cuffs or a single cable twisting up the front of a sweater, it's these little details that give a finished piece its personality.

What's really cool about the stitch patterns that I show you how to make in this chapter (and the jaw-dropping number of other stitch patterns that you can find in other books and online) is that they're often interchangeable. And swapping one stitch pattern for another is an easy way to create something that you can truly call your own. Altering the stitch patterns you use not only inspires your creativity, but it also keeps knitting interesting and fun, even if you want to rely on a set of tried-and-true patterns. Here are some suggestions to get you thinking about substitutions:

✔ Think of a sweater with classic 2 x 2 ribbing at the hems and cuffs. What if you used the two-stitch rib instead? Or what about using the two-stitch twist miniature cables? You don't have to alter the pattern's numbers; you simply use the directions given in this chapter in lieu of the ribbing directions in the pattern.

✔ Consider the loose rib wrap in Chapter 8. If you change the rib pattern or switch to a lace pattern, you've created your own design! For a piece like a wrap or scarf, it's fine to add or subtract a few stitches to the cast-on so that your pattern comes out even. Let your imagination (and the yarn you've chosen) inspire you to experiment.

Be aware, though, that different stitch patterns can behave quite differently. For example, using two-stitch twist miniature cables rather than 2 x 2 ribbing may result in a rib that pulls in slightly more. It's a good idea to swatch the different stitch patterns you're considering to see how they'll behave and to prevent unpleasant surprises.

If you're substituting stitch patterns, verify that you're working with a number of stitches that adds up correctly. Each stitch pattern in this chapter tells you how many stitches you need. For example, a multiple of 4 plus 2 means that you need a multiple of 4 (such as 12, 32, or 80) plus 2 extra stitches to keep the pattern symmetrical (so 14, 34, or 82).

## Lining Up with Ribs

Ribs, in some sense, belong with the simplest stitches in Chapter 5 because, like those stitches, they're made only of knit and purl stitches with no fancy footwork required. Whenever ribs are used, they create a strong (and flattering) vertical line that moves the eye up and down.

Ribs have function in addition to their form. They don't roll, so they make great scarves and wraps. Additionally, ribs are the best way to create an elastic fabric that stretches and contracts. Because of this stretch, ribs are the most traditional choice for cuffs, collars, and the bottoms of sweaters. And a whole top worked in rib, such as the shell in Chapter 10, stretches to hug your curves.

The steps to working a rib pattern are essentially the same, regardless of the rib. All ribs are made by working knits and purls in regular columns, and they're all easy to see or "read" once you get started. In other words, after you work the first couple of rows, it's easy to see where the knits and purls should go.

Generally speaking, ribs are worked on smaller needles than you would normally use to knit stockinette stitch with the same yarn; knitting with smaller needles helps ribs look tidy and do their job (keeping your cuff out of your dinner plate or keeping wrist warmers in place). Patterns usually tell you which needles to use, but if you're experimenting, remember that you may want to use smaller needles, typically two sizes smaller than you would for stockinette stitch.

Aside from getting off track and purling knits or knitting purls, the one common problem that comes up when knitters are learning to rib is that they bring the yarn *over* the needle rather than *under* when they're moving the yarn from the knit position to the purl position and back again. Bringing the yarn over the needle results in a *yarn over,* which creates a hole — called an *eyelet* — and an extra stitch. (See Chapter 7 for more on yarn overs.)

In the following sections, I show you how to create two types of ribs:

✔ **True ribs:** A *true rib* is a rib where the knits are always knit and the purls are always purled. True ribs can be broken down into two groups: even ribs, where the number of knits and purls is the same (knit 2, purl 2), and uneven ribs, where the number of knits and purls is different (knit 4, purl 2). Consider some of the differences:

   • Small even ribs, such as 1 x 1 rib and 2 x 2 rib, are the hands-down winners of any sort of ribbing popularity contest. They're both great at what they do: creating nice elastic fabrics that don't roll and that go well with just about anything you can dream up.

   You can make 3 x 3 ribs (as I have in the shawl collared coat in Chapter 10), 4 x 4 ribs, or even larger ribs, but the ribs will become less stretchy as they get larger.

   • Though even ribs win the popularity contest, there's no reason that the number of knits and purls must be the same in a rib pattern. Indeed, something a bit less regular is often more pleasing to the eye, especially if it's going to cover a large space (for example, the loose rib wrap in Chapter 8). Try uneven ribs, such as 3 x 1, 4 x 2, or 5 x 3, as nice variations.

   The larger your groups of stitches, the fewer ribs you'll make, which means that a 5 x 3 rib will be less elastic than a 2 x 2 rib.

✔ **False ribs:** Even though *false ribs* look like ribs, they don't have the elasticity of true ribs. They make great choices for allover patterns, or you can use them to substitute for 2 x 2 rib in places where you'd prefer a straight clean line to an edge that pulls in.

   While ribbing at the bottom of a sweater is a classic look, many times you don't really want your sweater to be tighter at the bottom. For women especially, a straighter line gives a more contemporary and flattering look. If you want to keep the classic ribbed look without it fitting like a cinched sack, use a false rib pattern like broken rib or two-stitch rib.

## 1 x 1 rib

A *1 x 1 rib* is a very elastic rib with a subtle texture. In its relaxed state, from both sides you see mostly the knit stitches with the purls hiding behind them. This rib is a great choice for the bottom of a hat or the cuff of a fine-gauged sweater. You can see a 1 x 1 rib in Figure 6-1.

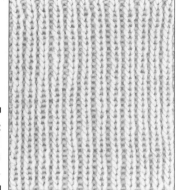

**Figure 6-1:**
Knit 1, purl 1 creates a classic rib.

Follow these steps to work 1 x 1 rib when you're knitting flat. To practice with a swatch, cast on any odd number of stitches:

**Right-side (RS) rows:** *K1, p1, repeat from * to last st, k1.

**Wrong-side (WS) rows:** *P1, k1, repeat from * to last st, p1.

Repeat these 2 rows for the pattern.

To knit 1 x 1 rib in the round (see Chapter 11 for details on knitting in the round), use any even number of stitches and knit as follows:

**All rounds:** *K1, p1, repeat from * to end of round.

## 2 x 2 rib

Knit 2, purl 2 rib, or *2 x 2 rib,* shown in Figure 6-2, is a great rib choice for scarves, hats, socks, and sweaters. This ribbing is elastic, so it easily stays snugly in place and stretches enough to allow you to put the garment on.

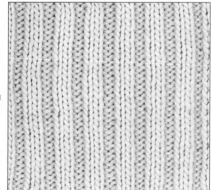

**Figure 6-2:**
2 x 2 rib adds stretch where you need it.

Follow these steps to work 2 x 2 rib when you're knitting flat. To practice with a swatch, cast on a multiple of 4 stitches plus 2 more (which makes your piece symmetrical, beginning and ending with 2 knits) and work as follows:

**Right-side (RS) rows:** *K2, p2, repeat from * to last 2 sts, k2.

**Wrong-side (WS) rows:** *P2, k2, repeat from * to last 2 sts, p2.

Repeat these 2 rows for the pattern.

If you're knitting in the round, you need a multiple of 4 stitches for things to work out evenly. Knit as follows:

**All rounds:** *K2, p2, repeat from * to end of round.

## 4 x 2 rib

An example of an uneven rib, *4 x 2 rib,* is shown in Figure 6-3. This rib isn't quite as stretchy as 1 x 1 or 2 x 2 rib, but it still performs nicely on a cuff or collar. It's also a great choice for any scarf, wrap, or stole that you care to dream up.

**Figure 6-3:** 4 x 2 rib creates strong vertical lines.

To work 4 x 2 rib when you're knitting flat, use a multiple of 6 stitches plus 4 to make it symmetrical and work as follows (you can make a swatch to practice):

**Right-side (RS) rows:** *K4, p2, repeat from *to last 4 sts, k4.

**Wrong-side (WS) rows:** *P4, k2, repeat from *to last 4 sts, p4.

Repeat these 2 rows.

To knit 4 x 2 rib in the round, use a multiple of 6 stitches and knit as follows:

**All rounds:** *K4, p2, repeat from * to end of round.

## Broken rib

Knitting has its share of stitches with poetic or funny names. For instance, how can you knit something called *broken rib* without suppressing a laugh? What's broken in this rib (which is a false rib) is the pattern. Only every other row is actually ribbed, making this one quicker and easier to knit than most ribs. It lays flat and has an interesting, though different, look on each side. See an example of broken rib in Figure 6-4.

**Figure 6-4:**
Broken rib
is a type of
false rib.

Follow these steps to work broken rib when you're knitting flat. To practice with a swatch, cast on a multiple of 4 stitches plus 2 and work as follows:

> **Row 1:** *K2, p2, repeat from * to last 2 sts, k2.
>
> **Row 2:** Purl.
>
> Repeat these 2 rows for the pattern.

To work broken rib in the round, use a multiple of 4 stitches and knit as follows:

> **Round 1:** *K2, p2, repeat from * to end of round.
>
> **Round 2:** Knit.
>
> Repeat these 2 rounds for the pattern.

## Two-stitch rib

*Two-stitch rib,* which is a false rib, is the love child of 2 x 2 rib and seed stitch (see Chapter 5 for more about this stitch). With this rib pattern, you work knit 2, purl 2 all the time, but you always knit the purls and purl the knits, just like you do in seed stitch. As you can see in Figure 6-5, the result is a highly textured pattern with a strong vertical element. The finished fabric from a two-stitch rib looks the same on both sides and lays flat, so it's a nice choice for a scarf. Its rugged look also makes it a great choice for men's knits.

Follow these directions to work two-stitch rib when you're knitting flat. To practice with a swatch, use a multiple of 4 stitches plus 2 and work as follows:

> **For all rows:** *K2, p2, repeat from * to last 2 sts, k2.

To work two-stitch rib in the round, use a multiple of 4 stitches and knit as follows:

> **Round 1:** *K2, p2, repeat from * to end of round.
>
> **Round 2:** *P2, k2, repeat from * to end of round.
>
> Repeat these 2 rounds for the pattern.

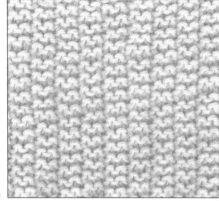

**Figure 6-5:**
Two-
stitch rib
combines
2 x 2 rib with
seed stitch.

# Twisting Away with Cables

Cables are one of the magic parts of knitting. They're beautiful to look at and are unique to the craft. Just think of those classic sweaters from the Aran Isles. Cables may look complicated, especially when they're grouped together, and you may feel intimidated by them. But the truth is that after you know the secret to cable construction, you're good to go — even rookie knitters can master basic cables in no time. Practice some of the cables presented in this section as swatches, or dive right into some of the cabled variations of the projects presented in this book: the cabled variation of the basic beanie in Chapter 11 or the kid's top with a horseshoe cable up the front in Chapter 13.

The secret to cables lies in knitting stitches out of order. This sleight of hand creates the twists and turns that make up all cables, from simple to complex. The tiniest cables, or twists, can be knit without any extra tools, but for most cables, it's easier if you use a *cable needle* (which may be abbreviated as "cn" in patterns). You can see the different types of cable needles in Chapter 1. Which one you use is only a question of personal preference or what you have on hand.

If you don't have a cable needle handy, use a short double-pointed needle of approximately the same gauge as the needles that you're knitting on. A pencil or an unbent paperclip will also do in a pinch!

Here are a few things to know about crafting cables:

- ✔ **Cable twists are usually made with an even number of stitches: 4, 6, 8, 12, or even more.** Half of the stitches cross in front (or behind) the other half each time you turn the cable.

- ✔ **A cable looks great on its own, but putting two or more next to one another leads to more intricate-looking designs.** Horseshoe cables and chain cables (both of which I describe later in this chapter) are composed of two basic cables that are placed directly next to each other.

- ✔ **You don't have to turn the cable every row; instead, you turn it every few rows.** Here's a rule of thumb: Turn your cable according to how many stitches are in it. For instance, if there are 4 stitches in the cable, turn it every 4th row. If there are 8 stitches in a cable, turn it every 8th row. And remember that you should always turn your cables on the right side (or public side) of your piece.

- ✔ **You control the twist of a cable by placing the stitches that are held on the cable needle to the front or the back of the work to wait their turn to be knit.** A cable that looks like it twists to the right is made by holding the stitches to the back. A left-twisting cable is made by holding the stitches to the front.

- **You don't need to do any extra twisting when it comes to cables.** So, remember to slip your stitches purlwise onto the cable needle, and be sure that the knit side of the stitches on the cable needle is showing when you go to knit them.

- **Cables show up best on light colors.** Imagine cream-colored Aran sweaters; the cables show up well on these. If you use black or a dark color, however, the cables are more difficult to see.

Cable directions, like other knitting instructions that have several steps, may be confusing to read the first couple of times. Honestly, deciphering the directions is more difficult for some people than actually turning the cable. Reading through the directions slowly, doing what they say while you read them, can be helpful. Some knitters find the written directions easiest to follow and others prefer the graphic representation of a chart, so I've included both for the cables in the following sections. (I discuss chart reading basics in Chapter 4.)

If you're having trouble managing the needles *and* reading the directions at the same time, have someone else read the directions aloud so you can concentrate on moving the needles. It's actually pretty funny to listen to a non-knitter read directions, so feel free to get any handy family member or friend to help you out.

## Two-stitch twist

The *two-stitch twist* is a total cheater cable. It's easy to work and makes an interesting stand-in for 2 x 2 rib (see it for yourself in Figure 6-6). Try it out in the wrist warmers project in Chapter 11.

**Figure 6-6:** Two-stitch twists worked in a rib pattern.

Because cables are made by knitting stitches out of order, with the two-stitch twist you knit with a slightly unorthodox technique that allows you to work without a cable needle. It feels a bit like a contortion act the first few times you do it, but soon you'll be making mini cables quickly.

The two-stitch twist technique creates a two-stitch left twist, which I abbreviate as "LT." Here's how to do it:

1. **Ignore the first stitch on the left-hand needle for a moment and put the right-hand needle into the back of the second stitch on the needle.**

   Knit this stitch through the back loop, but don't drop it off the left-hand needle.

2. **Bring the needle back around to the front and knit the first stitch normally through the front loop.**

3. **Drop both stitches from the left-hand needle.**

4. **Repeat Steps 1–3 each time you need to work a twist.**

Here's how to work the two-stitch twist rib pattern shown in Figure 6-6 (and charted in Figure 6-7). To practice, cast on a multiple of 4 stitches plus 2 to knit it flat and follow these steps:

> **Right-side (RS) rows:** *LT, p2, repeat from * to last 2 sts, LT.
>
> **Wrong-side (WS) rows:** *P2, k2, repeat from * to last 2 sts, p2.
>
> Repeat these 2 rows for the pattern.

To work the two-stitch twist pattern when knitting in the round (see Chapter 11 for details on knitting in the round), use a multiple of 4 stitches and knit as follows:

> **Round 1:** *LT, p2, repeat from * to end of round.
>
> **Round 2:** *K2, p2, repeat from * to end of round.
>
> Repeat these 2 rounds to form the pattern.

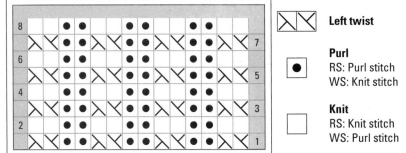

**Figure 6-7:** A chart of the two-stitch twist.

**Left twist**

**Purl**
RS: Purl stitch
WS: Knit stitch

**Knit**
RS: Knit stitch
WS: Purl stitch

## Four-stitch cables

*Four-stitch front and back cables* (abbreviated as C4F and C4B, respectively) are small enough that they can be used as an allover pattern without overwhelming the piece. Remember that C4F looks like it's twisting to the left and C4B looks like it's twisting to the right, as you can see in Figure 6-8.

**Figure 6-8:** Four-stitch front cable (on the left) and four-stitch back cable (on the right).

To work a four-stitch front cable, follow these steps when you come to the direction C4F in a pattern:

1. **Slip the next 2 stitches on the left-hand needle to the cable needle and hold the cable needle to the front of the work.**

2. **Knit 2 stitches from the left-hand needle.**

3. **Knit 2 stitches from the cable needle.**

Likewise, to turn a four-stitch back cable, follow these steps when you come to the direction C4B in a pattern:

1. **Slip the next 2 stitches on the left-hand needle to the cable needle and hold the cable needle to the back of the work.**

2. **Knit 2 stitches from the left-hand needle.**

3. **Knit 2 stitches from the cable needle.**

To knit a swatch and practice making these cables, cast on 20 stitches and follow these directions or the chart in Figure 6-9:

**Rows 1 and 3 (WS):** *K4, p4, repeat from * to last 4 sts, k4.

**Row 2 (RS):** *P4, k4, repeat from * to last 4 sts, p4.

**Row 4 (turning row) (RS):** P4, C4B, p4, C4F, p4.

Repeat these 4 rows until you get the hang of turning cables.

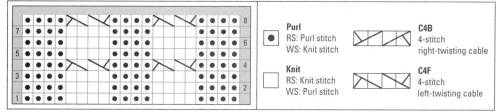

**Figure 6-9:**
C4F and
C4B,
charted.

## Six-stitch cables

A *six-stitch left-twisting cable* (abbreviated as C6F) and a *six-stitch right-twisting cable* (abbreviated as C6B) will be a piece of cake if you've already practiced with four-stitch cables because you follow the same basic steps (see the previous section for more information). Figure 6-10 shows a left-twisting cable; Figure 6-11 shows a right-twisting cable. In a bulky yarn, a single six-stitch cable can be enough to get attention on a scarf, or you can try several on the cabled beanie variation in Chapter 11.

Here's what you need to do to work a six-stitch cable when you come to the direction C6F or C6B in a pattern:

1. **Slip 3 stitches to the cable needle.**

2. **Bring the cable needle with its 3 stitches to the front of the work for C6F (or to the back for C6B).**

   Just let the needle hang there. You don't need to hold it. If your stitches begin to slip off the cable needle, use a larger one.

3. **Knit the next 3 stitches from the left-hand needle.**

Slide the stitches on the left-hand needle over a bit so they aren't in danger of falling off the tip, and then drop the left-hand needle.

4. **Pick up the cable needle with your left hand, and without twisting it (the knit side of the stitches will face you), knit the 3 stitches from the cable needle.**

5. **Put down the cable needle, pick up the left-hand needle, and finish the row.**

**Figure 6-10:**
A six-stitch left-twisting cable.

**Figure 6-11:**
A six-stitch right-twisting cable.

That's it! Repeat the cable as specified in your pattern. You can practice six-stitch cables by creating a swatch of the horseshoe cable in the following section.

## Horseshoe cable

Combining cables can lead to all sorts of interesting effects. For instance, by working a left cable and a right cable next to each other, you create the cool cable shown in Figure 6-12, called a *horseshoe cable*. If you work the right cable first, you make a horseshoe that points up; if you work the right cable last, you make a horseshoe that points down.

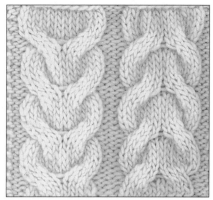

**Figure 6-12:**
Horseshoe
cables.

Horseshoes can be worked over larger or smaller groups of stitches, but 12 stitches (two six-stitch cables) or 8 stitches (two four-stitch cables) are typical choices. To make the horseshoe cable shown on the left in Figure 6-12, you need 12 knit stitches on a background of purl stitches. Even though there are 12 stitches total involved in the horseshoe, each cable uses 6 stitches, so you turn the cables every 6th row.

To practice this horseshoe, cast on 18 stitches. Follow the directions given here, or look at Figure 6-13:

**Rows 1 and 3:** P3, k12, p3.

**Rows 2 and 4:** K3, p12, k3.

**Row 5 (turning row):** P3, sl 3 sts to cn, hold cn to back, k3, k3 from cn, sl 3 sts to cn, hold to front, k3, k3 from cn, p3.

**Row 6:** K3, p12, k3.

To finish your swatch, repeat the 6 rows of the pattern until you've mastered the horseshoe cable.

To make your horseshoe cable point the other direction, as shown on the right side of Figure 6-12, work everything exactly the same, except for the turning row. At the turning row, you knit the cable the opposite way — that is, working the front cable first and the back cable second, like this:

**Row 5 (turning row):** P3, sl 3 sts to cn, hold cn to front, k3, k3 from cn, sl 3 sts to cn, hold to back, k3, k3 from cn, p3.

## Wave cable and chain cable

*Wave cables,* like the basic cables that I describe earlier in this chapter, can be worked singly, in pairs, or as an allover pattern. Instead of always twisting the cable one way, alternating front and back cable twists causes the line of stitches to wave back and forth. Two wave cables next to one another form a *chain cable* as shown in the center of Figure 6-14.

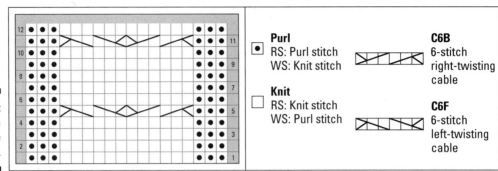

**Figure 6-13:**
Charting a
horseshoe
cable.

**Figure 6-14:**
Two wave
cables flank
a chain
cable.

Practice making a single wave cable by casting on 12 stitches (6 stitches for the cable and 3 purl stitches on either side). After casting on, follow these directions (the same information is presented in chart form at the right side of Figure 6-15):

**Rows 1 and 3:** P3, k6, p3.

**Rows 2, 4, and 6:** K3, p6, k3.

**Row 5 (turning row):** P3, sl next 3 sts to cn and hold to back, k3, k3 from cn, p3.

**Rows 7 and 9:** P3, k6, p3.

**Rows 8, 10, and 12:** K3, p6, k3.

**Row 11 (turning row):** P3, sl next 3 sts to cn and hold to front, k3, k3 from cn, p3.

Repeat these 12 rows for the wave cable pattern. After you've got it down, bind off.

To work a chain cable, as shown in the center of Figure 6-14, make two wave cables next to one another. To practice a chain cable, cast on 18 stitches and knit as follows (refer to Figure 6-15 for the charted directions):

**Row 1 and 3:** P3, k12, p3.

**Rows 2, 4, and 6:** K3, p12, k3.

**Row 5 (turning row):** P3, sl 3 sts to cn and hold to back, k3, k3 from cn, sl 3 sts to cn and hold to front, k3, k3 from cn, p3.

**Rows 7 and 9:** P3, k12, p3.

**Rows 8, 10, and 12:** K3, p12, k3.

**Row 11 (turning row):** P3, sl 3 sts to cn and hold to front, k3, k3 from cn, sl 3 sts to cn and hold to back, k3, k3 from cn, p3.

Repeat these 12 rows to create a chain cable. When you've got the hang of chain cables, bind off.

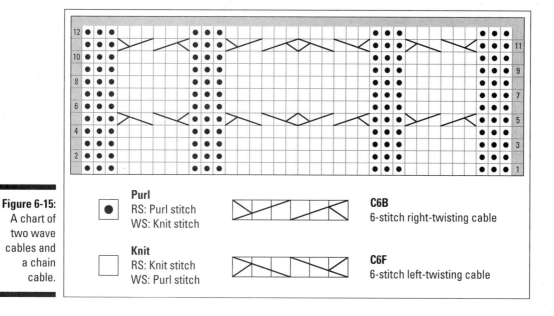

**Figure 6-15:** A chart of two wave cables and a chain cable.

**Purl**
RS: Purl stitch
WS: Knit stitch

**Knit**
RS: Knit stitch
WS: Purl stitch

**C6B**
6-stitch right-twisting cable

**C6F**
6-stitch left-twisting cable

# Seeing Through Your Knitting with Lace

Lace is a beautiful way to make your knitting spectacular. Lace patterns can range from simple to complex, but they all rely on the same basic maneuvers:

- *Yarn overs* (abbreviated as "yo") create the eyelets in lace. Because yarn overs are increases, using them without decreases causes your piece to grow, which is how a simple piece like the lacy shawl in Chapter 12 is created.

- Lace patterns typically combine yarn overs with decreases to balance out the extra stitches, keeping the stitch count constant. Lace usually uses k2tog (knit 2 together) to slant to the right and ssk (slip, slip, knit) to slant to the left. In some lace patterns the stitch count changes from row to row, but in the patterns I discuss in this section, the stitch counts don't change, which makes it easier to stay on track.

In the following sections, I explain how to make yarn overs, decreases, and double decreases — all important to making lace. I also show you how to make several different beautiful lace patterns: openwork, feather and fan, climbing vine lace, and arrowhead lace.

## Yarn overs

A *yarn over* is an increase that creates a hole. Knitters call this decorative hole an *eyelet* (check out Figure 6-16 for an example). Chances are you made lots of yarn overs when you first tried ribbing, but at that point you called them mistakes. The British call the yarn over "yarn forward." Knowing this fact may help you remember what to do with the yarn.

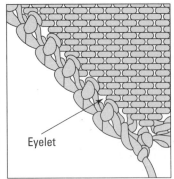

**Figure 6-16:**
A yarn over
creates a
hole called
an eyelet.

Eyelet

When you come to the spot in your pattern where you make a yarn over (abbreviated "yo" in pattern directions), follow these steps (and check out Figure 6-17):

1. **Between 2 knit stitches, bring the yarn forward, as if to purl.**

2. **Insert the needle into the next stitch knitwise, and knit it.**

   The working yarn comes up over the right-hand needle and lies diagonally between 2 stitches. You've made an extra stitch, and knit the next stitch. Note that the stitch after the yarn over may be something other than a knit, so be sure to look ahead and see what comes next before working your yarn over. The important thing is that you've formed a loop of yarn over your right-hand needle.

3. **In the next row, knit this new stitch normally.**

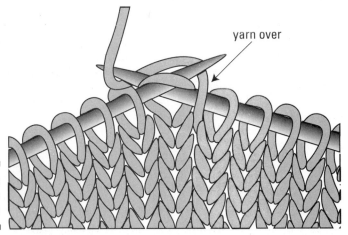

yarn over

**Figure 6-17:**
Making a
yarn over.

## Common decreases used in lace

To make a right-slanting k2tog (as shown in Figure 6-18), follow these steps:

1. **Insert the right needle through 2 stitches from left to right, just as you would to knit a single stitch.**

2. **Wrap the yarn around the right-hand needle as usual and knit the 2 stitches together.**

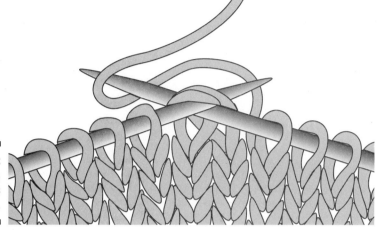

**Figure 6-18:**
The k2tog
stitch slants
to the right.

To make a right-leaning decrease when you're purling, you purl 2 stitches together (p2tog) as follows:

1. **Insert the right needle through 2 stitches from right to left, just as you would to purl a single stitch.**

2. **Wrap the yarn around the right-hand needle as usual and purl the 2 stitches together.**

Use these steps to decrease with a left-slanting ssk (slip, slip, knit):

1. **Slip 1 stitch knitwise.**

2. **Slip the next stitch knitwise.**

3. **Slip the left needle through both slipped stitches from the left so that it crosses in front of the right needle, and then wrap the yarn as usual and knit the 2 stitches together.**

You can see how an ssk is worked in Figure 6-19.

**Figure 6-19:**
Working the
left-slanting
ssk stitch.     A. Two stitches slipped knitwise.        B. Insert the LH needle into the front of the loops.

## Double decreases

In knitting, sometimes you need to get rid of 2 stitches at once, particularly in lace patterns. There are a couple ways to remove 2 stitches at once, but usually in lace patterns you see sk2p, which stands for slip 1, knit 2 together, pass the slipped stitch over. This technique combines a left- and right-slanting decrease to get rid of 2 stitches at once. To work this double decrease, you follow three steps:

**Slip 1:** Slip 1 stitch, as if to knit, to the right-hand needle without knitting it.

**K2tog:** Knit the next 2 stitches together.

**Psso (pass the slipped stitch over):** Use the tip of the left-hand needle to bring the slipped stitch (the second stitch on the right-hand needle) up and over the first stitch on the right-hand needle.

## Other essential lace know-how

Knitting lace requires you to pay attention. If you skip a yarn over or a decrease, your pattern won't line up; with lace, unfortunately, mistakes show. But for this book, I've chosen lace patterns that aren't so difficult to follow. There aren't that many stitches or rows in a pattern repeat, and I've intentionally picked patterns that have wrong-side rows without any increases or decreases. I find that plain wrong-side rows really help if you ever have to rip back to correct an error. Also, the patterns all have constant stitch counts. So, you can go through and count your stitches at any time to see if something has gone wrong. If you suspect an error, here's the general rule: One stitch too many usually means that you've skipped a decrease. One stitch too few, on the other hand, suggests that you've forgotten a yarn over.

Understanding how to read your knitting is an essential skill for correcting errors. Like anything else, reading your work takes practice. If your lace seems to have gone off track, start at the right-hand side of your row of knitting and read across. For example, your knitting might go something like this: "Knit 2, k2tog (you can see 2 stitches knit together), yarn over (the yarn lies diagonally over the needle), knit 3, yarn over (another diagonal stitch), ssk (2 stitches together) . . ." Compare your reading to the written pattern to keep yourself lined up. Reading your knitting takes time and effort at first, but the better you become at it, the easier it will be to find and correct errors — and then you'll become a more self-reliant knitter.

Like cables and color patterns, lace often is presented in chart form. Once knitters become familiar with the symbols used, many find that a chart is easier to follow than written directions for lace because you can visualize the lace and begin to understand how the yarn overs and decreases create the pattern. Both charts and line-by-line instructions are presented in this book, so use whichever one comes more naturally for you. If you haven't worked from charts before, you can find out the basics of chart reading in Chapter 4.

## Openwork

*Openwork* is made up of the simplest lace unit (a yarn over and a decrease) worked over and over again (see Figure 6-20). On its own, openwork can create a lovely shawl or scarf, or it can form part of a larger piece as it does in the box top pattern in Chapter 8.

Lots of openwork variations exist, but practice making the one pictured in Figure 6-20 (and charted in Figure 6-21) by casting on any odd number of stitches:

**Row 1:** K1, *yo, k2tog, repeat from * to end.

**Rows 2 and 4:** Purl.

**Row 3:** *K2tog, yo, repeat from * to last st, k1.

Repeat these 4 rows to form the pattern, and bind off your swatch when you have the hang of it.

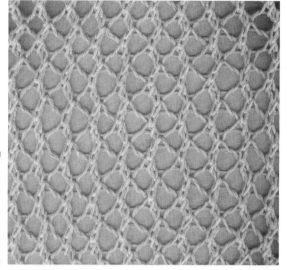

**Figure 6-20:**
Openwork is a good introduction to lace knitting.

## Feather and fan

*Feather and fan,* or Old Shale, creates an undulating line that's great for borders, blankets, or wraps. There are many variations, but they all rely on a group of increases followed by a group of decreases to form the waves of the pattern that you see in Figure 6-22. This pattern is lovely in any sort of yarn, but if you use a yarn that shifts colors, or if you change yarns at every pattern repeat, you accentuate the rippled effect of the pattern.

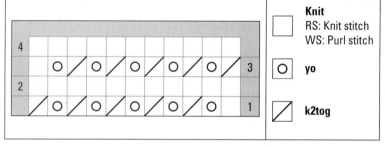

**Figure 6-21:**
A chart of the openwork pattern.

| | Knit |
|---|---|
| ▢ | RS: Knit stitch WS: Purl stitch |
| ◯ | yo |
| ╱ | k2tog |

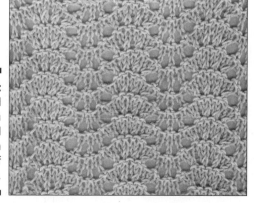

**Figure 6-22:**
Feather and fan is a beautiful pattern with dozens of variations.

Because the increasing and decreasing only happens every 4th row in this pattern, feather and fan gives you a chance to catch your breath between the lace rows, making it a good choice for beginners.

The following version of feather and fan, shown in Figure 6-22 and charted in Figure 6-23, requires a multiple of 11 stitches:

> **Row 1:** Knit.
>
> **Row 2:** Purl.
>
> **Row 3:** *K2tog, k2tog, yo, k1, yo, k1, yo, k1, yo, k2tog, k2tog, repeat from * to end.
>
> **Row 4:** Knit.
>
> Repeat these 4 rows for the pattern.

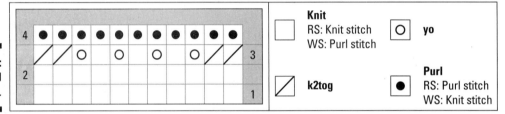

**Figure 6-23:** Feather and fan charted.

If you would like to practice this stitch pattern, cast on 22 stitches with a thicker yarn or 33 stitches with a thin one to make a beautiful, feminine scarf. Follow the directions until the piece measures 60 inches or the desired length.

## Climbing vine lace

The *climbing vine lace* pattern, shown in Figure 6-24, features a strong vertical element. You can use it as a substitute on the lacy V-neck top in Chapter 14, or you can use this lace pattern instead of the rib pattern on the loose rib wrap in Chapter 8. Because you need a multiple of 8 stitches plus 3 for climbing vine lace, try casting on 59 or 67 stitches for the wrap.

The pattern (charted in Figure 6-25) is composed of 4 rows. The wrong-side rows are plain with the exception of the single knit stitch in each repeat. The rest of the pattern is pretty straightforward, and with practice, you'll soon fall into its rhythm. Note the double decrease on Row 3; I explain how to make a double decrease earlier in this chapter. Here's how to knit the climbing vine lace:

> **Row 1 (RS):** K1, p1, *k2tog, yo, k3, yo, ssk, p1; repeat from * to last st, k1.
>
> **Row 2 (WS):** P1, *k1, p7; repeat from * to last 2 sts, k1, p1.
>
> **Row 3 (RS):** K1, p1, *k2, yo, sk2p, yo, k2, p1; repeat from *, k1.
>
> **Row 4 (WS):** P1, *k1, p7; repeat from * to last 2 sts, k1, p1.
>
> Repeat these 4 rows for the pattern.

To practice the climbing vine lace pattern with a swatch, cast on 27 stitches. Work through the 4 rows of the pattern until the swatch measures 6 inches, and then bind off.

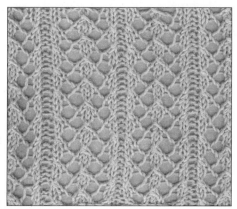

**Figure 6-24:**
Climbing
vine lace.

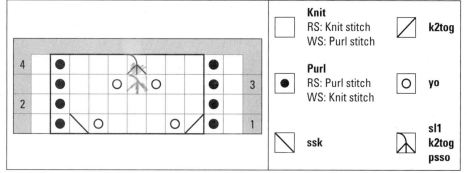

**Figure 6-25:**
Climbing
vine lace
chart.

# Arrowhead lace

*Arrowhead lace,* shown in Figure 6-26, features arches that recall leaves or arrowheads. This lace pattern can be substituted directly into the lacy V-neck top pattern in Chapter 14 to vary the look. Or you can try it alone to create a beautiful scarf or stole.

**Figure 6-26:**
Arrowhead
lace.

Note the double decrease in Row 6 (I explain how to make this decrease earlier in this chapter). Using a multiple of 8 stitches plus 3 (see Figure 6-27), follow these directions:

**Row 1 and all WS rows:** Purl.

**Row 2 (RS):** K2, *yo, ssk, k3, k2tog, yo, k1, repeat from * to last st, k1.

**Row 4 (RS):** K3, *yo, ssk, k1, k2tog, yo, k3, repeat from * to end.

**Row 6 (RS):** K1, p1, *k2, yo, sk2p, yo, k2, p1, repeat from * to last st, k1.

**Rows 8, 10, and 12 (RS):** K1, p1, *ssk, (k1, yo) twice, k1, k2tog, p1, repeat from * to last st, k1.

Repeat these 12 rows for the pattern.

To practice the arrowhead lace pattern and create a scarf, cast on 27 stitches with a fine or sport weight yarn and US 5 needles. Or consider making a stole by casting on 67 stitches. Repeat the 12 rows of the pattern until your scarf or stole measures 60 inches or your desired length, binding off after Row 12.

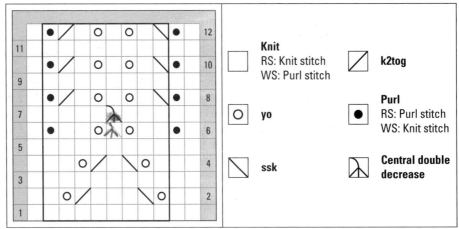

**Figure 6-27:**
Arrowhead
lace chart.

# Chapter 7

# Colorful Stitches

- - - - - - - - - - - - - - - - - - - - - - - - - - - - - - - - - - - - - - - - - - - - - - - - - - - - - - - - - - - - - - - - - - - - - -

## In This Chapter

▶ Adding different color combinations to your work

▶ Making stripes, Fair Isle patterns, and mosaics

▶ Discovering tricks to add color to finished pieces

- - - - - - - - - - - - - - - - - - - - - - - - - - - - - - - - - - - - - - - - - - - - - - - - - - - - - - - - - - - - - - - - - - - - - -

**K**nitting allows you to work with colors in unique ways, creating rich fabrics that are unlike those made by any other method. So why not experiment with these techniques and add some color to your knitting? In this chapter, I offer some tips on choosing colors and combining them in pleasing ways. Then, you find out how to work with color using three different knitting techniques: stripes, Fair Isle patterns, and mosaics. Once you understand the basics behind these techniques, you can use them to create colorful patterns on just about anything you knit. Finally, I offer a bit of how-to on duplicate stitch and surface crochet. Both of these methods allow you to add a bit of color to your knitting after it's done; they're perfect for personalizing or embellishing your finished projects.

## Combining Colors with a Careful Eye

Everything you knit has color — even if the piece is taupe or cream. But sometimes knitters are scared off from working with more than one color. Not because the actual color work techniques are difficult; these knitters don't trust themselves to put colors together. But everyone has a sense of what they like and don't like! I don't think that you can make mistakes with color; you only make choices. So trust yourself.

Here are a few ways to practice combining colors:

✔ **Experiment with color combinations at the yarn shop.** The next time you go into your local yarn shop, grab a skein of yarn in any color that you're drawn to. Don't overthink your choice; just grab one. Choose another and place the two skeins side by side. Add a third and a fourth. Which combinations do you like best? How does swapping one yarn for another change the look of things?

If it's okay with the people at the shop, snap some pictures of the different combinations. Sometimes looking at a photograph gives you different information than you get with your eye. And back home you may have a different reaction to the colors.

✔ **Think about color in terms of percentages.** Find a picture that you're drawn to. This picture might be a painting or postcard or even a newspaper clipping. Think about the colors in it. Does it have, for example, several neutral shades with a small amount of turquoise? Really study the picture and think about colors in terms of percentages. You might say to yourself, "It's about a third sand-colored, and maybe a quarter gray. The rest is a mix of neutral colors with some green tones and pink tones. And then there's that turquoise bucket. Maybe the bucket is only five percent of the picture, but that's definitely what makes the picture interesting."

When you're buying yarn and laying out your colors, use these percentages as guidelines for how much of which color to use. Just as the turquoise bucket "makes" the picture, a skinny stripe of turquoise here and there will really make an otherwise neutral sweater much more interesting.

- **Map out your color patterns on graph paper.** Knitter's graph paper (which you can find online or where you buy yarn) can help you draw the stripe, Fair Isle, and mosaic patterns presented in this chapter. Even designers who work with color patterns every day make sketches like these. You really can't skip this step if you want to know what you're going to get in the end. Use crayons or colored pencils to make your sketch.

If you use regular graph paper, your design will look taller on paper and will look shorter when it has been knit because knitting stitches are shorter than they are wide (knitting graph paper takes this into account). Still, regular graph paper is just fine for working out your colors.

- **Keep color value and contrast in mind.** Any time that you're using multiple colors you have to consider not just the hue of a color but the value of it too. (*Hue* is the "color," such as red or yellow; *value* is the lightness or darkness of the color.) Even if you use a dozen colors, if they're all the same value, the result will be boring or flat, and your hard work just won't show. Why? Dark colors appear to recede and light colors seem to come forward. In other words, having both light and dark colors adds the contrast that you need.

To practice identifying light and dark colors (and this can be more difficult than it seems like it should be), look at your colors and squint for a quick assessment of the differences in value. Better still, take a picture and look at it in black and white to see if you have chosen colors with enough contrast.

- **Use self-striping yarn.** If you don't want to think too hard about color choices, consider using one of the dozens of yarns that stripe themselves. You can knit these yarns on their own to get great stripes, but you can also use one self-striping yarn and one plain yarn in a stripe or mosaic pattern. You'll be pleasantly surprised by the results. If you're feeling even more daring, choose two different colorways of a self-striping yarn and make a piece that's wonderfully rich and colorful.

# Get in Line: Stripes

Stripes are the easiest way to make your knitting colorful. Just because they're easy to knit doesn't make them boring, though. Stripes can be narrow or wide, or you can use a combination of the two. You can knit stripes with two colors or four (or even 20!) to use up every last yard of leftover yarn you have. Allover stripes in bold colors can be great for a blanket or for kids' pieces. Choosing two similar colors can yield a more subtle but lively sense of style for a garment that's a little more sophisticated. And remember that stripes can be used sparingly and still have great effect. For instance, a couple of broad stripes across the chest makes a jaunty men's sweater; skinny stripes on the lower arm and torso makes a women's top fun without overwhelming the shape and structure of the garment.

You can add your stripes to any design — just follow the pattern as written, but change colors as needed to create the stripes you want. Remember to use yarns that meet the gauge requirements for that pattern. However, it's okay to throw a couple of rows in here and there in a yarn that's a little thicker or narrower.

In the following sections, I show you how to make three different types of stripes: two-row stripes, regularly repeating stripes, and random stripes. If you want to get a handle on them, why not create a playful sampler scarf that uses them all? Choose a stitch pattern that doesn't roll, such as garter stitch, seed stitch, or rib. Then cast on enough stitches to create a scarf that's 6 inches wide (go to Chapter 2 to read up on gauge and figure out the correct cast-on number for the weight of yarn you want to use). Follow the stripe patterns laid out here to create your scarf (I give specific scarf instructions after each set of stripe steps). You need at least three colors of yarn for your scarf.

## Two-row stripes

*Two-row stripes* (see Figure 7-1) are easy to work and can be applied to any pattern. A baby sweater knit in two-row stripes has a nautical look. And a two-row striped scarf knit with two self-striping yarns has a lot of visual appeal.

**Figure 7-1:**
Two-row stripes are the easiest kind of stripe to make.

You can make two-row stripes knitting flat or in the round with these directions. With two colors (color A and color B), follow these steps:

1. **With color A, cast on the number of stitches called for in the pattern that you're making.**

2. **Work 2 rows with color A following your pattern.**

3. **Drop color A and start knitting with color B.**

   Don't cut color A; just leave it hanging. (See Chapter 8 for tips on changing colors.)

4. **Work 2 rows with color B.**

5. **Drop color B and pick up color A.**

   Don't cut color B.

6. **Repeat Steps 2 through 5 as you follow the knitting directions in your pattern.**

   Because the stripes are only 2 rows long, you don't need to cut the yarn between stripes and you won't have extra ends to weave in.

For your sampler scarf, continue with the 2-row stripes until the scarf measures about 12 inches. Leave the stitches on the needle, and carry on with the regularly repeating stripes in the following section.

## Regularly repeating stripes

Stripes can be as wide or narrow as you like. If you're knitting back and forth between different widths of stripes, however, it's easiest if your stripes cover an even number of rows. That way, you're always changing yarn at the same edge and minimizing the number of ends you need to weave in.

Just as you can make two-row stripes (see the previous section for the basics of knitting these stripes and changing colors), you also can knit four- or eight-row stripes. But it's often more interesting to knit (and look at) something with a little more variety. For example, the knit sample in Figure 7-2 uses four-row stripes in the darkest color (color C) and eight-row stripes in a medium color (color B), which are always separated by two rows in the lightest color (color A).

**Figure 7-2:**
A pattern
of regular
stripes.

The knit sample in Figure 7-3 uses the same stripes (2 rows, 4 rows, 2 rows, 8 rows), but instead of the color sequence A, B, A, C, A, B, A, C, it uses the sequence A, B, C, A, B, C. As you can see, you can get different looks by using the same yarn and stripes in different ways. Use your graph paper and colored pencils to make a quick sketch before you start knitting (see the earlier section "Combining Colors with a Careful Eye" for tips on trying out different groups of colors).

When making your sampler scarf, work 12 inches with each of the regular stripe sequences described. That is, 12 inches with the color sequence A, B, A, C . . . and 12 inches with the color sequence A, B, C . . . Your scarf now measures 36 inches. Leave the stitches on the needles; you'll finish your scarf with random stripes in the following section.

**Figure 7-3:**
A different
arrange-
ment of
colors on
the same
stripe
pattern.

## *Random stripes*

TIP

Sometimes you may want more chaos and less order. Stripes that aren't repeated in any regular way can give you great results. You can alternate regularly between three or five colors and have their widths vary, or you can let chance tell you which color to use *and* how wide to make the stripes. But how do you introduce randomness? Here are some options:

- ✔ Roll dice. Whatever number you roll is the number of rows you knit in the next color.

- ✔ Flip through a book and use the last digit of a page number to determine the width of your stripe.

- ✔ Do a Web search for a random stripes generator. Yes, there really is such a thing!

- ✔ Put all the yarns that you're willing to use in a paper bag (they should all knit to the same gauge), and pull one out at random each time you're ready to change colors. Then, to determine how many rows to knit, roll the dice and knit away. With this technique, you'll come up with something totally unique. Besides, it's fun to be surprised!

See an example of random stripes in Figure 7-4; it uses five different colors in stripes of varying widths.

Complete your sampler scarf with random stripes, continuing until the scarf measures 60 inches or the length you desire. Bind off and weave in the remaining loose ends (see the appendix for more about these tasks).

**Figure 7-4:**
Random
stripes
create
visual
interest.

# *Classic Color: Fair Isle Patterns*

*Fair Isle,* or stranded, knitting patterns are made up of repeated multicolor motifs. These patterns are named after the Scottish islands where they were developed (even if the particular pattern you're working on actually comes from the British Isles, Scandinavia, or your own imagination). There can be any number of colors in a Fair Isle pattern, but usually just two colors are used in each row. And thank goodness for that!

While you knit with one color, you carry the other color along (or *strand* it along the back), creating what knitters call *floats*. So, you need to figure out a way to carry both yarns comfortably across the row. Some knitters put both yarns in their right hand. Others find it easier to carry one yarn in their right hand and carry the second yarn in their left hand. If, at first, you find that you can hold only one yarn at a time, alternating which yarn you hold, don't worry; this technique works fine. You'll get more comfortable holding the yarn as you go along.

Keep one ball of yarn on your left and one on your right so they don't become tangled as you knit.

Don't pull the yarn tightly when you knit the first stitch with a new color. The float you're creating needs to span the back of as many stitches as it passes over. As you knit, take a moment to look at the back of your work, and be mindful of making your floats long enough. Some knitters find it useful to spread out the stitches on the right needle rather than bunching them up. Try working back and forth on a circular needle to give yourself more room to stretch the stitches out if you need to.

The following sections contain a few Fair Isle motifs that you can use to practice or to include in a few different patterns in this book. If you're new to knitting from charts or need a quick refresher, have a look at Chapter 4.

## Simple stranded pattern

This simple stranded pattern creates little polka dots of color. Use white on a dark background to suggest snowflakes (as you see in Figure 7-5). You only carry both colors on those rows with the dots (that is, Rows 1 and 5 of the eight-row pattern repeat).

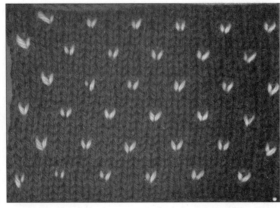

**Figure 7-5:** A simple stranded pattern creates dots of color.

You can read stranded patterns from a chart like the one in Figure 7-6. When reading the chart, remember to read right-side rows from right to left and wrong-side rows from left to right.

To practice making a flat swatch with this simple stranded pattern, you need two colors, the main color (MC) and the contrasting color (CC). Cast on 27 stitches (or any multiple of 8 stitches plus 3) with MC, and then purl 1 row. Then check out Figure 7-6, repeating the 8 rows of the chart to form the pattern. Bind off when your swatch reaches the desired length, ending after Row 8.

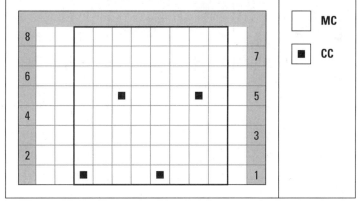

**Figure 7-6:**
A chart of the simple stranded pattern.

# Small Fair Isle motif

A small Fair Isle motif, like the one in Figure 7-7, can be used as a simple border or as an allover pattern. For example, try it as a design for the throw pillows in Chapter 9. To do so, cast on 67 or 75 stitches (a multiple of 8 plus 3). You can also use this motif as a border on either the lacy V-neck top or the women's scoop neck pullover in Chapter 14. The numbers for this pattern work out just right; you won't have to modify the number of stitches you cast on for your top.

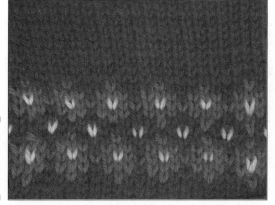

**Figure 7-7:**
A simple Fair Isle motif.

To practice this pattern, cast on 27 stitches (or any multiple of 8 plus 3) with color A. Color A is the same as the main color (or MC) if you intend to use this pattern as a detail on a larger project. Before you begin the chart, create a plain-colored border with color A. To do so, knit for 1 inch, ending with a wrong-side row. Then follow the chart in Figure 7-8. Repeat the 7 rows for the pattern. If you're using this as a border stripe, repeat the 7 rows as many times as desired, ending the last repeat after Row 5, and then continue with color A only.

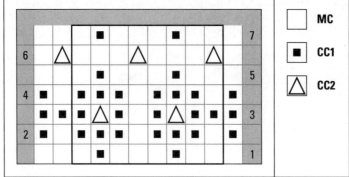

| | MC |
| | CC1 |
| | CC2 |

**Figure 7-8:**
A chart of
the small
Fair Isle
motif.

If you're making a swatch, work a few more rows with color A, and then bind off.

# Fair Isle border

Figure 7-9 shows a classic-looking Fair Isle border pattern. Because this pattern uses five colors, it's worth experimenting a bit with your graph paper and colored pencils (as I explain in the earlier section "Combining Colors with a Careful Eye") to get the look that you're after (whether that's a vintage ski sweater or a more contemporary take on this classic). In fact, I think someone should create a Fair Isle coloring book; if you're like me, you'll be fascinated by how different the same pattern can look when you simply exchange one color for another! Put your favorite Fair Isle border color combination into action on the women's scoop neck pullover in Chapter 14.

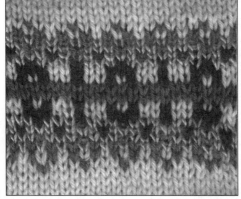

**Figure 7-9:**
A Fair Isle
border
pattern.

The same knitting principles for any stranded color work apply, whether it's a simple two-color pattern or something more ambitious like Fair Isle. Even though five colors are used, remember that you're only using two colors in any row. So the knitting will be the same. Reading the chart may demand a little more attention though; using a ruler or sticky note to mark what row of the pattern you're on can help. See Chapter 4 for more on deciphering patterns and working from charts.

Before you start on a new row, take a moment to see what two colors are used in it. Cut the yarn for any color you won't be using in the next couple of rows and leave a tail to weave in. Taking time to keep your yarns tidy helps prevent irritating tangles down the road.

It's always smart to make a swatch with a Fair Isle pattern because you want to make sure that your gauge is right. Swatching also gives you a chance to see what the pattern will really look like knit up. To make your swatch of this pattern, cast on 27 stitches (or any multiple of 8 plus 3) with color A (which should be your main or background color), and work a few rows. Then follow the chart in Figure 7-10.

After completing the 18 rows of the pattern continue on with color A only. Work at least 4 inches in color A if you're using this piece as a swatch to measure, and then bind off. That way you can be sure that your gauge over the color work section and the single color section are the same.

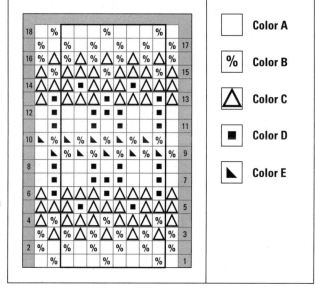

**Figure 7-10:**
A chart of a Fair Isle border.

# Slip in Some Color: Mosaics

When it comes to color patterns, I love mosaics. Why? Their repeating geometric patterns are pleasing, and I find them much easier to knit than other multicolor techniques. If you can knit two-row stripes (which I discuss earlier in this chapter) and can slip a stitch, you're more than halfway there. In mosaic knitting, instead of knitting with two strands of yarn, you only use one at a time. On right-side rows, any stitch that needs to be the "new" color (the color of yarn you're holding), you knit. Any stitch that's supposed to stay the old color (the color from the previous row), you slip, bringing the new color along on the wrong side of the work. (Chapter 4 has the basics of reading mosaic charts.) And wrong-side rows are even easier: If the stitch is the same color as the yarn in your hand, purl it; if it isn't the same, slip it.

Here are a few things to remember about mosaic knitting:

✔ Choose yarns that have the same weight. If one yarn is thicker than the other, the design won't look its best.

✔ When it comes to yarn color, contrast is vital to a pleasing final result. Choose two colors that have different values (that is, one darker and one lighter) so that the pattern pops out. To get more complex color results without the fuss of changing yarns all the time, choose a plain-colored yarn and a variegated yarn. A bright multicolored foreground with a black background, for example, looks almost like stained glass.

✔ Work two rows in the first color and then two rows in the second color. Repeat. In the second row of a color, knit or purl the stitches that were worked in the previous row, and slip the slipped stitches. No stitches change color in this row.

✔ Always slip stitches purlwise with the yarn held to the wrong-side of the work. (See Chapter 5 for how-to on slipping stitches.)

✔ Mosaic patterns that are knit flat usually include some extra stitches for the edges so that the patterns stay evenly centered. For example, you're likely to see directions that ask you to use, say, a multiple of 16 stitches plus 3. When you knit a mosaic in the round, though, throw out those extra stitches and stick to the even multiple only.

✔ Stitches are slipped exactly twice. If you find yourself slipping a stitch more (or fewer) times, back up and read your knitting to see what went wrong.

✔ If you tend to knit tightly, remember that the yarn carried behind the slipped stitch should be as wide as the normal stitches. Keep the stitches on the right needle stretched out a bit to help you overcome the tendency to pull too tight. Use a needle long enough to do so; working back and forth on a circular needle may help.

In the following sections, I give you two 16-stitch mosaics and three 8-stitch mosaics. Here are some general facts about each of them:

✔ Mosaics with 16 stitches, like the puzzle piece mosaic and woven cord mosaic, can be substituted directly into the mosaic bags pattern in Chapter 11. The pattern for this eye-catching bag is a good one to help you get comfortable with mosaic knitting. Because you're knitting in the round, you'll find it easy to keep things lined up.

The written directions for both 16-stitch mosaics in this chapter are designed for knitting in the round (so they're easy to use in the mosaic bags pattern); if you're using this pattern to knit flat, add the 3 selvedge stitches shown in the charts (1 at the beginning of the row and 2 at the end of the row) to complete the pattern. If you're using the charted pattern to work in the round, read only the outlined 16-stitch pattern repeat.

✔ Smaller mosaics, such as the little mosaic, little boxes mosaic, and miniature mosaic are 8 stitches wide, which makes them perfect for the women's scoop neck pullover and lacy V-neck top patterns in Chapter 14 (if you want to use a mosaic pattern in lieu of Fair Isle or lace). You can also use these smaller mosaics in the mosaic bags pattern. Just remember to throw out the 3 selvedge stitches given in the directions for knitting flat; you won't need them to work in the round. Or try them on the throw pillows in Chapter 9, using 67 or 75 stitches.

If you want to get your hands on more mosaic patterns, any of the brilliant treasuries by Barbara G. Walker offer lots of inspiring options.

## Puzzle piece mosaic

The *puzzle piece mosaic,* as the name suggests, looks a bit like jigsaw puzzle pieces. You can see this mosaic in Figure 7-11. You'll find this mosaic to be quite predictable: After you get going with it, you'll be able to see what should come next and will soon fall into its rhythm.

You can get a feel for this mosaic by making a swatch with 35 stitches. You'll use two colors. I call them main color (MC) and contrasting color (CC), but the colors will be used equally. Cast on 35 stitches with CC and knit 2 rows, and then follow the chart in Figure 7-12 or the upcoming written directions. Remember, because you're knitting flat, you need to use those 3 edge stitches!

**Figure 7-11:**
Puzzle piece
mosaic.

**Set-up rounds:** Knit 2 rounds with CC.

**Round 1:** With MC, *(k1, sl 1) 8 times, repeat from * to end.

**Round 2 and all even-numbered rounds:**

If a stitch was knit in the previous row (it will be the same color as the yarn in your hand), knit it (or purl it if you're working back and forth).

If a stitch was slipped in the previous row (it won't be the color of the yarn in your hand), slip the stitch purlwise with the yarn held to the wrong-side of the work.

**Round 3:** With CC, *k2, sl 1, k11, sl 1, k1, repeat from * to end.

**Round 5:** With MC, *k1, sl 1, k3, sl 1, k5, sl 1, k3, sl 1, repeat from * to end.

**Round 7:** With CC, *k4, sl 1, k1, sl 1, k3, sl 1, k1, sl 1, k3, repeat from * to end.

**Round 9:** With MC, *k1, sl 1, k5, sl 1, k1, sl 1, k5, sl 1, repeat from * to end.

**Round 11:** With CC, *k2, sl 1, k1, sl 1, k7, sl 1, k1, sl 1, k1, repeat from * to end.

**Round 13:** With MC, *k3, sl 1, k3, sl 1, k1, sl 1, k3, sl 1, k2, repeat from * to end.

**Round 15:** With CC, *k6, sl 1, k3, sl 1, k5, repeat from * to end.

**Round 17:** With MC, *(k1, sl 1) 8 times, repeat from * to end.

**Round 19:** Repeat Round 15.

**Round 21:** Repeat Round 13.

**Round 23:** Repeat Round 11.

**Round 25:** Repeat Round 9.

**Round 27:** Repeat Round 7.

**Round 29:** Repeat Round 5.

**Round 31:** Repeat Round 3.

Repeat Rounds 1–32 for pattern.

When your swatch is large enough to measure accurately and you feel comfortable knitting the mosaic pattern, bind off.

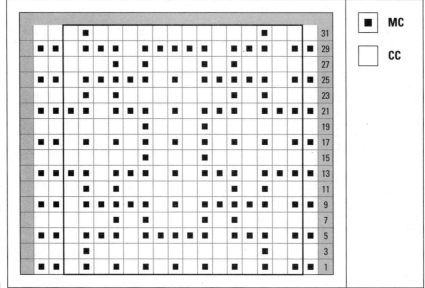

■ MC

□ CC

**Figure 7-12:**
Puzzle piece mosaic chart.

# Woven cord mosaic

The *woven cord mosaic,* shown in Figure 7-13, creates a dynamic design with strong diagonal elements. Try it with the mosaic bags pattern as I have (see Chapter 11).

If you're knitting flat, remember that you need the 3 edge stitches shown in the chart. If you're knitting in the round, ignore the selvedge stitches and use only the 16-stitch pattern repeat outlined by the dark box. The written directions describe how to work the pattern in the round, so they're easy to use with the mosaic bag pattern. But remember not to include the 3 edge stitches.

**Figure 7-13:**
The woven cord mosaic.

You can practice this mosaic by making a swatch that's made with 35 stitches or any multiple of 16 plus 3. Choose two colors, referred to as MC and CC. MC is the foreground color, represented as black in the chart in Figure 7-14. CC is the background color, represented by white in the chart. To begin your swatch, cast on 35 stitches, knit 2 rows with CC, and then follow the chart or these written directions:

**Set-up rounds:** Knit 2 rounds with CC.

**Round 1:** With MC, *k8, sl 1, k1, sl 1, k5, repeat from * to end.

**Round 2 and all even-numbered rounds:**

If a stitch was knit in the previous row (it will be the same color as the yarn in your hand), knit it (or purl it if you're working back and forth).

If a stitch was slipped in the previous row (it won't be the color of the yarn in your hand), slip the stitch purlwise with the yarn held to the wrong-side of the work.

**Round 3:** With CC, *k1, sl 1, k5, sl 1, k8, repeat from * to end.

**Round 5:** With MC, *k2, sl 1, k1, sl 1, k1, sl 1, k3, sl 1, k1, sl 1, k1, sl 1, k1, repeat from * to end.

**Round 7:** With CC, *k9, sl 1, k5, sl 1, repeat from * to end.

**Round 9:** With MC, *sl 1, k1, sl 1, k13, repeat from * to end.

**Round 11:** With CC, *k3, sl 1, k9, sl 1, k2, repeat from * to end.

**Round 13:** With MC, *sl 1, k13, sl 1, k1, repeat from * to end.

**Round 15:** With CC, *k1, sl 1, k5, sl 1, k8, repeat from * to end.

**Round 17:** With MC, *k2, sl 1, k1, sl 1, k1, sl 1, k3, sl 1, k1, sl 1, k1, sl 1, k1, repeat from * to end.

**Round 19:** With CC *k9, sl 1, k5, sl 1, repeat from * to end.

**Round 21:** With MC, *k6, sl 1, k1, sl 1, k7, repeat from * to end.

**Round 23:** With CC, *k5, sl 1, k5, sl 1, k4, repeat from * to end.

Repeat Rounds 1–24 for pattern. To complete your swatch, repeat the 24 rows of the chart, and then bind off.

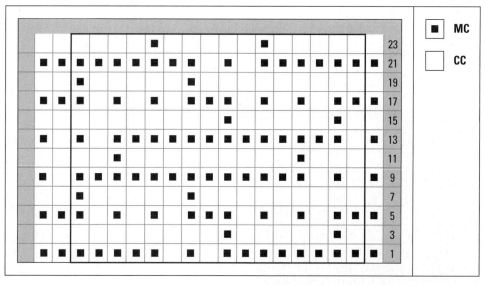

**Figure 7-14:** The woven cord mosaic, charted.

## Little mosaic

The *little mosaic* is shown at the bottom of Figure 7-15. Use it instead of the Fair Isle pattern on the women's pullovers in Chapter 14 or try it on a throw pillow using 67 or 75 stitches and worsted weight yarn (see the throw pillow pattern in Chapter 9).

**Figure 7-15:**
Three 8-stitch mosaics from top to bottom.

To practice the little mosaic, use two colors, referred to as MC and CC. Cast on 27 stitches with MC and follow these directions to get started (or check out Figure 7-16 for a chart):

**Set-up rows:** With MC, knit a row, purl a row.

**Row 1:** With CC, k1, *k4, sl 1, k3, repeat from * to last 2 sts, k2.

**Row 2 and all wrong-side rows:** Purl the sts knit in the previous row and slip the sts slipped in the previous row.

**Row 3:** With MC, k1, *k3, sl 1, k1, sl 1, k1, sl 1, repeat from * to last 2 sts, k2.

**Row 5:** With CC, k1, *sl 1, k1, sl 1, k1, sl 1, k3, repeat from *to last 2 sts, sl 1, k1.

**Row 7:** With MC, k1, *k3, sl 1, k4, repeat from * to last 2 sts, k2.

**Row 9:** With CC, k1, *sl 1, k7, repeat from * to last 2 sts, sl 1, k1.

**Row 11:** With MC, k1, *k1, sl 1, k1, sl 1, k3, sl 1, repeat from * to last 2 sts, k2.

**Row 13:** With CC, k1, *sl 1, k3, sl 1, k1, sl 1, k1, repeat from * to last 2 sts, sl 1, k1.

**Row 15:** With MC, k1, *k7, sl 1, repeat from * to last 2 sts, k2.

Repeat Rows 1–16 for pattern. To complete your swatch, repeat the 16 rows once more and then bind off.

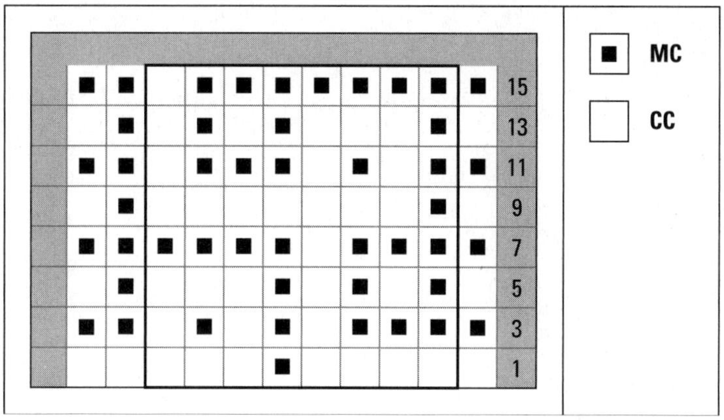

**Figure 7-16:**
Little mosaic
chart.

# Little boxes mosaic

The *little boxes mosaic* is a miniaturized version of the larger pinbox mosaic in Chapter 11. This mosaic is shown in the center of Figure 7-15 and charted in Figure 7-17.

To practice the little boxes mosaic, use 27 stitches to make a swatch. Use two colors, referred to as MC and CC. For your swatch, cast on 27 stitches with MC and follow these directions (or the chart in Figure 7-17):

**Set-up rows:** With MC, knit a row, purl a row.

**Row 1:** With CC, knit.

**Row 2 and all wrong-side rows:** Purl the sts knit in the previous row and slip the sts slipped in the previous row.

**Row 3:** With MC, k1, *k4, sl 1, k3, repeat from * to last 2 sts, k2.

**Row 5:** With CC, k1, *k3, sl 1, k1, sl 1, k2, repeat from * to last 2 sts, k2.

**Row 7:** With MC, k1, *k2, sl 1, k1, sl 1, k1, sl 1, k1, repeat from * to last 2 sts, k2.

**Row 9:** With CC, k1, *k1, sl 1, k1, sl 1, k1, sl 1, k1, sl 1, repeat from * to last 2 sts, k2.

**Row 11:** With MC, k1, *k2, sl 1, k1, sl 1, k1, sl 1, k1, repeat from * to last 2 sts, k2.

**Row 13:** With CC, k1, *k3, sl 1, k1, sl 1, k2, repeat from * to last 2 sts, k2.

**Row 15:** With MC, k1, *k4, sl 1, k3, repeat from * to last 2 sts, k2.

**Row 17:** With CC, knit.

**Row 19:** With MC, k1, *sl 1, k7, repeat from * to last 2 sts, sl 1, k1.

**Row 21:** With CC, k1, *k1, sl 1, k6, sl 1, repeat from * to last 2 sts, k2.

**Row 23:** With MC, k1, *sl 1, k1, sl 1, k3, sl 1, k1, repeat from * to last 2 sts, sl 1, k1.

**Row 25:** With CC, k1, *k1, sl 1, k1, sl 1, k1, sl 1, k1, sl 1, repeat from * to last 2 sts, k2.

**Row 27:** With MC, k1, *sl 1, k1, sl 1, k3, sl 1, k1, repeat from * to last 2 sts, sl 1, k1.

**Row 29:** With CC, k1, *k1, sl 1, k6, sl 1, repeat from * to last 2 sts, k2.

**Row 31:** With MC, k1, *sl 1, k7, repeat from * to last 2 sts, sl 1, k1.

Repeat Rows 1–32 for pattern. If you're making a swatch, bind off after Row 32.

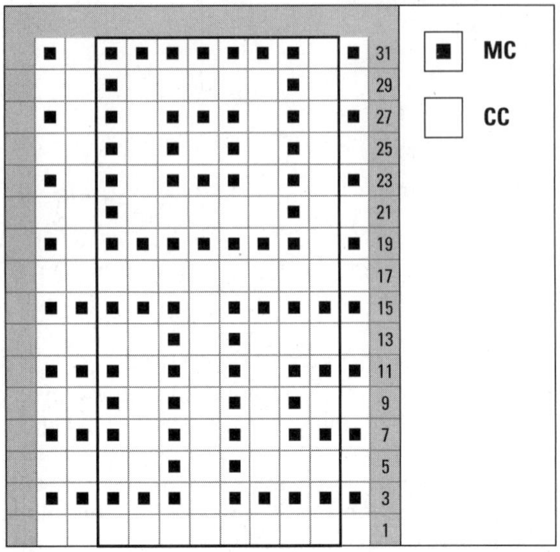

**Figure 7-17:**
The chart for the little boxes mosaic.

## Miniature mosaic

The *miniature mosaic,* another 8-stitch mosaic pattern, can be used in the same places as the other small mosaic patterns. It's also a great allover pattern; try it on a throw pillow (see Chapter 9 for the throw pillow pattern). Or you can knit it as a scarf using garter stitch instead of stockinette stitch — just remember to keep the yarn to the wrong-side when you slip your stitches! This mosaic is shown at the top of Figure 7-15 and is charted in Figure 7-18.

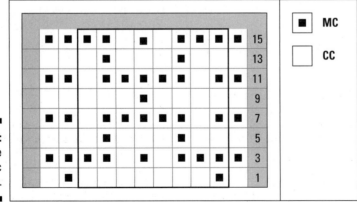

**Figure 7-18:**
Miniature mosaic chart.

To practice this mosaic pattern with a swatch, cast on 27 stitches with MC and follow these directions (or the chart in Figure 7-18):

> **Set-up rows:** With MC, knit a row, purl a row.
>
> **Row 1:** With CC, k1, *sl 1, k7, repeat from * to last 2 sts, sl 1, k1.
>
> **Row 2 and all wrong-side rows:** Purl the sts knit in the previous row and slip the sts slipped in the previous row.
>
> **Row 3:** With MC, k1, *k3, sl 1, k1, sl 1, k2, repeat from * to last 2 sts, k2.
>
> **Row 5:** With CC, k1, *k2, sl 1, k3, sl 1, k1, repeat from * to last 2 sts, k2.
>
> **Row 7:** With MC, k1, *k1, sl 1, k5, sl 1, repeat from * to last 2 sts, k2.
>
> **Row 9:** With CC, k1, *k4, sl 1, k3, repeat from * to last 2 sts, k2.
>
> **Row 11:** With MC, k1, *k1, sl 1, k5, sl 1, repeat from * to last 2 sts, k2.
>
> **Row 13:** With CC, k1, *k2, sl 1, k3, sl 1, k1, repeat from * to last 2 sts, k2.
>
> **Row 15:** With MC, k1, *k3, sl 1, k1, sl 1, k2, repeat from * to last 2 sts, k2.

Repeat Rows 1–16 for pattern. To complete your swatch, repeat the 16 rows once more and then bind off.

# Color for Cheaters: Adding Details after You Finish Knitting

So what do you do when you want to add a bit of color or personalization to a hand-knit after the fact? Or what do you do if you're reaching despair with the line of duck-ies that you're supposed to have in a row on that sweater? My answer: cheat. Well, it's not really cheating, but in the following sections, I show you two great ways to add little bits of color detail *after* the piece has been knit: duplicate stitch and surface cro-chet. I find these techniques particularly useful for things like monogramming a baby's name or initial onto an already knit piece after he or she arrives. That way, you can have the hat or blanket done in a neutral color, and just add the details (in whatever you deem to be a gender-appropriate color) at the last minute.

Here's a little secret: You don't actually even have to knit the thing that you're person-alizing. These techniques work just fine on purchased knits too.

## Duplicate stitch

*Duplicate stitch,* also called Swiss Darning, allows you to go back over your stitches with a different color. When done carefully, you can't even tell that the stitches weren't knit in the contrasting color (or at least not without scrutiny).

To work duplicate stitch, you need a finished piece in stockinette stitch, a good yarn needle, and some contrasting yarn of the same weight as the knitted piece. Tape or ribbon yarns work very nicely. Also consider a yarn with some variegation; this type of yarn adds shading to your finished work.

Before you start working the duplicate stitch, decide what you want to stitch, where you want to stitch it, and how big it should be. Say, for example, that you want to make letters that are about 2 inches tall. To figure out how many stitches you have to work with vertically, multiply your row gauge by 2. (See Chapter 2 for gauge basics.) At 5 rows per inch, for example, that's 10 stitches. So, using knitter's graph paper, draw out your design so that it's ten spaces tall.

From here, duplicate stitch is a bit like counted cross-stitch and a bit like weaving in your ends. Thread your needle with the contrasting yarn, and, looking at your chart, begin stitching (following the steps I provide later in the section). The trick to duplicate stitch is to follow the serpentine path that the yarn takes: up, over, down, over, up, over, down, over (which makes little horseshoes).

The technique that you use for duplicate stitch is also a tidy way to weave in ends. When worked from the wrong side, the ends are almost invisible and have the same stretch as the finished knitting.

To work duplicate stitch, follow these steps:

1. **Insert the needle from the wrong-side to the right-side at the base of the first stitch (you see the yarn come out the front of the piece in Figure 7-19).**

2. **Follow the line of the stitch and put the needle back in at the top of the stitch (that is, in the row above the stitch that you're duplicating) as shown in Figure 7-19.**

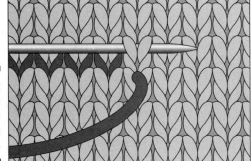

**Figure 7-19:**
Starting the duplicate stitch technique.

3. **Go under the full stitch (two legs) in the row above, and then bring the needle back out to the right side.**

4. **Put the needle back in where you came out, at the bottom of the stitch.**

5. **Go under one full stitch (two legs) in the row below the stitch you're duplicating, and then bring the needle back out to the front as shown in Figure 7-20.**

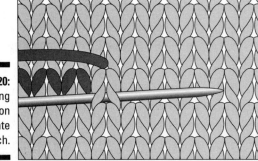

**Figure 7-20:**
Showing progress on duplicate stitch.

**6. Follow Steps 2–5 for each stitch that you want to duplicate.**

If the stitches aren't consecutive, it's fine to skip spaces. However, always begin by bringing the needle from back to front at the base of the stitch to be duplicated.

To practice duplicate stitching, first make a swatch that's about 20 stitches wide and about 30 rows tall and bind it off (or use a leftover swatch from another project). On graph paper, sketch out your initial, no more than 10 stitches wide or 20 stitches tall. With a contrasting yarn, duplicate stitch your initial onto the swatch. When practicing this technique, you may find it useful to have a swatch knit in a variegated yarn; this makes following the path of the yarn easier. Be sure the yarn you're stitching with contrasts strongly with the yarn of the swatch.

## Surface crochet

Like duplicate stitch, *surface crochet* is a great way to add colorful details to a finished piece. However, it's a little more free-form than duplicate stitch and it has a different look. It's a fun technique to experiment with and can be used on top of any stitch pattern. In other words, unlike duplicate stitch, surface crochet doesn't require your finished piece to be knit in stockinette stitch.

To try surface crochet, you need your finished knit, some contrasting yarn, and a crochet hook. Before you start, you should have a rough idea of what sort of designs you want to add and where. But because surface crochet is pretty easy to redo, feel free to experiment with the technique, adding flowers, geometric motifs, or abstract designs as the spirit moves you. You can work with a single color or with many.

To surface crochet, follow these steps:

**1. Insert your crochet hook through a purl bump or the ladder rung between columns of stitches.**

Grab the contrasting yarn with the hook and pull it through, forming your first loop or crochet chain.

**2. Stick the hook under the next purl bump or ladder rung.**

Wrap the yarn around the hook and pull it through the loop on the hook. See Figure 7-21 to see what this step looks like.

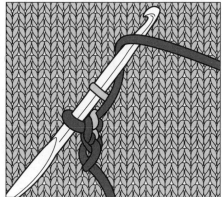

**Figure 7-21:**
Adding detail with surface crochet.

3. **Continue in this way until your design is done.**

You can move up, down, sideways, or diagonally. Figure 7-22 shows a finished surface crochet design.

As you're working, take care to keep your stitches loose enough that you don't cause the finished piece to pucker. Try a larger hook or work 1 chain stitch between stitches if you have trouble keeping your stitches loose.

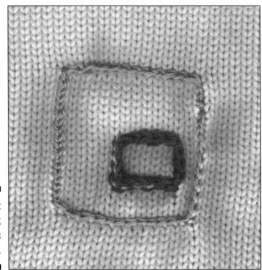

**Figure 7-22:**
A quick design adds personality.

Experiment with surface crochet techniques using spare swatches and scrap yarn. Try your hand at making circles, triangles, letters, or abstract designs using one color or several.

# Part III
# Patterns with Rectangles and Related Shapes

The 5th Wave                    By Rich Tennant

"She started knitting oven mitts and toaster cozies. Then, one day she saw Snowball shivering next to her drinking bowl, and well, her tail's still wagging in there, so I don't see the harm."

# In this part . . .

**W**hen I first started thinking about basic designs for this book, I, of course, thought of rectangles; they're the easiest to knit, after all. But what can you do with a rectangle that you'd actually want to knit and would want to wear or use? A bunch, as you find out in this part. Chapters 8 and 9 feature patterns and variations for scarves, wraps, hats, slippers, blankets, pillows, and more. And when I say that they're all rectangles, I mean it. Brand-new knitters can pull off any of these projects; more experienced knitters will enjoy their ease and versatility. Chapter 10 is full of projects that call for "almost rectangles" — these patterns are just a baby step up. There's very little shaping to do in these patterns, and even the more complex-looking projects in this chapter are straightforward knits. In fact, with this chapter you can comfortably consider leaving the land of the scarf in favor of a great knit coat or messenger bag. And throughout this part, remember to read through the variations. These may inspire you to move in new directions.

# Chapter 8

# Rectangles to Wear

. . . . . . . . . . . . . . . . . . . . . . . . . . . . . . . . . . . . . . . . . . . . . . . . . . . . . . . . . . . . . . . . . .

. . . . . . . . . . . . . . . . . . . . . . . . . . . . . . . . . . . . . . . . . . . . . . . . . . . . . . . . . . . . . . . . . .

*W*hen I first started thinking about writing a book of straightforward patterns based on simple shapes, I joked about rectangles and that classic first knitting project: the garter stitch scarf (and yes, I've come up with a version of it). But the more I thought about the knitted rectangle, the more I came to like it. The rectangle lying flat may seem boring, but when it's draped over your body or filled with a bit of stuffing, it takes on form and style.

On the surface, knitting rectangles is about casting on the appropriate number of stitches and just knitting away. But varying the yarns you use, the gauge you knit them at, the stitch pattern, or the size of the rectangle can turn this basic shape into a thousand beautiful things. Anyone who has successfully knitted a few rows can happily knit the most basic versions of these patterns. You don't increase or decrease (see Chapters 11 and 12 for more about these skills), and each project can be knit in a simple stitch pattern. However, just because these patterns are simple doesn't mean that seasoned knitters can't enjoy them! Those of you who are ready for more adventure in your knitting should try some of the variations given at the end of each pattern; they offer plenty of options for color and stitch work. And, of course, knitters of all skill levels can use these basic ideas as templates for their own improvisations.

With this chapter, you can make oodles of scarves using the patterns and variations for the garter stitch scarf, ribbed scarf, and box stitch scarf. You'll also find a hat pattern that's sized for the whole family and slippers that are sure to bring back waves of knitted nostalgia with each wearing. I also include two wraps, both of which are stunning and no more difficult to knit than a scarf. I especially love how the loose rib wrap can make a great updated poncho or a sleeves-only shrug. I round out the chapter with a project that I call the box top. While the knitting in this project is purely rectangular, by using a wisely placed combination of simple stitches, the top recalls a 1940s pin-up girl.

## Garter Stitch Scarf

If you've ever knit anything before, chances are you have at least started a garter stitch scarf. The pattern for it is sort of like a recipe for toast — it barely merits writing down. But the thing is, even after centuries of knitting, you can still do a bunch of cool things with a garter stitch scarf. Try my pattern (see Figure 8-1), or use it as a jumping off point to find your own special recipe. (For the basics on garter stitch, head to Chapter 5.)

This scarf pattern is enormously flexible. Cast on more or fewer stitches. In fact, any number is fine. Try adding in a quadruple or even quintuple wrap, or if you want, change the spacing between the elongated rows.

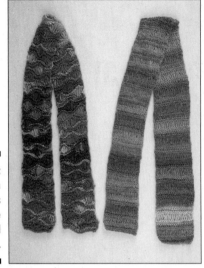

**Figure 8-1:** Garter stitch scarves feature elongated stitches.

# New skill: The double wrap (and beyond)

A *double wrap* is a shockingly easy way to get a lacy look. It works with any number of stitches and can add a bit of visual interest to the bottom of a sweater, a shawl, or, in this case, a scarf.

To work the double wraps, follow these instructions:

1. **On the row specified in the pattern, insert the needle into the stitch as if to knit, but instead of wrapping the yarn once around the needle as you usually do, wrap it around a second time as shown in Figure 8-2.**

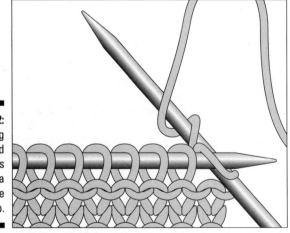

**Figure 8-2:** Making elongated stitches with a double wrap.

2. **Do the same on the next stitch and on each stitch across the row.**

   At the end of the row, you'll end up with what looks like a lot of stitches on the needle.

3. **On the next row, insert the needle into the first wrap of the first stitch normally, and knit it, wrapping the yarn only once.**

Even though you have lots of wraps on the needle, the bottom of the stitch should look the same as a normal knitted stitch.

**4. As you complete the stitch, let the extra wraps fall as shown in Figure 8-3.**

Dropping these wraps creates the elongated stitches.

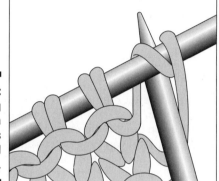

**Figure 8-3:** Dropping the extra wraps forms elongated stitches.

 A triple wrap is worked the same way (and you can extend this number as far as you want, wrapping four, five, or more times). Wrap each stitch in the row three times, and then let the extra wraps fall on the next row. The more times you wrap, the longer your stitches will be.

## Materials and vital statistics

- **Yarn:** Trendsetter Tonalita (50% wool, 50% acrylic); 100 yards (91 meters) per 50 grams; 2 balls; color: 2348
- **Needles:** US 7 (4.5 mm) needles, or the size needed to match gauge
- **Other materials:** Yarn needle for weaving in ends
- **Size:** 5 inches wide by 62 inches long
- **Gauge:** 16 stitches and 32 rows per 4 inches in garter stitch (matching gauge precisely isn't critical for this project)

This scarf features rows of elongated stitches that are made by wrapping the yarn around the needle multiple times. This allows light to shine through and really show off your yarn. Combine these airy rows with a self-striping yarn, and you'll have yourself something quite eye-catching. This scarf is quick to knit and won't deplete your yarn stash — a boon to the knitter in need of a speedy project that won't break the bank.

## Directions

Cast on 20 sts.

Rows 1, 2, and 3: Knit.

Row 4: Knit, wrapping the yarn twice around the needle for each st. It will look like there are 40 sts on the needle.

Row 5: Knit, dropping extra wraps. You will have 20 sts.

Rows 6, 7, and 8: Knit.

Row 9: Knit, wrapping the yarn 3 times around the needle for each st. It will look like there are 60 sts on the needle.

Row 10: Knit, dropping the extra wraps. You will have 20 sts.

Repeat Rows 1–10 until you're nearly out of yarn or until your scarf is as long as you like, ending with Row 3 or Row 8. Bind off and weave in ends.

## Variation: Using beautiful yarns

 Chances are that you've had a ball of yarn that looked better on the coffee table than it did when it was knit up. Some yarns, like hand-spun yarn, are beautiful on the skein, but their beauty gets lost when they're knit because you don't see enough of the yarn in any one place. If I ever have a small amount of a beautiful yarn that can't seem to find its rightful place, I try using it with this garter stitch scarf pattern or the lovely seafoam stitch variation in the next section. Use needles of whatever size are right for the yarn. (See Chapter 2 for more on gauge and needle size.)

## Variation: Creating a seafoam stitch scarf

This kicked-up version of the garter stitch scarf uses the same idea of wrapping the yarn two, three, and four times around the needle, but it uses these different numbers of wraps all in the same row, creating an undulating pattern of elongated stitches.

Here are the directions to knit this very quick and pretty variation:

Cast on 27 sts (try 17 sts with very fat yarn or 37 sts with thinner yarns). You don't need to use a larger needle to make the stitches loose; the extra wraps take care of that.

Rows 1 and 2: Knit.

Row 3: K1, *k1 wrapping twice, k1 wrapping 3 times, k1 wrapping 4 times, k1 wrapping 3 times, k1 wrapping twice, k5, repeat from * to last st, ending the last repeat with k1 instead of k5.

Row 4: Knit, dropping extra wraps as you go.

Rows 5 and 6: Knit.

Row 7: K6, *k1 wrapping twice, k1 wrapping 3 times, k1 wrapping 4 times, k1 wrapping 3 times, k1 wrapping twice, k5, repeat from * to last st, k1.

Row 8: Knit, dropping extra wraps as you go.

Repeat these 8 rows to form the seafoam stitch. Continue until the scarf measures approximately 60 inches, or desired length, ending with Row 6.

Bind off and weave in ends.

# Ribbed Scarf

A ribbed scarf is an undeniably classic knit. You see them in stores, in magazines, and around dozens of necks in cooler weather. In this section, I offer a pattern for a Fibonacci ribbed scarf (which you can see in Figure 8-4). A basic pattern in the variation section allows you to create scads of scarves with any yarn you choose. For the fundamentals of making ribs, see Chapter 6.

**Figure 8-4:**
A Fibonacci
ribbed scarf
is classic.

## New skill: Switching from knit to purl and back again

Many new knitters make a common mistake: When they're working a row that has both knit and purl stitches in it, they bring the yarn *over* the needle between stitches, which creates a yarn over and an extra stitch. If you look closely, you'll be able to spot the yarn overs because they'll sit diagonally on the needle.

This mistake is an easy one to remedy, though. Just remember to move the yarn from back to front *between and under the needles* as shown in Figure 8-5. Practice knitting *2 x 2 rib* by following these steps:

1. **Knit 2 stitches and then bring the yarn from back to front between and under the needles.**

2. **Purl 2 stitches and then bring the yarn from front to back between and under the needles.**

3. **Repeat these two steps across the row.**

To find out more about making yarn overs on purpose, go to Chapter 6.

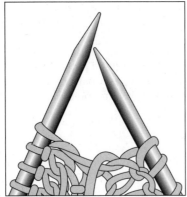

**Figure 8-5:**
Bring the yarn between and under the needles when switching from knits to purls.

## Materials and vital statistics

- ✔ **Yarn:** Baby Alpaca Chunky (100% baby alpaca); 108 yards (99 meters) per 100 grams; 3 skeins; color: 551 Pink
- ✔ **Needles:** US 13 (9 mm) needles, or the size needed to match gauge
- ✔ **Other materials:** Yarn needle for weaving in ends
- ✔ **Size:** 6 inches wide by 60 inches long
- ✔ **Gauge:** 11 stitches and 14 rows per 4 inches in stockinette stitch

Ribs don't always have to be even. In fact, they're often more interesting to look at if they aren't. You can choose almost any combination of knits and purls to create your ribs. In this pattern, I use the numbers of the Fibonacci sequence.

## Directions

Cast on 19 sts.

Row 1: K1, p1, k2, p3, k5, p3, k2, p1, k1.

Row 2: P1, k1, p2, k3, p5, k3, p2, k1, p1.

Repeat these 2 rows until scarf measures 60 inches, or your desired length.

Bind off and weave in ends.

If you want to use a yarn that knits to a gauge between 4 and 5 stitches to the inch, follow these instructions instead:

Cast on 32 sts.

Row 1: K1, p1, k2, p3, k5, p8, k5, p3, k2, p1, k1.

Row 2: P1, k1, p2, k3, p5, k8, p5, k3, p2, k1, p1.

Repeat these 2 rows until scarf measures 60 inches, or your desired length.

Bind off and weave in ends.

## *Variation: Ribbed scarves with any yarn*

The variations on ribbed scarves are endless. This section walks you through the steps needed to make a ribbed scarf with any yarn you choose.

First, make a swatch in stockinette stitch with your chosen yarn to check your gauge. You want to make a looser fabric for a scarf than for a sweater because you want the scarf to fall becomingly around your neck. So, use needles about two sizes larger than those suggested on the yarn label. (See Chapter 2 for information on getting your gauge right, if you're unsure.)

After you've come up with the right gauge for your yarn, consult Table 8-1 to decide how many stitches to cast on. Then follow the directions for 1 x 1 rib, 2 x 2 rib, broken rib, or two-stitch rib in Chapter 6. Bind off when your scarf measures 60 inches or the desired length.

| Table 8-1 | The Cast-On Numbers for Different Gauges |
|---|---|
| *Your Gauge per Inch* | *Stitches to Cast On* |
| 2½ | 18 |
| 3 | 22 |
| 3½ | 26 |
| 4 | 30 |
| 4½ | 34 |
| 5 | 38 |

Remember that scarves are forgiving projects. It doesn't matter if your gauge is exactly right, and a scarf that's skinnier or wider than my suggested 6 inches is still a great scarf.

# *Box Stitch Scarf*

Just like the garter stitch scarf or the ribbed scarf, which are both described earlier in this chapter, the basic box stitch scarf has so many variations that it's always sure to be fresh and interesting. Try the stitch by holding two yarns together, or have a go with my twins scarf, which is a variation that features two different takes on box stitch. See a box stitch scarf in Figure 8-6, and head to Chapter 5 for more about box stitch.

**Figure 8-6:**
A box stitch scarf is always fresh.

## Materials and vital statistics

- **Yarn:** Rowan Kid Classic (70% lambswool, 26% kid mohair, 4% nylon); 151 yards (140 meters) per 50 grams; 2 balls; color: Straw
- **Needles:** US 9 (5.5 mm) needles, or the size needed to match gauge
- **Other materials:** Yarn needle for weaving in ends
- **Size:** 6 inches wide by 60 inches long
- **Gauge:** 18 stitches and 24 rows per 4 inches in stockinette stitch

Working box stitch is a lot like knitting ribs — you're regularly alternating between knits and purls. See the earlier section "New skill: Switching from knit to purl and back again" if you find you're having trouble.

## Directions

Cast on 28 sts.

Rows 1, 3, and 5: *K4, p4, repeat from * to last 4 sts, k4.

Rows 2 and 4: *P4, k4, repeat from * to last 4 sts, p4.

You now switch so that the boxes that were purled are now knit and vice versa.

Rows 6, 8, and 10: *K4, p4, repeat from * to last 4 sts, k4.

Rows 7 and 9: *P4, k4, repeat from * to last 4 sts, p4.

Repeat these 10 rows until scarf measures 60 inches, or your desired length, ending with Row 5 or Row 10.

Bind off and weave in ends.

# Variation: Twins scarf

Work the first half of the scarf exactly the same as the basic pattern. When your scarf measures 30 inches, or half the desired length, end with Row 10 of the box stitch pattern, and switch to the leaning box stitch as follows:

Row 1: *K4, p4, repeat from * to last 4 sts, k4.

Row 2: K1, *p4, k4, repeat from * to last 3 sts, p3.

Row 3: K2, *p4, k4, repeat from * to last 2 sts, p2.

Row 4: K3, *p4, k4, repeat from * to last st, p1.

Row 5: *P4, k4, repeat from * to last 4 sts, p4.

Now the boxes switch from knit to purl *and* switch to lean the opposite direction.

Row 6: P4, *k4, p4, repeat from * to end.

Row 7: P1, *k4, p4, repeat from * to last 3 sts, k3.

Row 8: P2, *k4, p4, repeat from * to last 2 sts, k2.

Row 9: P3, *k4, p4, repeat from * to last st, k1.

Row 10: *K4, p4, repeat from * to last 4 sts, k4.

Repeat Rows 1–10 of leaning box stitch until scarf measures 60 inches, or your desired length, ending with Row 5 or Row 10.

Bind off and weave in ends.

# Variation: Two-yarns scarf

This variation uses two yarns — a mohair yarn and a ribbon yarn — held together. Why not give it a try? It's a great way to make something totally unique because you're making your own multistrand yarn. Not only are you doing something interesting with the texture of the scarf, but you're also playing with color. For example, a yarn that's too bright can be toned down when paired with a subdued mohair. Or a novelty yarn can gain both structure and substance when you use it with a more conventional yarn.

When trying out this variation, hold both strands of yarn together and treat them as a single strand of yarn (see Figure 8-7). Be sure to pick up both strands of yarn for each stitch. If you're worried that the strands will tangle, put each yarn in its own zippered sandwich bag. And don't limit yourself to two yarns: You can use three, five, or even a dozen yarns held together!

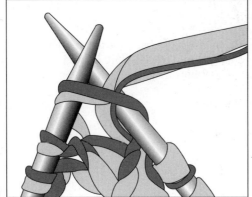

**Figure 8-7:**
Knitting with
two yarns
held
together.

To get an idea of what needles to use, add the needle sizes (in millimeters) that are recommended for each yarn. (This information is found on the yarn's label.) The resulting number of millimeters tells you what size needles to use. For example, if you want to use a yarn that suggests a US 6 (4 mm) needle paired with a yarn that suggests a US 8 (5 mm) needle, you should knit them on a 9 mm needle (4 mm + 5 mm = 9 mm). A 9 mm needle is a US 13 needle. It's handy to have a needle gauge close by when you're making this sort of calculation (see Chapter 1 for more about this tool).

Remember, though, this calculation gives you only a suggestion for needle size. Cast on a few stitches, knit a few rows, and see if you like the fabric you're creating. Switch to smaller or larger needles to get the look and feel that you're after.

Ready to knit? Use one strand of Crystal Palace Deco Ribbon and one strand of Crystal Palace Kid Merino held together. (Or try any ribbon combined with a mohair blend, depending on the look you want.) Use a US 13 (9 mm) needle, or the needle that makes a fabric you like.

Cast on 20 stitches and follow the earlier basic pattern. You can also try 28 or 36 stitches if you want something even larger and more dramatic.

## Flat Hat

A flat hat (shown in Figure 8-8) is so simple to make. It may look a little goofy just sitting there, but put it on a baby's head and you'll swoon at its cuteness. The hat looks great in a single color or striped. The basic pattern is knit in stockinette stitch, but if you'd prefer garter stitch, check out the variation that follows the basic pattern.

Knit this flat hat in gender-neutral colors and then add embellishment after the baby is born. Gender-neutral colors, in my book, include all those that aren't pink or baby blue. Babies look darned cute in red or grey — and this way they'll stand out from the rest of the baby crowd.

**Figure 8-8:**
Flat hats
work great
for babies.

## Materials and vital statistics

- **Yarn:** RYC Cashsoft Aran (57% merino wool, 33% microfiber, 10% cashmere); 95 yards (87 meters) per 50 grams; 1 skein; color: 001 Oat
- **Needles:** US 9 (5.5 mm) needles, or the size needed to match gauge; US 7 (4.5 mm) needles for rolled edge and three-needle bind-off
- **Other materials:** Yarn needle for weaving in ends
- **Size:** Newborn (toddler, child)
  - **Finished circumference:** 14 (16, 18) inches
  - **Finished length:** 5 (6, 6½) inches
- **Gauge:** 18 stitches and 24 rows per 4 inches in stockinette stitch

This hat is worked flat and then seamed up the side. When knit in a plain color, it's a great backdrop for all kinds of adornment, whether it's tassels, buttons, or embroidery. Or try your hand at duplicate stitch, which is outlined in Chapter 7, to personalize a baby's hat. Pair the hat with the baby blanket in Chapter 9 and you have a memorable gift.

## Directions

Cast on 64 (72, 82) sts with the smaller needles.

Work in stockinette stitch (knit RS rows, purl WS rows) for 1 inch. The edge will roll.

Switch to larger needles and continue working in stockinette stitch until the hat measures 5 (5½, 6) inches with the edge rolled, ending with a purl row.

**Finishing:** Knit across 32 (36, 41) sts so that half the stitches are on each needle.

Fold the hat in half, with the RS facing you and the needles held parallel in your left hand.

Use the three-needle bind-off to close the top of the hat. (See Chapter 10 for directions on this bind-off if you're unfamiliar with it.) Cut the yarn and pull it through the last stitch to secure.

Turn the hat right side out and use mattress stitch to sew up the side seam. (See the appendix for the how-to on mattress stitch.) Weave in ends.

If desired, decorate the two top corners of the hat with pompoms, tassels, jingle bells, or O-rings covered in contrasting yarn.

## Variation: Knitting a garter stitch flat hat

For this variation of the basic flat hat, you use the same yarn and needles as in the basic pattern, plus small amounts of two contrasting colors (CC1 and CC2). With a garter stitch, you should have a gauge of 16 stitches and 32 rows per 4 inches. The following hat pattern covers the same sizes as the previous stockinette stitch version:

Cast on 56 (64, 72) sts with CC2.

Work in garter stitch (knit all rows) for 1 inch.

Switch to CC1 and continue in garter stitch for 2 inches.

Switch to the main color and continue in garter stitch until your hat measures 5 (5½, 6) inches.

**Finishing:** Work across half of the stitches, and then use the three-needle bind-off to close the top of the hat as in the main pattern.

Sew up the side seam and weave in ends. (See the appendix for information on seaming up garter stitch.)

# Retro Slippers for Baby

This retro slipper (see Figure 8-9) is hardly more than a swatch. Still, if you grew up around knitters, chances are they'll fill you with nostalgia. Just because these slippers are labeled as "nostalgic" and "retro," however, doesn't mean that they aren't cute! You can adorn them with old-school pompoms, bows, or buttons that match the ones you use on the one piece baby sweater in Chapter 10 for an oh-so-cute matching ensemble.

**Figure 8-9:**
Try these easy slippers for baby — and the whole family!

## Materials and vital statistics

- **Yarn:** Cascade 220 Superwash (100% superwash wool); 220 yards (203 meters) per 100 grams; 1 skein; color: 860 Gray Heather
- **Needles:** US 7 (4.5 mm), or the size needed to match gauge
- **Other materials:** Yarn needle
- **Size:** Newborn (6–12 months, 1–2 years), 4 (5, 6) inches square
- **Gauge:** 18 stitches and 36 rows per 4 inches in garter stitch

These slippers are a cinch to make. They're quick to knit and a great way to use up left-over yarn. Essentially, all you have to do is knit your rectangle and then sew it up. After making some for baby, why not try making some for yourself? See the variations that follow.

## Directions

Make 2 slippers with the following pattern:

Cast on 18 (22, 26) sts.

Work in garter stitch (knit all rows) for 3 (3½, 4) inches.

Switch to rib as follows:

Row 1 (RS): K2, *p2, k2, repeat from * to end of row.

Row 2 (WS): P2, *k2, p2, repeat from * to end of row.

When slipper measures 4 (5, 6) inches, stop knitting, but don't bind off.

**Finishing:** Cut the yarn, leaving a 12-inch tail.

Thread the end of the tail through the yarn needle, and then pass the yarn through all the stitches on the needle. Pull snugly to gather the stitches, and then draw the yarn through the stitches again to secure. This creates the toe.

Without breaking the yarn, use mattress stitch to sew the edge of the slipper from the end of the toe about halfway up the edge of the work to form the top of the slipper.

Cut the yarn and weave in the end.

Fold the cast-on edge of the slipper in half and sew together to form the back of the slipper, as shown in Figure 8-10.

## Variation: Using different yarns

You can knit these slippers with any sturdy yarn. But, unless you're knitting for a baby whose feet will never touch the ground, I'd recommend a washable yarn. For babies learning to walk, use caution: Slippers can be slippery!

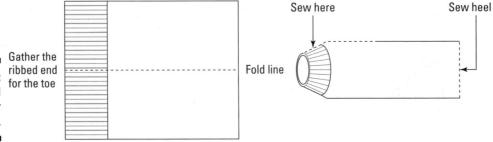

**Figure 8-10:**
Folding and sewing your slippers.

Gather the ribbed end for the toe

Fold line

Sew here

Sew heel

Yarn labels give an estimated gauge in stockinette stitch, but you're knitting these slippers in garter stitch. The perfectionists will swatch. But if you're making baby slippers, you're more or less making a swatch anyway. So just go for it. A typical worsted weight yarn that knits at 20 stitches per 4 inches in stockinette stitch will give you the garter stitch gauge that you're after.

## Variation: Sizing up

Sure these slippers are cute on baby feet, but you can easily scale them up to fit anyone. Use Table 8-3 to find the correct cast-on number.

You're better off making the slippers a little smaller if you're in doubt of the proper size — they'll stretch, and you don't want them to slip off.

| Table 8-3 | Cast-On Chart for Adult Retro Slippers | |
|---|---|---|
| *Size* | *Cast on* | *Foot Length* |
| 4–6 years | 30 stitches | 7 inches |
| 6–10 years | 34 stitches | 8 inches |
| Small adult | 38 stitches | 9 inches |
| Medium adult | 42 stitches | 10 inches |
| Large adult | 46 stitches | 11 inches |

Cast on the number of stitches specified for your size.

Knit in garter stitch until your slipper measures 5 (6, 7, 8, 9) inches.

Knit 2 (2, 3, 3, 3) inches in rib as described in the baby slipper pattern, and then follow the finishing directions there.

# Longways Multiyarn Stole

This multiyarn stole lets a collection of beautiful yarns do the work for you — the knitting could hardly be simpler, yet the result is stunning. I've chosen a mohair yarn, a thick and thin wool, and a shiny ribbon with glints of silver for mine. But choose any combination of yarns with a variety of textures and colors you love, and you'll create a showstopping stole that's guaranteed to bring drama to any outfit. See what I mean in Figure 8-11.

**Figure 8-11:** A longways multiyarn stole is breath-taking.

## New skill: Changing colors

Many new knitters have angst about changing from one yarn to the next, but really you have nothing to worry about. When a pattern asks you to join a new yarn, here's what to do:

1. **Knit to the end of the row with the first color. Cut the yarn, leaving a 6-inch tail.**

2. **Insert the needle into the first stitch, ready to start the next row.**

3. **Pick up the second color of yarn and lay it across the back (right-hand) needle with a 6-inch tail on the left and the working yarn on the right.**

   This step is equivalent to wrapping the first stitch. See Figure 8-12 to see how this step should look.

4. **Bring the yarn through the first stitch, giving both tails a gentle tug to tighten up the stitch.**

   If you want to, at this step you can tie the two tails in a single knot — just like the first step in tying a shoelace.

That's all there is to it. Later, weave in the ends with a yarn needle.

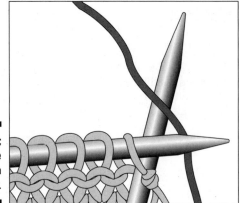

**Figure 8-12:**
Knitting the first stitch in a new color.

# New skill: Making fringe

Adding fringe to a piece of clothing can totally change its personality. Fringe can be long or short, widely or narrowly spaced, knotted, beaded, or plain. Fringe showcases particularly well yarns that vary in color, texture, or size, but any yarn adds movement and visual interest to a finished piece. Fringe also adds length to knitting projects that come up a little short. If you've run out of yarn, consider adding fringe in a contrasting color or texture.

You may typically think of fringe as being on the two short ends of a scarf, but you can also consider fringing two short sides *and* one long side of a stole for something more out of the ordinary. Or you might consider fringing the edges of a shawl or poncho, the cuff of a mitten, or the hem of a sweater.

To make fringe, begin by calculating how many pieces of fringe you want and how long you want the fringe to be. The lengths of yarn used to make fringe are doubled over, so use two strands of yarn to make four lengths of fringe in one spot. You can use just a couple of strands for each group and space them closer together or hold several strands together for tassel-like fringe and space them further apart. You don't have to follow any rules — just experiment to your heart's content.

The fringe lengths need to be twice as long as you want your fringe to be, plus about an inch for the knot at the top. As you can imagine, fringe can use a lot of yarn. So, plan for it in the yarn-buying phase. A quick way to make uniform lengths of fringe is to wrap your yarn around an appropriately sized book, and then make a single cut along the spine of the book.

To attach your fringe:

1. **Stick your crochet hook through the edge of the work from the wrong side to the right side.**

2. **Grab the center of the length of fringe with the hook, and then pull through a loop of yarn about 1 inch long.**

3. **Using your fingers or the crochet hook, pull the tails of the fringe through the loop and give them a gentle tug to secure them.**

## Materials and vital statistics

- **Yarn:** You need the following three types of yarn:
  - **Yarn A:** Divé Mohair Kiss Ombre (73% mohair, 22% wool, 5% polyamide); 98 yards (90 meters) per 50 grams; 3 skeins; color: 40377
  - **Yarn B:** Divé Fiamma (100% wool); 55 yards (50 meters) per 50 grams; 2 skeins; color: 40377
  - **Yarn C:** Divé Luxus (91% nylon, 9% polyester); 51 yards (47 meters) per 50 grams; 2 skeins; color: 40377
- **Needles:** US 15 (10 mm) circular needle, 24-inch length or longer, or the size needed to match gauge (if you tend to cast on tightly, use an even bigger needle to cast on and bind off)
- **Other materials:** Large crochet hook; yarn needle to weave in ends
- **Size:** 65 inches long by 16 inches wide, without fringe
- **Gauge:** 8 stitches and 12 rows per 4 inches in garter stitch

In this pattern, you have to change yarns, but don't worry — it isn't as difficult as it sounds. Just remember that when making this wrap, you should carry the mohair (yarn A) loosely up the side of the work since you're using it every other stripe. The other two yarns are cut and rejoined as indicated in the pattern.

## Directions

With yarn B (the thick and thin wool), cast on 130 sts loosely.

Knit 1 row. Cut yarn B.

Rows 1 and 2: Join yarn A (the mohair) and knit 2 rows. Don't cut yarn A.

Rows 3 and 4: Join yarn C (the ribbon) and knit 2 rows. Cut yarn C.

Rows 5 and 6: Knit 2 rows with yarn A. Don't cut yarn A.

Rows 7 and 8: Join yarn B and knit 2 rows. Cut yarn B.

Repeat these 8 rows until your stole measures approximately 16 inches, ending with Row 7. Bind off loosely with yarn B.

Weave in any loose ends.

**Finishing:** From the remaining yarn, cut 20-inch lengths for the fringe. Cut 18 pieces each from yarn B and yarn C. Cut 36 pieces from yarn A. Divide the pieces of fringe into 18 groups with 2 strands of A, 1 strand of B, and 1 strand of C in each group. Attach fringe every 2 inches along each short side of the stole.

If you like, use scissors to give the ends of your fringe a trim.

## Variation: Changing yarns

The sky's the limit in selecting yarns for your multiyarn stole. Choose any three yarns you like — or choose more than three. Just be sure to stick to the basic formula of going back to yarn A between the other yarns you've chosen. This formula gives your project the continuity it needs. I've chosen a monochromatic palette for my stole, but you can vary the look by going for greater contrast in color as well as texture. Even yarns that don't "go" together at first glance can create a pleasing result. Don't be afraid to experiment!

# Loose Rib Wrap

If you knit this simple ribbed wrap (see Figure 8-13) with a sumptuous yarn at a loose gauge, it can add glamour to any outfit. Even though the knitting creates only a simple rectangle, the way you put the rectangle together allows you to create many different garments — a wrap, a poncho, or a fun sleeves-only shrug. That the humble rectangle can do so much is really one of the marvels of knitted fabric! Mohair, thin ribbon, and hand-dyed silk all make great choices for this project that you'll want to do again and again.

**Figure 8-13:**
A loose rib wrap is a glamorous accessory to any ensemble.

## Materials and vital statistics

- ✔ **Yarn:** S. Charles Collezione Rittrato (28% mohair, 53% viscose, 10% polyamid, 9% polyester); 198 yards (183 meters) per 50 grams; 3 skeins; color: 73

- ✔ **Needles:** US 8 (5 mm) needles, or the size needed to match gauge

- ✔ **Other materials:** Yarn needle for weaving in ends

- ✔ **Size:** 14 (16) inches wide by 60 inches long after blocking

- ✔ **Gauge:** 16 stitches and 20 rows per 4 inches over rib pattern, lightly stretched

This delightful wrap is worked from one short side to the other. If you plan to wear it as a wrap, you can make either size. The first size will fit any small- to medium-sized woman as a shrug or poncho (see the later variations). If you have larger arms or want a bit more coverage, make the larger size.

# Directions

Cast on 61 (71) sts.

Row 1: K2, *p2, k3, repeat from * to last 4 sts, p2, k2.

Row 2: P2, *k2, p3, repeat from * to last 4 sts, k2, p2.

Repeat these 2 rows until your wrap measures 60 inches.

Bind off loosely and weave in ends.

**Finishing:** Block the wrap to the measurements given in the "Materials and vital statistics" section (see the appendix for more details on blocking).

# Variation: Make your wrap a poncho

From the basic rectangle of the loose rib wrap, you can create a fantastic poncho. This poncho shape is my favorite — it's a bit more contemporary looking and its unconventional shape allows you to wear it in lots of different ways. I love the drape and hint of sparkle in this feather-light yarn. It looks terrific with your favorite little black dress or even with jeans and a T-shirt!

To make the wrap into a poncho, follow these steps:

1. **After blocking the basic wrap, place markers or pins 15 inches in from each end of one long side of the rectangle to mark the placement of the seam.**

2. **Fold the wrap into a horseshoe shape with the two short ends closest to you and the markers you've just placed touching (as shown in Figure 8-14).**

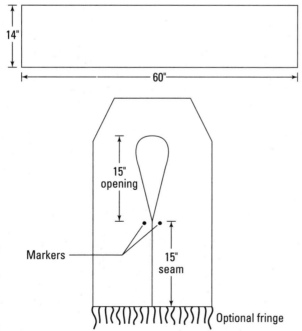

**Figure 8-14:** Putting the poncho together.

3. **Using mattress stitch, sew from the outside edge to the markers, creating a seam about 15 inches long and leaving an opening for the head.**

You can create fringe for the straight side if you want. (See the section "New skill: Making fringe" earlier in this chapter for details.) Fringe draws attention to the great asymmetrical shape of this poncho.

## Variation: Make your wrap a shrug

Another fun way to use the basic rectangle is to create a little shrug. Even though you start with just a rectangle, it actually does create sleeves and a bit of a back — the perfect thing to wear with a halter top or a sleeveless dress. But you can also layer it over a T-shirt or turtleneck to add a bit of warmth and fun. Just follow these steps:

1. **After blocking the basic wrap, fold the piece in half lengthwise as shown in Figure 8-15.**

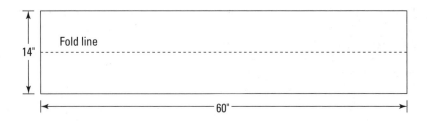

**Figure 8-15:**
Turning a rectangle wrap into a shrug.

2. **Starting at the outside (where your wrist will be), use mattress stitch to sew a seam toward the center that's about 15 inches long.**

3. **Do the same on the other side, leaving an opening in the center that's about 30 inches wide.**

Be sure to try on the shrug before finishing the seams, and adjust as necessary for a perfect fit.

## Box Top

From the looks of Figure 8-16, it's hard to believe that this boat neck top is really just a pair of rectangles, but it is! You don't have to do any increasing or decreasing — it's just changing from the simplest of lace patterns, to rib, to stockinette stitch that makes the difference.

This box top is lovely and a little out of the ordinary. It's perfect with a skirt or pants, and you can wear it in the office or on the town. You can knit this top in bamboo or a cotton blend, but the pure silk yarn that I use in this pattern drapes beautifully on the body and is a pleasure to wear.

**Figure 8-16:**
The unboxy
box top.

Check out the schematic in Figure 8-17 to see how using stitch patterns that knit at different gauges adds shaping to the garment. To me, this top recalls a 1940s pin-up girl with its capped sleeves and nipped waist. If you want to skip the lace, you can just make the ribbed section longer and have a different, but equally elegant, look (see the variation at the end of the pattern for details).

## Materials and vital statistics

- ✔ **Yarn:** Curious Creek Fibers Isalo (100% silk); 262 yards (238 meters) per 95 grams; 3 (3, 4, 4, 5, 6) skeins; color: Sunrise on Daffodils

- ✔ **Needles:** US 6 (4 mm) needles, or the size needed to match gauge; US 4 (3.5 mm) needles for the ribbing

- ✔ **Other materials:** Stitch markers or safety pins; yarn needle for weaving in ends

- ✔ **Size:** Women's XS (S, M, L, 1X, 2X) or actual chest size of 30 (34, 38, 42, 46, 50)

    - • **Finished chest circumference:** 30 (34, 38, 42, 46, 50) inches

    - • **Finished length:** 23 (23, 24, 25, 26, 27) inches

    Figure 8-17 is a schematic of the finished dimensions

- ✔ **Gauge:** 20 stitches and 28 rows per 4 inches in stockinette stitch

This top is worked from the lower edge to the shoulder in two pieces, and the front and back are the same. Keep track of the numbers of rows you work over the openwork and ribbed sections as you knit the back. That way, when you knit the front you can make it exactly the same.

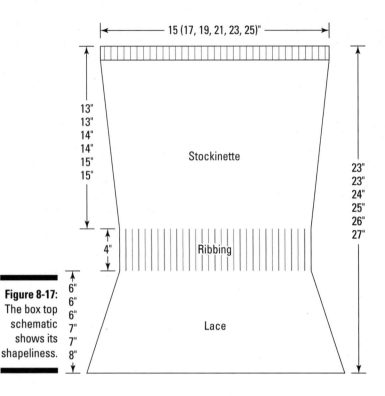

**Figure 8-17:**
The box top
schematic
shows its
shapeliness.

## Starting with the back

Cast on 75 (85, 95, 105, 115, 125) sts with larger needles and begin the lacy openwork pattern:

Row 1 (RS): K2, *yo, k2tog, repeat from * to last st, k1.

Row 2: Purl.

If you haven't tried a yarn over (yo) before, you can read all about this lace basic in Chapter 6. You also find out about knitting 2 stitches together (k2tog) in Chapter 6.

Repeat these 2 rows until the lace section measures 6 (6, 6, 7, 7, 8) inches. (Note that this lace pattern has a bias. Don't fret though: When you block the fabric and sew the pieces together, it will turn out just right.)

Switch to smaller needles and begin ribbing as follows:

Row 1 (RS): K1, *p1, k1, repeat from * to end.

Row 2: P1, *k1, p1, repeat from * to end.

Repeat these 2 rows until the ribbed section measures 4 inches (for all sizes).

Switch to stockinette stitch (knit a row, purl a row) and work until the bodice measures 13 (13, 14, 14, 15, 15) inches from the end of the ribbing.

Work 1 inch in ribbing, and then bind off all sts.

## Moving to the front

Make the front the same as the back.

## Finishing your top

Weave in ends.

Block the two pieces, but don't stretch the ribbing out too much; you want this top to be shapely (see the appendix for more details on blocking). Find the center of the neck, measure 6 inches out from this point to either side, and place a marker or safety pin. Sew each shoulder seam from the outside edge to the marker.

Because you don't have to shape the neck, you can make the head opening wider or narrower to suit your own style. If you work both shoulder seams at once, you can try the top on as you go.

Starting at the bottom, sew up the side seams up leaving the upper 8 (8, 9, 9, 9½, 9½) inches open for the armhole. Again, because you don't have to shape any part of this top, simply make the armhole the right size for you by trying it on before you finish the seam. See the appendix for more on finishing.

## Variation: Short and simple

This shorter top (see the schematic in Figure 8-18) is meant to hug the body and to end just below the waist. The total length will be 22 (22, 23, 23, 24, 24) inches.

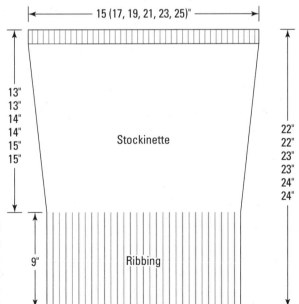

**Figure 8-18:** The box top made short and simple.

For the front and the back of this variation follow these instructions:

Cast on as described in the basic pattern, but use the smaller needles, skip the lace section, and start right in with the ribbing. Continue the ribbed section until it measures 9 inches (for all sizes).

Switch to stockinette stitch and continue as described in the basic pattern.

# Chapter 9

# Rectangles for the Home

*T*here are so many rectangles worth knitting that they've spilled over into a second chapter! Like the projects in Chapter 8, these knits for the home appeal to knitters at all skill levels. Any of the knits in this chapter make wonderful gifts. But that doesn't mean you shouldn't consider knitting them for yourself too.

The felted potholders are quick to knit and are a great way to use up your scrap wool. Pair them with matching coasters and you've got a perfect housewarming gift. The baby blanket knit as a set of nested squares will keep a newborn warm with style. Knit it larger to cover the back of your sofa or favorite chair. Hand-knit throw pillows are great to update your home décor. And finally, check out the journal cover. Knit the larger size for a loose-leaf binder and the smaller one for your diary or appointment book.

## Felted Potholders

The potholders in Figure 9-1 are fun to make and are a great way to practice some new skills. Knit them with three colors and miters as I do in the basic pattern and you'll add pizazz to any kitchen. You can also make your potholders plain or striped. You'll find directions for these following the main pattern. Make a set to match your friend's kitchen for an out-of-the-ordinary hostess gift. You can use the same techniques to make coasters or even a great blanket. Read the variation sections to find out how.

**Figure 9-1:** Felted potholders (and coasters) are quick and easy to make.

Wool is a good choice for potholders because it insulates well and is slow to ignite. Still, always use caution when handling hot things, and test your potholders before you rely on them to remove your 20-pound turkey from the oven.

## New skill: Making miters

A *miter* is simply a corner where the two edges come together at a diagonal. Think of the edge of a picture frame or window. With the felted potholders, you'll be making a square by casting on the stitches for two adjacent sides and working diagonally to finish with a single stitch at the opposite corner. It may be tough to wrap your mind around, but this technique isn't difficult to do. After you get the hang of it, you'll be able to extend the technique to create not only potholders, but beautiful dishcloths or even afghan squares (as I show you in the later variation sections).

To make a mitered square, follow these instructions:

1. **Cast on an even number of stitches that's equal to the length of two sides of your finished square.**

   For the potholder, you cast on 64 stitches (32 stitches for each of the two sides of the square).

2. **Place a marker between the 2 center stitches.**

3. **On Row 1 and all wrong-side rows: Knit.**

4. **On Row 2 and all right-side rows, decrease twice in the center as follows: Knit to 2 stitches before the marker, k2tog, slip the marker, ssk, knit to the end of the row.**

   If you're unfamiliar with decreasing using k2tog and ssk, see Chapter 6 for details.

5. **Repeat Rows 1 and 2 until you have only 2 stitches left, and then knit these last 2 stitches together on the last wrong-side row.**

   Change colors every few rows as described in the pattern.

Place a safety pin or some other little marker on the right side of your square. Then, when you can see the safety pin, you know that you've reached a decrease row.

## Materials and vital statistics

- ✔ **Yarn:** Cascade 220 (100% wool); 220 yards (201 meters) per 100 grams

  - **Color 1:** 8686 Brown; 1 skein

  - **Color 2:** 8907 Teal; 1 skein

  - **Color 3:** 8400 Gray; 1 skein

  You can use any worsted weight yarn that's 100% wool. However, don't use a wool that's labeled "superwash," because this type of yarn has been specially treated to resist felting.

- ✔ **Needles:** US 10½ (6.5 mm) needles, or the size needed to match gauge

- ✔ **Other materials:** Stitch markers; large crochet hook; yarn needle for weaving in ends

- ✔ **Size:** The measurement before felting is about 9¾ inches wide by 13 inches long; the measurement after felting is about 7 inches wide by 7 inches long

✔ **Gauge:** 14 stitches and 20 rows per 4 inches in garter stitch before felting; 18 stitches and 36 rows per 4 inches after felting

These potholders are a great way to get your feet wet with felting. You may not be familiar with the technique, but if you've ever accidentally put a sweater through the laundry, you've unwittingly experimented with felting. When you do it intentionally though, the results can be great. You use the same approach (a washing machine with hot water, agitation, and soap) to turn your loosely knit potholder into a sturdy, dense fabric. Flip to the appendix for felting tips and techniques.

## Directions

The felted potholders are worked in garter stitch. It's difficult to see the rows in garter stitch, but it's easy to see what knitters call *garter ridges*. Each ridge is made up of 2 rows.

With color 3, cast on 64 sts, placing a marker in the center of the row between the 32nd and 33rd sts.

Row 1 (WS): Knit.

Row 2 (RS): Knit to 2 sts before the marker, k2tog, slip marker, ssk, knit to the end of the row.

Repeat these 2 rows 5 more times for a total of 12 rows.

Switch to color 1 and work Rows 1 and 2 10 times. There will be 20 rows or 10 garter ridges in color 1. (If you need a refresher on changing colors, see Chapter 8.)

Switch to color 2 and continue repeating Rows 1 and 2 until there are only 2 sts left.

Next row: K2tog. There is 1 st on the needle. Place this st on your crochet hook and make a chain about 5 inches long. Slip stitch through the last knit stitch to form a loop. (See the appendix for crochet chain basics.) Cut the yarn and weave in the ends.

**Finishing:** To felt, place your potholders in a zippered pillowcase or lingerie bag and run it through the washing machine along with a pair of jeans for added agitation. Set the machine for a hot wash and a small load. You may need to run the wash cycle more than once to felt your items completely.

When the potholders look like felt and measure about 7 inches square, remove them from the washer. They may need to be wrestled into shape, but you can't hurt them, so be rough if you need to. Allow the potholder to dry thoroughly before using them.

## Variation: Single-color potholders

With the color of your choice, cast on 32 sts.

Knit 64 rows or until you can see 32 garter ridges.

Bind off all your stitches, but don't cut the yarn or pull it through the last stitch. Instead, using your crochet hook, make a chain about 5 inches long. Slip stitch through the last knit stitch to form a loop, and then cut the yarn and weave in the end. Finish your potholder as I describe in the earlier directions.

## *Variation: Striped potholders*

Cast on 32 sts with color 1.

With color 1, knit 8 rows.

Switch to color 2 and knit 4 rows.

Switch to color 3 and knit 8 rows.

Switch to color 2 and knit 4 rows.

Switch to color 1 and knit 16 rows.

Switch to color 2 and knit 4 rows.

Switch to color 3 and knit 8 rows.

Switch to color 2 and knit 4 rows.

Switch to color 1 and knit 8 rows.

Bind off all your stitches, but don't cut the yarn or pull it through the last stitch. Instead, using your crochet hook, crochet a chain about 5 inches long. Slip stitch through the last knit stitch to form a loop, and then cut the yarn and secure the end. Finish your potholder as I describe in the earlier directions.

## *Variation: Coasters*

You can use the earlier mitered, single-color, and striped patterns to make coasters that measure 4 by 4 inches. For the striped and mitered coasters, I've made suggestions for pleasing color layouts, but let your imagination guide you. A set of six or eight coasters stacked together and tied like a present with a bit of yarn makes a great gift for any home. Here are the basic instructions for the different types of coasters:

- ✔ **Mitered coasters:** Cast on 36 stitches, placing a marker in the center of the row, between stitches 18 and 19.

   Follow the earlier directions for the mitered potholder, switching colors every 6th row.

   When there are 2 stitches left, k2tog, and then cut the yarn and pull the tail through the last stitch.
- ✔ **Single-color coasters:** Cast on 18 stitches. Knit 36 rows, and then bind off all stitches.
- ✔ **Striped coasters:** Cast on 18 stitches. Work 12 rows in each color for a total of 36 rows (or 18 garter ridges), and then bind off.

Follow the directions for felting the potholders to felt your coasters.

## *Variation: Mitered square afghan*

To make a wonderful blanket that's tons of fun to knit, choose a yarn that recommends a gauge between 3½ and 4 stitches to the inch, and use needles that are one size larger than recommended on the yarn label. But, remember, because blankets don't need to be an exact size, don't worry too much about gauge. Instead, use the needles and yarn needed to create a fabric that you like. (See Chapter 2 for more on gauge.)

While it's important to use a yarn that will felt for the potholders and coasters, you'll likely want a yarn that's more washable when you're making a blanket. Take that into consideration when you're buying yarn.

You need approximately 600 yards (550 meters) of yarn for a baby blanket or lap quilt. A blanket made with 2,400 yards will cover the bed of the truly ambitious. Use three colors or a self-striping yarn to get the look that you're after.

To get started on your blanket, follow the basic potholder pattern to make 16 squares, but bind off the final stitch of each square and leave off the crocheted loop. You can make more or fewer squares depending on the size of blanket you want. When you're finished with your squares, don't felt them. Instead, lay them out in an arrangement that you like, and then sew the edges together. You can see from Figure 9-2 that both regular and haphazard placement of the squares can yield interesting results. Find tips on sewing things up in the appendix.

**Figure 9-2:** How you arrange your squares makes a dramatic difference in style.

# Throw Pillows

Use this pattern to create some great throw pillows for your sofa or bed (check some out in Figure 9-3). A couple of new pillows can really liven up your décor, and the knitting will give you a chance to hone some new skills. The basic pattern creates a simply textured pillow in a single color; the later variations give you two different options for slip-stitch color patterns.

**Figure 9-3:** Spruce up your living space with throw pillows.

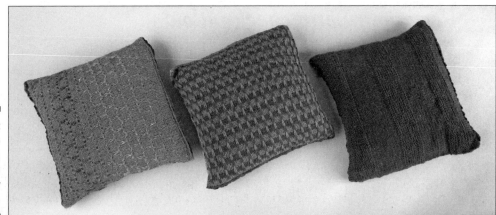

## Materials and vital statistics

- ✔ **Yarn:** Berrocco Ultra Alpaca (50% alpaca, 50% wool); 215 yards (198 meters) per 100 grams; 2 skeins; color: 6282 Cranberry
- ✔ **Needles:** US 7 (4.5 mm) needles, or the size needed to match gauge
- ✔ **Other materials:** Yarn needle; 14-inch pillow form
- ✔ **Size:** 14 inches square
- ✔ **Gauge:** 20 stitches and 26 rows per 4 inches in stockinette stitch

This throw pillow is worked in two pieces and then stitched up. If you want more pillows with less knitting, use cloth for the backs of your pillows. Cut the fabric into a 15½-inch square, and then hem the edges so that the backing measures 14 inches square. Then you can attach the fabric to your knitted piece with a needle and thread.

## Directions

Make 2 pieces the same. To make the simplest pillow, make the back piece exactly the same way as you made the front. But, if you want to vary the sides, follow one of the later variations.

Cast on 70 sts and work 1 inch in stockinette stitch (knit RS rows, purl WS rows).

Work in garter stitch (knit all rows) for 2 inches.

Work in stockinette stitch for 3 inches.

Work in garter stitch for 2 inches.

Work in stockinette stitch for 3 inches.

Work in garter stitch for 2 inches.

Work in stockinette stitch for 1 inch.

Bind off and weave in ends.

**Finishing:** Block your finished pieces to measure 14 inches square. Using the working yarn and a yarn needle, sew three sides together. Insert the pillow form and sew the last side closed. You can find details on blocking and sewing seams in the appendix.

## Variation: Retro check pillow

Lots of knitting abbreviations look funny, and to my eye, wyif and wyib (featured in this variation and the next) are right near the top of the list! Here's what they mean:

- ✔ **Wyif stands for "with yarn in front."** What this phrase means is that you need to bring the yarn to the front (or into the purl position) before you perform the next step. If your yarn is already in front, don't do anything; just carry on with the next instruction.
- ✔ **Wyib stands for "with yarn in back."** This phrase means that you need to bring the yarn to the back of the work (or into the knit position) before you perform the next step. If your yarn is already in back, you don't have to move it.

When you change your yarn's position to the front or back, remember to bring it *between* and *under* the needles and not up over the needle. (Chapter 8 has a figure of how to perform this task.)

Usually wyif and wyib accompany slipped stitches (I cover the basics of slipping stitches in Chapter 5). The position of the yarn, at the front or the back of the work, dictates where the horizontal *float* will be. You create floats when dragging the yarn over an unworked stitch. If the float is in the front on the right side, or in the back on the wrong side, it shows and becomes part of the decoration. Check out wyif and wyib stitches in Figure 9-4.

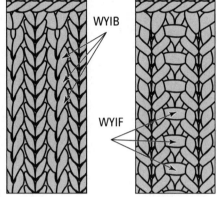

WYIB

WYIF

**Figure 9-4:** Stitches made with yarn in back and with yarn in front.

For the retro check pillow, you need two colors of yarn. Choose two colors with high contrast like orange and avocado green for a retro look. Or choose two shades of the same color if you're looking for a more subtle pattern. For each side of the pillow, you need one skein of each color.

Because you're alternating colors every 4 rows, you don't need to cut the yarn each time you switch colors. Just carry the unused color loosely up the side.

Cast on 71 sts with the first color.

Purl 1 row.

Row 1 (RS): With the second color, k3, *slip 1 st wyib, k3, repeat from * to end.

Row 2 (WS): With the second color, p3, *slip 1 st wyif, p3, repeat from * to end.

Row 3 (RS): With the second color, repeat Row 1.

Row 4 (WS): With the second color, purl.

Row 5 (RS) With the first color, k3, *slip 1 st wyib, k3, repeat from * to end.

Row 6 (WS): With the first color, p3, *slip 1 stitch wyif, p3, repeat from * to end.

Row 7 (RS): With the first color, repeat Row 5.

Row 8 (WS): With the first color, purl.

Repeat these 8 rows 11 more times or until piece measures 14 inches.

Bind off and weave in ends.

Make a second piece the same.

Follow the directions for finishing in the main pattern.

## *Variation: Bean sprout pillow*

Barbara Walker, a famous collector of stitch patterns and a profoundly influential knit-ter, calls this color pattern "bean sprouts." Whatever you call it, it's a fun slip stitch pattern to try. A strong contrast like black and white will definitely make this pattern stand out, but a combination like orange and red will also create a wonderful result. Or, for an effect that looks almost like stained glass, use a self-striping yarn for one yarn and a plain color for the other. To make both sides of a pillow, you need two balls of the main color (MC) and one ball of the contrasting color (CC). You can see this pillow in the color photo insert.

In this pattern, you work 6 rows in the main color between the rows you work in the contrasting color. You can carry the contrasting yarn up the side, twisting it with the main color at the beginning of each odd-numbered row. But take care not to pull it too tight, because if you do, that side of the pillow will pucker. If you prefer, cut the con-trasting color each time and weave in the ends when you're finished. You don't need to cut the main color yarn because the contrasting color is only worked for 2 rows. (You can find more information about changing colors in Chapter 8.)

Cast on 71 sts with MC.

Row 1 (RS): With MC, knit.

Row 2 (WS): With MC, purl.

Row 3 (RS): With CC, k2, *slip 1 st wyib, k1, repeat from * to last st, k1.

.Row 4 (WS): With CC, k1, *k1, slip 1 st wyif, repeat from * to last 2 sts, k2.

Note that this WS row (Row 4) is knit rather than purled.

Rows 5 and 7 (RS): Using MC, k5, *slip 1 st wyib, k5, repeat from * to end.

Rows 6 and 8 (WS): Using MC, p5, *slip 1 st wyif, p5, repeat from * to end.

Rows 9 and 10: Repeat Rows 1 and 2.

Row 11 (RS): With CC, k1, *slip 1 st wyib, k1, repeat from * to end.

Row 12 (WS): With CC, k1, *slip 1 st wyif, k1, repeat from * to end.

Again, this WS row (Row 12) is knit rather than purled.

Rows 13 and 15 (RS): With MC, k2, *slip 1 st wyib, k5, repeat from * to last 3 sts, slip 1 st wyib, k2.

Rows 14 and 16 (WS): With MC, p2, *slip 1 st wyib, k5, repeat from * to last 3 sts, slip 1 st wyib, k2.

Repeat these 16 rows until the pillow measures approximately 14 inches. End with Row 2 or Row 10 of the pattern repeat. Bind off and weave in ends. Make a second piece the same, and then follow the directions for finishing in the earlier pattern.

# Journal Cover

Knitted journal covers, like the one in Figure 9-5, are fun to knit, and like the other items in this chapter, are nothing more than simple rectangles. The basic pattern is for a journal cover that's worked in stockinette stitch with a simple seed stitch edging. It's sized to fit a standard three-ring binder with a 2-inch wide spine. The variation is for a smaller half linen stitch journal cover that fits a standard 5-by-8-inch blank book.

Even though you can keep just about anything inside your binder, I think this one is particularly well-suited for use as a knitter's journal. You can use it to keep track of your projects.

**Figure 9-5:**
Journal covers that fit blank books or standard loose-leaf binders.

# Materials and vital statistics

- ✔ **Yarn:** Schaefer Yarns Miss Priss (100% merino wool); 280 yards (256 meters) per 115 grams; 1 skein; color: Jane Adams
- ✔ **Needles:** US 9 (5.5 mm) needles, or the size needed to match gauge
- ✔ **Other materials:** Three-ring binder with a 2-inch spine; yarn needle for finishing
- ✔ **Size:** Fits a standard 10-by-12-inch three-ring binder
- ✔ **Gauge:** 18 stitches and 22 rows per 4 inches in stockinette stitch

The journal cover is worked from side to side, starting with a 4-inch flap that will be turned under to form the inside of the cover. I love the way the variegation plays across this journal cover, but you might also consider a plain-colored cover with duplicate stitch initials or doodling.

## Directions

Cast on 57 sts.

Work the flap in seed stitch as follows (Chapter 5 gives more details on seed stitch):

All rows: K1, *p1, k1, repeat from * to end.

Repeat this row until the flap measures 4 inches.

Knit 1 WS row to form a turning ridge.

Begin working in stockinette stitch (knit RS rows, purl WS rows) with a three-stitch seed stitch border for the front of the journal cover as follows:

Row 1 (RS): K1, p1, k1, knit to last 2 sts, p1, k1.

Row 2 (WS): K1, p1, k1, purl to last 3 sts, k1, p1, k1.

Repeat these 2 rows for 21 inches.

Knit 1 WS row to create a turning ridge.

Switch back to seed stitch and work 4 more inches before binding off.

**Finishing:** Block the piece so that it measures 12 by 29 inches and the edges are square. (See the appendix to find out about blocking.) When the piece is dry, fold the flaps toward the WS and sew the flap in place along the top and bottom edges. See the appendix for more information on finishing. Insert your binder by opening it and inserting the front and back covers into the pockets that you've created with the flaps.

## Variation: Small journal cover in half linen stitch

To make this easy variation, use the same yarn and needles specified in the basic pattern. Your gauge should be approximately 17 stitches and 28 rows per 4 inches in half linen stitch (see Chapter 5 for details on working half linen stitch). Change needles if necessary to match gauge. If you're having trouble with the gauge, remember this: It's more important to match the stitch gauge than the row gauge. This pattern makes a journal cover that fits an 8-by-5-inch blank book.

Should you slip stitches knitwise or purlwise? The short answer: When in doubt, slip purlwise. Slipping a stitch knitwise twists the stitch. So, you only want to slip knitwise when you actually want the stitch twisted (ssk and skp decreases, for instance; see Chapter 6 for more about ssk and Chapter 12 for more about skp). Slipping purlwise is neutral and leaves the stitch in the normal position, ready for the next row. If you're simply moving the stitch from one needle to the other, as you are with half linen stitch, slip purlwise.

Cast on 37 sts.

Work for 2½ inches in seed stitch to form the first flap:

For all rows: K1 *p1, k1, repeat from * to end.

Knit 1 WS row to create a turning ridge.

On the next RS row, begin working half linen stitch with a three-stitch seed stitch border on each side as follows:

Row 1 (RS): K1, p1, k2, *slip 1 st purlwise wyif, k1, repeat from * to last 3 sts, k1, p1, k1.

Row 2 (WS): K1, p1, k1, purl to last 3 sts, k1, p1, k1.

Row 3 (RS): K1, p1, k1, slip 1 st purlwise wyif, *k1, slip 1 st purlwise wyif, repeat from * to last 3 sts, k1, p1, k1.

Row 4 (WS): K1, p1, k1, purl to last 3 sts, k1, p1, k1.

Repeat these 4 rows until the journal cover measures 11 inches from the turning ridge.

Knit 1 WS row to create the second turning ridge.

Work in seed stitch until the second flap measures 2½ inches.

Bind off and weave in ends.

**Finishing:** Block the piece so that it measures 8¼ by 16 inches and the edges are square (see the appendix for more about blocking). When it's dry, fold the flaps toward the wrong side and sew them in place along the top and bottom edges. Insert your blank book by opening it and inserting the front and back cover into the pockets that you've created with the flaps.

# Nested Squares Baby Blanket

This blanket (see Figure 9-6) features a center panel framed by contrasting colored stripes. With a blanket made of nested squares, you can easily extend the technique to create a larger blanket if you like.

## New skill: Picking up stitches along a garter stitch edge

When you're knitting something with blocks or stripes of different colors, you have several options. For example, you could work this blanket with *intarsia,* working the outer stripe in one color, the inner stripe in a second color, and the central panel in a third color. But that means you're stuck juggling yarns and managing all the colors at once.

Instead, I've chosen to work this blanket out from the center. If you look at Figure 9-7, you can see that the panels are numbered. You start with Section 1, switch yarns and knit Section 2, and then switch yarns again for Section 3. These directions are all pretty straightforward. To knit the other panels, though, you turn the work on its side and pick up stitches along the edge of the piece that you've already made. This technique is especially great for blankets because you can continue adding on as the spirit moves you, expanding in any direction.

**Figure 9-6:**
A paneled blanket makes a perfect gift for baby.

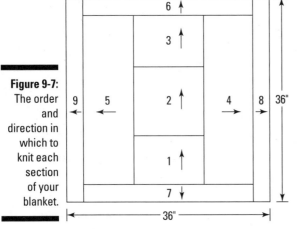

**Figure 9-7:**
The order and direction in which to knit each section of your blanket.

Fear not, though, because in garter stitch, picking up stitches is easy to do (which is another reason to embrace garter stitch!). If you look at a piece that was knit in garter stitch, you'll see that it has prominent ridges, one for each two rows of knitting. Notice also that a bit of each ridge sticks out a smidge at the edge — that's the loop of the edge stitch, as you can see in Figure 9-8.

To pick up stitches along the edge of a garter stitch, following these steps:

1. **Make sure that the right side (the public side) is facing up and that the edge you're working on is at the top.**

2. **Beginning at the left edge of the piece, stick your needle through the edge stitch of the first ridge.**

3. **Continue picking up each of these edge stitches, putting one stitch on the needle for every garter ridge, as shown in Figure 9-8.**

4. **When you get to the right edge, attach your yarn and knit the stitches that you've picked up, carrying on with the pattern as directed (see Chapter 8 for more on switching colors).**

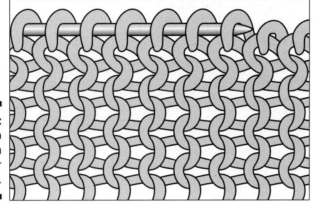

**Figure 9-8:**
Picking up stitches on a garter edge.

Note that picking up stitches on a garter edge is slightly different from the technique usually called "pick up and knit." Pick up and knit means that you're picking up *and* knitting at the same time. (See Chapter 10 for details on this technique.)

## Materials and vital statistics

✔ **Yarn:** RYC Cashsoft Aran (57% merino wool, 33% microfiber, 10% cashmere); 95 yards (87 meters) per 50 grams

  • **Main color (MC):** 001 Oat; 2 balls

  • **Contrasting color 1 (CC1):** 003 Mole; 9 balls

  • **Contrasting color 2 (CC2):** 006 Bud; 5 balls

  • **Contrasting color 3 (CC3):** 008 Tornado; 1 ball (for optional edging and surface details)

✔ **Needles:** US 9 (5.5 mm) circular needles, 36-inch length or longer

✔ **Other materials:** Two extra circular needles to use as holders (US 9 or smaller); US H (5 mm) crochet hook (for optional edging)

✔ **Size:** 36 inches square

✔ **Gauge:** 16 stitches and 32 rows per 4 inches in garter stitch

This blanket is worked out from the center, using one color at a time. Refer to Figure 9-7 to see the order and direction in which to knit the panels of the blanket.

## Directions

For Section 1: With CC1, cast on 48 sts very loosely and knit 72 rows (9 inches). Cut CC1.

You're going to pick up these stitches later, so make it easier on yourself by casting on loosely (use a larger needle if you need to). See the appendix for more about cast-on methods.

For Section 2: Attach MC and knit 96 rows (12 inches). Cut MC.

For Section 3: Attach CC1 and knit 72 rows (9 inches).

Up to this point, the pattern isn't at all unusual. But now comes the twist: Transfer the stitches to one of the holder needles. Cut the yarn leaving a tail that's long enough to convince you that your stitches won't unravel — at least 6 inches.

For Section 4: With the RS facing you, turn the blanket 90 degrees (clockwise or counterclockwise — it doesn't matter!).

Start at the left edge and pick up 120 sts along the edge — 36 sts from each of the CC1 sections and 48 sts from the center MC section.

When picking up stitches in this pattern, it's okay to use a needle that's a different size from your working needle. Just be sure to switch to the working needle when you begin working the picked-up stitches.

Reattach CC1 and knit 72 rows (9 inches). Cut the yarn and slip the stitches to a holder needle.

For Section 5: Turn the blanket 180 degrees and repeat the instructions for Section 4.

For Section 6: Go back to the top of the piece where 48 sts remain on the holder needle (Section 3). Use the ends of the needle to pick up 36 sts from the CC1 sections (Sections 4 and 5) on each end. There are now 120 sts on the needle.

With RS facing, attach CC2 and knit 24 rows (3 inches), and then bind off.

For Section 7: Turn the blanket 180 degrees. Working from left to right, pick up 36 sts from Section 4, 48 sts from the cast-on edge (pick up 1 st for every cast on st), and 36 sts from Section 5. There are now 120 sts on the needle.

Attach CC2 and knit 24 rows, and then bind off.

For Section 8: Turn the blanket 90 degrees. With the circular needle that's attached to this side, pick up 12 sts from the CC2 section (from Sections 6 and 7) on each end. There are now 144 sts on the needle.

With RS facing, attach CC2 and knit 24 rows, and then bind off.

For Section 9: Turn the blanket 180 degrees and repeat the instructions for Section 8.

**Finishing:** If desired, work a row of single crochet around the edges of the blanket with CC3. Crocheting around the edge not only adds a splash of another color, it also provides added strength to the spots that get the most strain. Read up on basic crochet skills in the appendix.

Consider crocheting some surface detailing onto the blanket, such as a baby's name or initials. (See Chapter 7 for the scoop on surface crocheting.)

## Variation: Substituting yarns

Most people are looking for very specific colors when they make a baby blanket, whether it's classic pink and baby blue or some other colors that the mother-to-be or knitter favors. Luckily with this blanket, you can use any aran weight yarn that you think is appropriate (see Chapter 1 for more about this weight). Gauge isn't critical for a blanket, so if you follow the directions exactly at a tighter or looser gauge, you'll get a blanket that's smaller or larger. Twice as big may be a problem, but an inch or two here or there isn't significant. Just remember that fatter yarns will require more yardage.

# Chapter 10

# Almost Rectangles

· · · · · · · · · · · · · · · · · · · · · · · · · · · · · · · · · · · · · · · · · · · · · · ·

## In This Chapter

▶ Shaping a fabulous bag and a sweet baby sweater
▶ Knitting a simple shell and great coats for women

· · · · · · · · · · · · · · · · · · · · · · · · · · · · · · · · · · · · · · · · · · · · · · ·

*T*he patterns in this chapter use slightly more complex shapes than the rectangles in Chapters 8 and 9. They're "almost rectangles," as you'll notice from looking at the schematics. These patterns feature simple shaping largely accomplished by casting on and binding off in the right places — and they all have plenty of style. Looking at the photographs, what you see are great clothes and accessories that you're sure to get a lot of use out of. I firmly believe that simple patterns can be both stylish and fun to knit. So, if you're done knitting scarves and other strictly rectangular shapes, why not try a bag, a shell, or a coat? Or how about making a sweater for the new baby on the block? If you can knit, purl, cast on, and bind off, you're ready to dive into these projects.

## Felted Messenger Bag

This stylish bag can go everywhere with you — it has plenty of room and a stylish strap that you can adjust to fit your needs. The matching buckle closure adds panache and keeps your belongings safely inside. You can see this great bag in Figure 10-1.

**Figure 10-1:** The felted messenger bag has linen stitch straps.

# New skill: The cable cast-on

This messenger bag, like the other patterns in this chapter, relies on casting on and binding off to create its shape. But because you cast on in the middle of the project instead of just at the beginning, you can't use the long-tail cast-on (you won't have a long tail; indeed, you won't have any tail at all!). So what do you do? There are several ways, but my favorite is the cable cast-on.

If you want to try the cable cast-on, here's how:

1. **If you're at the beginning of a project, make a slip knot and put it on the left needle.**

   To make a slip knot, lay the yarn over the first two fingers of your left hand with the tail hanging down over your palm. Wrap the yarn loosely around your two fingers one time ending with the working yarn at the back of your hand. With your right hand, reach through the loop you've made, grab the working yarn, and pull it though the loop. Tug gently on both ends to form the slip knot. Place it on your needle and tighten the knot so that it loosely hugs the needle; this is your first cast-on stitch.

2. **Knit 1 stitch in the loop of the slip knot, but don't drop the slip knot from the left-hand needle.**

   There will be 1 stitch on each needle as shown in Figure 10-2. Transfer the new stitch to the left needle. I like to insert the left needle into the stitch on the right needle from right to left to transfer it, which twists the stitch and gets my needles into position for the next stitch. But the left needle can also be inserted from left to right. Feel free to experiment to see what works best for you.

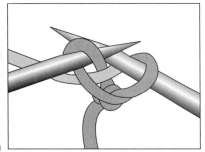

**Figure 10-2:** The first step of the cable cast-on.

3. **Instead of putting the right needle into the next stitch as if to knit, put it _between_ stitches as shown in Figure 10-3.**

   Knit a new stitch, again without dropping any stitches from the left-hand needle, and then transfer the new stitch to the left needle.

4. **Repeat Step 3 until you have cast on as many stitches as you need.**

**Figure 10-3:** Putting your needle between the stitches.

# New skill: Working linen stitch by slipping stitches

*Linen stitch* creates a beautiful woven texture that resists stretching, lays obediently flat, and looks great on both the front and the back. So this stitch makes a great choice for things like the straps on a bag. The stitch is also compact; you'll get a very firm gauge even on big needles. The reason linen stitch acts as it does is that each stitch is knit only every other row, which means that stitches are slipped as often as they are knit.

As you might guess, linen stitch has a lot in common with half linen stitch. With linen stitch, you slip stitches every row. In half linen stitch, you slip stitches only on right-side rows. So, half linen stitch is stretchier and less dense than true linen stitch. You can read about half linen stitch in Chapter 5.

The linen stitch pattern is composed of 2 rows: a right-side row and a wrong-side row. The pattern works over any odd number of stitches.

Starting with the right-side row, follow these steps:

1. **Knit 1 stitch.**

2. **Bring the yarn to the front as if to purl.**

   Be sure to bring the yarn between and under the needles when you do this; see Chapter 8 for more details.

3. **Slip the next stitch purlwise. That is, put the right needle into the stitch as though you were going to purl and transfer the stitch to the right needle without purling it.**

4. **Bring the yarn back between stitches to the knit position.**

   This step leaves a horizontal float across the front of the slipped stitch.

5. **Repeat these four steps until you've reached the last stitch. Knit the last stitch.**

Wrong-side rows are a bit more difficult to describe because you're slipping the first and last stitches of the row. Do it as you read it and the steps will fall into place!

1. **With the yarn in front as if to purl, slip the first stitch purlwise.**

2. **Bring the yarn around the outside of the work to the back and then between the first and second stitch, returning it to the purl position.**

   You've wrapped the yarn around the edge stitch counterclockwise (see Figure 10-4).

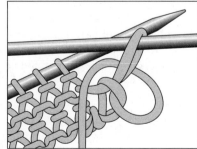

**Figure 10-4:**
Wrapping the yarn around the edge stitch.

3. **Purl the next stitch.**

4. **Bring the yarn to the back of the work, as if to knit.**

5. **Slip the next stitch purlwise.**

6. **Bring the yarn back to the front of the work.**

7. **Repeat Steps 3 through 6 until you've reached the last stitch.**

8. **Bring the yarn to the back of the work.**

9. **Slip the last stitch purlwise.**

10. **Bring the yarn to the front of the work, wrapping the last stitch and putting the yarn in the correct position to knit the first stitch of the next row.**

Continue repeating these 2 rows (right-side and wrong-side) as directed in the pattern you're working.

## Materials and vital statistics

- ✔ **Yarn:** You need two kinds of yarn for this project:
  - **For the bag:** Cascade 128 (100% wool); 128 yards (118 meters) per 100 grams; 4 skeins; color: 627 Grey Tweed
  - **For the straps:** Schaefer Yarns Miss Priss (100% merino wool); 280 yards (256 meters) per 115 grams; 1 skein; color: Rosa Parks
- ✔ **Needles:** You need two types of needles for this project:
  - **For the bag:** US 13 (9 mm) needles
  - **For the straps:** US 10½ (6.5 mm) needles

It is easiest to work with short straight needles or 2 double-pointed needles for the straps and a long circular needle for the bag, but any straight or circular needles of the appropriate size will work.

- ✔ **Other materials:** Two D-rings, 2 inches wide; 2 buckles, 2 inches wide; yarn needle; sewing needle and matching heavy-duty thread to attach the straps to the bag
- ✔ **Size:** See a schematic of the bag in Figure 10-5
  - **Before felting:** 18½ inches wide, 17 inches tall, and 3½ inches deep
  - **Finished size:** 15 inches wide, 12 inches tall, and 3 inches deep
- ✔ **Gauge:** You'll work at two different gauges on this project:
  - **For the bag:** 9 stitches and 18 rows per 4 inches in garter stitch before felting; 11 stitches and 26 rows per 4 inches in garter stitch after felting
  - **For the straps:** 26 stitches and 40 rows per 4 inches in linen stitch

This bag is knit in one piece starting with the front. From there you cast on a few stitches on each side to form the sides of the bag, which are knit at the same time as the back. After you bind off the side gusset stitches, you continue working the flap. When the knitting is complete, you sew the bag together and felt it in the washing machine. While it's drying, cast on for the eye-catching straps.

## Knitting the bag

Cast on 42 sts with a US 13 (9 mm) needle and the Cascade 128 yarn.

Knit 94 rows in garter stitch (knit all rows); 47 garter ridges will be visible.

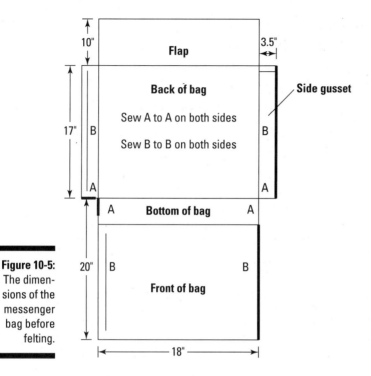

**Figure 10-5:**
The dimen-
sions of the
messenger
bag before
felting.

### Side gussets and back

To give the bag depth, stitches are cast on each side of the work. The sides are created as you knit the back of the bag.

Using the cable cast-on, cast on 8 sts at the beginning of the next 2 rows. There are 58 sts on the needles.

Knit 76 rows. There are 39 garter ridges visible from the beginning of the side gussets.

Bind off 8 sts at the beginning of the next 2 rows. There are 42 sts on the needle. (The appendix has details on binding off.)

### Flap

Knit 44 rows. There will be 22 garter ridges visible after the last bind-off.

Bind off remaining 42 sts.

## Creating the straps

Using US 10½ (6.5 mm) needles and the Miss Priss yarn, cast on 13 sts.

Begin working in linen stitch.

Row 1: *K1, slip 1 purlwise wyif, repeat from * to last st, k1.

Row 2: *Slip 1 purlwise wyib, purl 1, repeat from * to last st, slip 1 purlwise wyib.

The abbreviation "wyif" stands for "with yarn in front"; the abbreviation "wyib" stands for "with yarn in back." Find out more about these terms in Chapter 9.

Repeat these 2 rows until the piece measures 45 inches.

Bind off and weave in ends.

For the buckle closure you need 2 more straps:

For each one, cast on 13 sts and work in linen stitch. Make one piece that's 5 inches long and another piece that's 3 inches long.

## Finishing your bag

Using Cascade 128 and the yarn needle, sew the bottom of the side gusset to the front (the sections marked A on Figure 10-5) using mattress stitch. Sew the long vertical edges of the gussets to the sides of the front (the sections marked B), being sure that the top edge of the bag front is aligned with the top (bound-off) edges of the gussets. (You can read up on finishing in the appendix.)

Now it's time to felt your bag. Felting, which will make your bag smaller and sturdier, is accomplished by exposing the knitted bag to hot water and agitation in the washing machine. See the appendix for step-by-step felting instructions.

Don't felt the beautiful straps you've made! Only put the bag itself in the washing machine!

When the bag is dry (which may take a couple of days depending on your climate) attach the straps by following these steps:

1. **Sew the two D-rings to the top edges of the side gussets using a sewing needle and matching thread.**

2. **Slip one end of the longest strap through a D-ring from the outside toward the bag, making sure that the right side of the strap is out.**

3. **Fold an inch of the loose end of the strap over the D-ring and stitch it down.**

4. **Thread one buckle onto the long strap, placing it roughly in the middle of the strap.**

   Because it's adjustable, it doesn't matter where you put it for now.

5. **Insert the free end of the strap through the D-ring on the opposite side of the bag, putting it through from the outside toward the bag and bringing the free end up along the wrong side of the strap.**

6. **Bring the strap under the center bar of the buckle and fold it over the bar, and then stitch it down using a sewing needle and thread.**

7. **Attach the 5-inch-long strap to the center of the front flap as shown in Figure 10-6. Attach the first 2 inches of the strap to the flap itself, with the remaining 3 inches hanging down from the edge of the flap.**

8. **Attach one end of the 3-inch-long strap to the center bar of the second buckle using a sewing needle and thread.**

   The buckle will be at the top of the strap. Be sure that the right side of the strap faces out.

9. **Thread the strap from the flap through the buckle to determine the correct placement of the strap with the buckle on the front of the bag.**

10. **Close the bag and sew the last strap in place.**

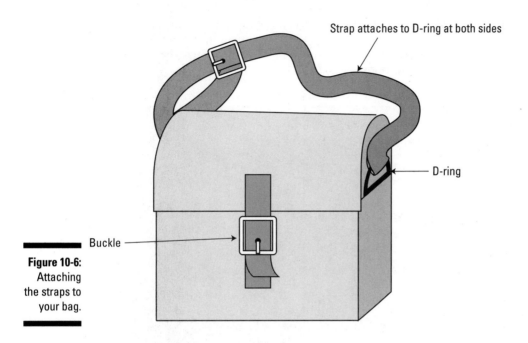

Strap attaches to D-ring at both sides

D-ring

Buckle

**Figure 10-6:**
Attaching
the straps to
your bag.

# One-Piece Baby Sweater

Legions of baby sweater patterns claim to be quick and easy. Here's an updated take on the classic kimono that suits both boys and girls (see Figure 10-7). It's unrealistic to expect to finish this sweater in one day, but you can still finish it pretty quickly. Pair this sweater with a set of retro slippers (see Chapter 8) and one of the great hats in Chapter 8 or Chapter 11, and baby's got a fantastic layette.

## New skill: Making a buttonhole

There are lots of ways to make a buttonhole when you knit. For a small buttonhole, for instance, you can simply use a yarn over and a single decrease and be done with it (see Chapter 6 for more about these stitches). For anything larger, I like to use a simple two-row buttonhole, which I explain later in this section. This type of buttonhole can be 2 or 3 (or more) stitches wide, though I find that it's better to underestimate the number of stitches you use; most times you can get a bigger button than you think through your buttonhole. However, I still like to make the buttonholes before I buy my buttons. I find that it's a lot easier to find a button that fits the hole than to make a hole that fits the button.

Here are a few tips to bear in mind when making your buttonholes:

✔ **Be sure to place them far enough in from the edges.** You don't want the button to hang over the edges of the sweater. So, for example, if you're using a 1-inch-diameter button, give yourself at least an inch on all sides of the buttonhole. That gives you half an inch for the button's radius, plus half an inch beside it. The bigger the buttonhole, the more room you should leave around it.

✔ **Buttonholes do stretch out.** If you find that your buttons are slipping out of their holes, replace the buttons with bigger buttons. This solution is particularly helpful when a sweater has been passed down to its fourth baby.

✔ **Buttonholes aren't just for buttons.** The two-row buttonhole technique can be used any time you need to create a slit in something that's knitted. I use it to make a thumbhole in the wrist warmers pattern and a purse handle in the mosaic bags pattern (both in Chapter 11).

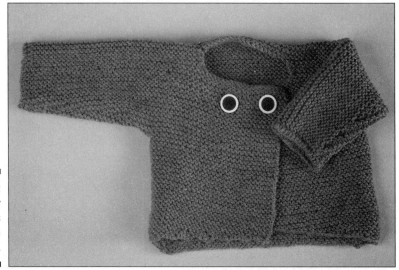

**Figure 10-7:**
This baby
sweater is
knit all in
one piece.

Are you ready to go? If you're working from a pattern, work to the spot directed, and then make your two-row buttonhole by following these steps:

1. **Bind off 2 stitches (or more for a larger buttonhole).**

   Continue knitting across the row.

2. **In the next row, knit to the gap created by your bound off stitches and cast on 2 stitches (or as many as you bound off in the first row).**

   You won't be able to use the long-tail cast-on here because you won't have a tail. Use the cable cast-on to get the job done. (See more on the cable cast-on earlier in this chapter.)

3. **Knit to the end of the row.**

   Your buttonhole is complete.

## Materials and vital statistics

✔ **Yarn:** Cascade 220 Superwash (100% superwash wool); 220 yards (201 meters) per 100 grams; 2 (2, 3) skeins; color: 860 Gray Heather

✔ **Needles:** US 7 (4.5 mm), or the size needed to match gauge

✔ **Other materials:** Two 1-inch buttons; sewing needle and thread to match buttons; yarn needle for sewing up seams

✔ **Size:** Newborn (6–12 months, 1–2 years)

   • **Finished chest circumference:** 18 (22, 26) inches

   • **Finished length:** 9 (11, 13) inches

   See the schematic in Figure 10-8.

✔ **Gauge:** 18 stitches and 36 rows per 4 inches in garter stitch

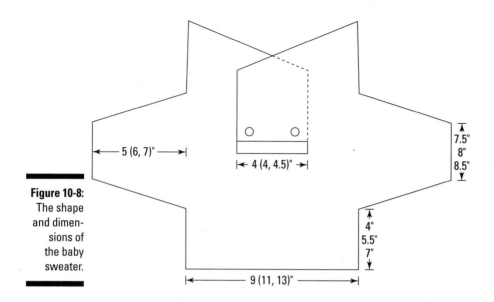

**Figure 10-8:**
The shape and dimensions of the baby sweater.

This sweater is worked in one piece. You start at the lower edge of the back and knit straight to the beginning of the sleeves, which are increased gradually. When you get to the shoulders, you bind off stitches for the neck opening, and then work each side of the front separately, casting on stitches for the front neckline. When you're done knitting, you have just one seam to sew on each side from the cuff to the waist. Then you attach the buttons.

# Directions

Cast on 36 (44, 54) sts.

Work in garter stitch (knit all rows) until the sweater measures 4 (5½, 7) inches.

### Sleeves

You'll cast on gradually for both sleeves. Using the cable cast-on (see the earlier section "New skill: The cable cast-on" for details) or your preferred method, cast on 4 sts at the beginning of the next 12 (14, 16) rows. There are now 84 (100, 118) sts on the needle.

Work even until the sweater measures 9 (11, 13) inches. The back is now complete.

### Neck

You now bind off stitches for the neck and work the left front and right front separately.

Next row: Knit 33 (41, 49) sts; bind off the center 18 (18, 20) sts; knit to the end of the row. You now have 2 sets of 33 (41, 49) sts.

Continue working on the set of stitches with the yarn attached. If you want, you can slip the other set of stitches to a holder. You can also just leave them on the needle and ignore them.

### Left front

Knit 6 rows on the 33 (41, 49) sts for the left front.

Knit across the 7th row, and at the end (the neck edge), turn the work and cast on 18 (18, 20) sts using the backward-e or cable cast-on. There are 51 (59, 69) sts on the needle.

Work even on these sts for 1 inch, ending with the yarn at the sleeve edge.

Now work buttonholes over the next 2 rows as follows:

Next row: K37 (45, 53) sts, bind off 2 sts, k5 (5, 7) sts, bind off 2 sts, k3. There are 6 (6, 8) sts between the 2 buttonholes.

Next row: K4, cast on 2 sts, k6 (6, 8) sts, cast on 2 sts, knit to end.

Work even until the left side measures 10¾ (14, 17¼) inches from the cast-on edge, ending with the yarn at the sleeve edge.

Next WS row (at the wrist edge): Bind off 4 sts, knit to end.

Next row: Knit.

Repeat the previous 2 rows 5 (6, 7) more times. There are 27 (31, 37) sts.

Work even until the sweater measures 2½ (3¾, 5) inches from the bottom of the sleeve, ending with the yarn at the front (tummy) edge.

Next row: Bind off 4 sts, knit across.

Next row: Knit.

Repeat the previous 2 rows 6 (7, 8) more times, and then bind off the remaining sts.

Some people care which side their sweaters button on (for example, right over left or left over right). This sweater has buttons on two sides, and the left side of the lapel goes on top. But if you want the right side of the lapel to go on top, turn the sweater inside out before you do the finishing.

### Right front

Reattach the yarn at the neck edge and knit 5 rows on the 33 (41, 49) sts for the right front.

Knit across the 6th row, and at the end (the neck edge), cast on 18 (18, 20) sts using the backward-e, knitted, or cable cast-on. There are 51 (59, 69) sts on the needle.

Work even until this side of the sweater measures 10¾ (14, 17¼) inches from the cast-on edge, ending with the yarn at the sleeve edge.

Next RS row (at the wrist edge): Bind off 4 sts, knit to end.

Next row: Knit.

Repeat the previous 2 rows 5 (6, 7) more times. There are 27 (31, 37) sts.

Work even until the sweater measures 2½ (3¾, 5) inches from the bottom of the sleeve, ending with the yarn at the tummy edge.

Next row: Bind off 4 sts, knit to end.

Next row: Knit.

Repeat the previous 2 rows 6 (7, 8) more times, and then bind off the remaining stitches.

### Finishing

Block the sweater so the edges are smooth and the side seams are the same length. Sew the seam on each side from cuff to underarm to hem. Using the buttonholes as guides, place the buttons on the opposite lapel and then sew them firmly in place using a needle and thread. (Read more on blocking and sewing seams in the appendix.)

You can make a good sweater great with the right buttons. So, I like to wait until the sweater is done to pick them. This way I know I've chosen the right ones. Even if I think I know how the sweater's going to look, I find I almost always pick a different button when the sweater's done.

# Deceptively Simple Shell

Like the box top in Chapter 8, this shell has an incredibly simple shape, but when worn on the body, it looks much more interesting. By simply splitting the front in half for the last couple of inches (think of making a slit in the front of a tight-fitting T-shirt), and then binding off all the neck stitches in one go, you get plenty of va-va-voom! This top has *negative ease,* which means that when worn it stretches to hug your curves. See the top in Figure 10-9.

**Figure 10-9:**
The deceptively simple shell is curve-hugging.

## Materials and vital statistics

- ✔ **Yarn:** Cascade Venezia (70% merino wool, 30% silk); 102 yards (94 meters) per 100 grams; 4 (5, 5, 5, 6) balls; color: Melon

- ✔ **Needles:** US 10 (6 mm) needles, or the size needed to match gauge

- ✔ **Other materials:** Yarn needle; stitch holder

- ✔ **Size:** XS (S, M, L, 1X)

  - **Finished chest circumference (unstretched):** 20 (22, 24, 27, 30) inches

  - **Finished chest circumference (stretched):** 30 (34, 38, 42, 46) inches

  - **Finished length:** 22 (23, 23, 24, 24) inches

  See Figure 10-10 for a schematic.

✔ **Gauge:** 22 stitches and 20 rows over 2 x 2 rib (unstretched); 14 stitches and 20 rows over 2 x 2 rib (stretched)

This top is a quick knit that you'll love to wear. Wear it on its own in summer or under a jacket year-round. It's knit in two easy pieces and is a cinch to sew up.

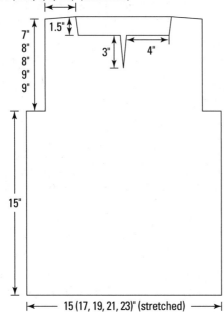

3.75 (4.25, 5, 5, 5.5)" (stretched)

**Figure 10-10:**
The dimensions of the deceptively simple shell.

15 (17, 19, 21, 23)" (stretched)

# Starting with the back

Cast on 54 (62, 66, 74, 82) sts.

Begin 2 x 2 rib as follows:

Row 1 (RS): K2, *p2, k2, repeat from * to end.

Row 2 (WS): P2, *k2, p2, repeat from * to end.

Repeat these 2 rows until the back measures 15 inches (all sizes).

### Shape armholes

Bind off 2 (4, 4, 6, 8) sts at the beginning of the next 2 rows. There are 50 (54, 58, 62, 66) sts.

Continue with the rib pattern, knitting the knit sts and purling the purl sts, until the back measures 22 (23, 23, 24, 24) inches.

Bind off all sts.

## Moving to the front

Work the front the same as the back through the armhole shaping.

Continue with the rib pattern until the front measures 17½ (18½, 18½, 19½, 19½) inches, ending with a RS row.

You now divide the left and right halves of the neck and work them separately.

### Right neck

Next row (WS): Work 25 (27, 29, 31, 33) sts in rib pattern. Do not complete the row; place the remaining stitches on a stitch holder.

Continue in rib pattern on these 25 (27, 29, 31, 33) sts until this side measures 3 inches from the beginning of neck shaping, ending with a WS row.

Next row (RS): Bind off 12 (12, 12, 14, 14) sts, work in rib pattern to the end of the row. There are 13 (15, 17, 17, 19) sts on the needle.

Work 1½ inches in rib pattern, measuring from the last bind off.

Bind off.

### Left neck

Replace the held stitches on the needle with the WS facing and rejoin the yarn. Work these 25 (27, 29, 31, 33) stitches in rib pattern as set for 3 inches, ending with a RS row.

Next row (WS): Bind off 12 (12, 12, 14, 14) sts at the neck edge, and then work in rib pattern to the end of the row. There are 13 (15, 17, 17, 19) sts on the needle.

Work 1½ inches in rib pattern as set.

Bind off.

## Finishing your shell

Using mattress stitch, sew the shoulder seams together, matching the outer edges of the front and back shoulders and lining up the rib pattern. Sew the side seams from the bottom of the armhole to the hemline. Weave in any loose ends and block if desired.

Leave the edges unfinished for a somewhat deconstructed look as I have (refer to Figure 10-9), or finish them with a row of single crochet if desired. (See the appendix for more about blocking and crocheted edging.)

# Shawl-Collared Coat

After finding a beautiful vintage hand-knit coat, I got a bee in my bonnet about creating my own. A knitted coat may not be the first thing you think of when you're looking for a simple project, but trust me, while the scale is a bit larger than a scarf or purse, the knitting itself couldn't be simpler. And while you can't really convince yourself that it's okay to wear the same pullover every day, you're justified in wearing the same coat all season long — so it's well worth making.

The basic version of this coat (see Figure 10-11) is just three simple rectangles joined at the shoulders with a three-needle bind-off. From there, stitches are picked up all the way around the front panels and back neck to make a shawl collar. The sleeve caps aren't shaped, so knitting and attaching the sleeves is straightforward.

**Figure 10-11:**
The shawl-collared coat can be worn in all seasons.

# New skill: The three-needle bind-off

Okay, so it's awkward to say, difficult to hyphenate properly, and doesn't have a catchy abbreviation. But the three-needle bind-off is lovable nonetheless. It allows you to attach two knitted pieces together tidily and sturdily without sewing. It's perfect for shoulder seams.

To use the three-needle bind-off, you need two pieces of knitting that are still on the needles, with an equal number of stitches on each, and a spare needle of the same size.

If you don't have three needles that are the same size, put one set of stitches on a smaller needle and bind off with the correctly sized one.

Follow these steps for a seamless three-needle bind-off:

1. **Hold the two pieces with their right sides (public sides) together and both needle tips parallel and pointing to the right as shown in Figure 10-12.**

   If the stitches on one needle are facing the wrong way, slip the stitches onto a circular needle and then back to the working needle so that they're facing the right way. Hold both needles in your left hand.

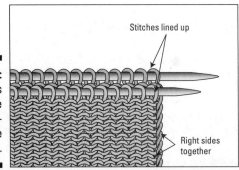

**Figure 10-12:**
Lining things up for the three-needle bind-off.

Stitches lined up

Right sides together

2. **Take the third needle in your right hand and stick it into the first stitch on the front needle as you would to knit it.**

   Continue through to the first stitch on the back needle, and then stick the needle through this stitch knitwise.

3. **Wrap the yarn as shown in Figure 10-13 and knit these 2 stitches together.**

   There's 1 stitch on the right-hand needle.

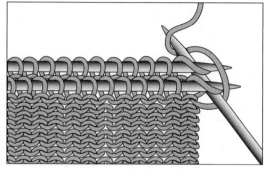

**Figure 10-13:**
Knitting the first stitch from both needles together.

4. **Knit together the next stitch from the front needle with the next stitch from the back needle.**

   There are 2 stitches on the right needle.

5. **Bring the rightmost stitch on the right needle over the stitch that you just worked (as you do when you bind off normally).**

   Check out Figure 10-14 to see how to bind off the first stitch.

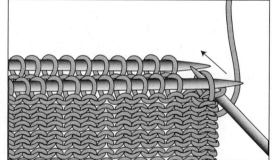

**Figure 10-14:**
Binding off the first stitch.

6. **Repeat Steps 4 and 5 until all the stitches are bound off.**

   Cut the yarn and pull the tail through the last stitch to secure.

## New skill: Pick up and knit vertically

To pick up stitches along a vertical edge, like the front edges of this shawl-collared coat, you need the smaller-sized knitting needles to knit the collar, the working yarn, and maybe a crochet hook.

Look closely for a moment at the edge of your knitted piece, comparing it to Figure 10-15. Between the first and second stitches on the edge, you should see a series of running threads that look like the rungs of a ladder; this is where the action is — just like when you're sewing something up with mattress stitch (see the appendix for details).

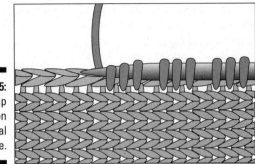

**Figure 10-15:** Picking up stitches on a vertical edge.

With the right (public) side facing up, start at the right edge of the work and follow these steps:

1. **Stick your needle between the first two rungs of the ladder from the front to the back of the piece.**

2. **Wrap the working yarn around the needle as you would if you were working a knit stitch and pull it through.**

3. **Continue picking up stitches in the same way until you've picked up the correct number of stitches.**

If you find the previous steps awkward, you can use a crochet hook and the following steps instead:

1. **Stick the crochet hook between the ladder rungs from the front of the piece to the back.**

2. **Grab the working yarn and pull through a loop.**

   Transfer the loop to your knitting needle and give the yarn a gentle tug to snug it up.

3. **Continue picking up stitches in the same way until you've picked up the correct number of stitches.**

To compensate for the difference between the number of stitches and the number of rows per inch, you need to skip spaces in the ladder regularly as shown in Figure 10-15. If you're knitting 3 stitches and 4 rows per inch, for example, you need to pick up 3 stitches for every 4 rows. Or, said more simply, you need to pick up and knit stitches in the next 3 spaces, skip 1 space, pick up and knit stitches in the next 3 spaces, skip 1, and so on across the piece.

A moment to flex the math brain gives you the specific information needed for this project. Verify your gauge from your swatch for the collar and the body of the coat. But remember to be honest with yourself about your gauge! Like buying pants based on the listed size rather than on how they fit, fudging your gauge is a mistake. If your gauge is different than mine, now's the time to deal with it. So, you need to plan *your* pick up based on what *you've* actually knit. Here's what you do for this particular pattern:

✔ The collar is knit in rib at 5¼ stitches per inch.

✔ The body of the coat is knit in half linen stitch at 6 rows per inch.

✔ Given these facts, you need to pick up 5¼ stitches for every 6 rows. Because you can't pick up a quarter stitch, you need to noodle a bit with fractions. For instance, 5¼ divided by 6 is 0.875, which is the same as ⅞. So, you have to pick up 7 out of every 8 stitches.

If you don't want to think through the math, place markers every 2 inches around the edges where you'll be picking up stitches, and then pick up your stitch gauge per inch times 2 between each set of markers. Using the previous example, 5¼ × 2 = 10½, so you pick up 10½ stitches between each set of markers. And, again, because you can't pick up half a stitch, compensate by picking up 10 stitches between the first set of markers, 11 stitches between the second set markers, and so on.

## New skill: Pick up and knit horizontally

Turn the coat so that the back is up with the right side facing you. You'll see a row of stitches, like little Vs, just below the bound-off edge along the neck. This is where you'll be picking up stitches horizontally, as shown in Figure 10-16.

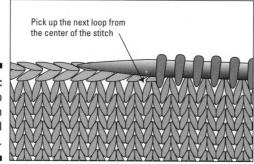

**Figure 10-16:** Picking up stitches on a horizontal edge.

Pick up the next loop from the center of the stitch

Still working from right to left, use your knitting needle or crochet hook as you did along the vertical edge in the previous section. Make sure that you're inserting your needle into whole stitches and not into the bound-off edges.

If you're picking up stitches along a horizontal edge and working your add-on at the same gauge as the body of the garment, you simply pick up 1 stitch in every bound-off stitch. But because you're working with two gauges in this project (half linen stitch versus rib), you have to do some math. But I promise that I've made it easy to get right. Choose the option that makes the most sense to you, and then do it:

- ✔ Pick up 5 stitches for every 4 stitches.
- ✔ Pick up 2 stitches in every 4th stitch.
- ✔ Pick up 9½ stitches for every 2 inches.
- ✔ Pick up 39 stitches across the back of the neck.

Generically, pick up as many stitches per inch as you're knitting for the new piece in every inch of the existing piece.

## Materials and vital statistics

- ✔ **Yarn:** Cascade Jewel (100% hand-dyed Peruvian wool); 142 yards (130 meters) per 100 grams; 10 (11, 12, 13, 13, 14) skeins; color: 9969
- ✔ **Needles:** US 10 (6 mm) needles, or the size needed to match gauge; US 8 (5 mm) needles for ribbing and hem facings; one very long circular needle or two or three shorter ones to work the collar

✔ **Other materials:** Stitch holders or spare needles; US H (5 mm) or smaller crochet hook; stitch markers or safety pins; yarn needle for finishing

✔ **Size:** Women's XS (S, M, L, 1X, 2X)

   • **Finished chest circumference:** 36 (40, 44, 48, 52, 56) inches, with front edges overlapped about 2 inches

   • **Finished length:** 30 inches (all sizes)

   See Figure 10-17 for the schematic

✔ **Gauge:** 15 stitches and 24 rows per 4 inches in half linen stitch on US 10 (6 mm) needles; 21 stitches and 24 rows per 4 inches in 3 x 3 rib on US 8 (5 mm) needles

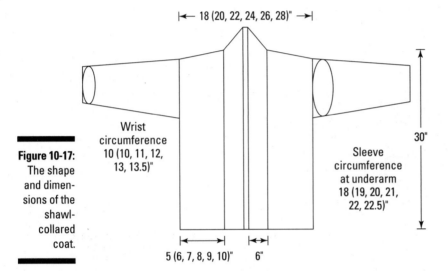

**Figure 10-17:** The shape and dimensions of the shawl-collared coat.

This coat is worked in half linen stitch (see Chapter 5), which creates a wonderful, almost woven-looking fabric. Because this technique involves slipping stitches, it minimizes vertical stretch, which is perfect for a longer, heavier garment like a coat. The coat also features a hem that's knit in. This type of hem may sound fancy, but it's easy to work and makes the edges of your coat sit properly. It also allows the half linen stitch pattern to continue all the way to the edges without being interrupted.

## Starting with the back

With smaller needles, cast on 69 (75, 83, 91, 99, 105) sts.

Work 10 rows in stockinette stitch (knit RS rows, purl WS rows) to form the hem facing, ending with a WS row.

Purl 1 RS row to create a turning ridge.

Next row: Switch to larger needles and purl.

Begin half linen stitch as follows:

Row 1 (RS): K2, *sl 1 purlwise wyif, k1, repeat from * to last 3 sts, sl 1 purlwise wyif, k2.

Row 2 (WS): Purl.

Row 3: K3, *sl 1 purlwise wyif, k1, repeat from * to last 4 sts, sl 1 purlwise wyif, k3.

Row 4: Purl.

Repeating these 4 rows, continue in pattern until the back measures 29.5 inches from turning ridge, or desired length, ending with a WS row.

### Shoulder and neck shaping

The shoulders on your coat are worked with simple short rows. I didn't wrap the stitches at the turning points, but if you want to wrap them, see Chapter 12.

Next row (RS): Work across in half linen stitch to last 9 (11, 13, 15, 17, 19) sts. Turn work, leaving remaining sts unworked.

Next row (WS): Slip first st, and then purl to last 9 (11, 13, 15, 17, 19) sts. Turn work, leaving remaining sts unworked.

Next row: Slip first st, and then work across, maintaining the half linen stitch pattern, to last 19 (22, 26, 30, 34, 37) sts. Turn work, leaving remaining sts unworked.

Next row (WS): Bind off the center 31 sts and cut the yarn. There are 19 (22, 26, 30, 34, 37) shoulder sts on either side awaiting three-needle bind-off. Slip these sts to holders or spare needles while you knit the front panels.

# Moving to the left front panel

For this coat, you make two front panels, each of which is only as wide as the shoulder sections of the back. The center portion of the front is worked later as a wide shawl collar.

Cast on 19 (23, 27, 31, 35, 37) sts with smaller needles.

Work 10 rows in stockinette stitch to form the hem facing, ending with a WS row.

Purl 1 RS row to create a turning ridge.

Next row (WS): Switch to the larger needles and purl.

Work in half linen stitch as you did for the back until the front measures the same as the back to the shoulder shaping, ending with a WS row.

### Shoulder shaping

Work the first row of shoulder shaping appropriate for your size as follows:

Next row for sizes XS and 2X only (RS): Work in pattern.

Next row for sizes S, M, L, 1X only (RS): Work in pattern to last 4 sts, k2tog, k2. There are now 19 (22, 26, 30, 34, 37) sts on the needle.

All sizes continue:

Next row (WS): Purl to last 9 (11, 13, 15, 17, 19) sts. Turn work, leaving the remaining sts unworked.

Next row (RS): Slip first st and then work across row, maintaining the half linen stitch pattern. Do not bind off; cut the yarn, leaving a tail that's at least 4 feet long. Slip all sts to holders or spare needles.

# Continuing with the right front panel

Work the right front the same as the left front to shoulder shaping ending with a RS row.

### Shoulder shaping

Work the first row of shoulder shaping appropriate for your size as follows:

Next row for sizes XS and 2X only (WS): Work in pattern.

Next row for sizes S, M, L, 1X only (WS): Work in pattern to last 4 sts, p2tog, p2. There are now 19 (22, 26, 30, 34, 37) sts on the needle.

All sizes continue:

Next row (RS): Work in half linen stitch to last 9 (11, 13, 15, 17, 19) sts. Turn work, leaving remaining sts unworked.

Next row (WS): Slip first st and then purl to end. Don't bind off or cut yarn.

# Attaching the front and back panels

Slip sts from the back right shoulder to a needle so that the RS faces up and the needle points toward the neck.

Place right front, WS up, on top of the back so that the needles are parallel. Use the three-needle bind-off described earlier in this chapter to attach the two pieces.

Repeat the three-needle bind-off to attach the second shoulder.

# Making the sleeves

Make 2 sleeves that are the same as follows:

With smaller needles, cast on 37 (37, 43, 45, 49, 51) sts.

Work 6 rows in stockinette stitch to form the hem facing, ending with a WS row.

Next row (RS): Switch to the larger needles and purl.

Work 6 rows in half linen stitch as you did for the back.

Begin increases for sleeves.

Row 1 (Increase Row): K1, m1, sl 1, k1, *sl 1 purlwise wyif, k1, repeat from * to last 2 sts, sl 1, m1, k1.

The abbreviation "m1" stands for "make 1." For more details, see Chapter 14.

Row 2 (WS): Purl.

Row 3 (RS): K3, *sl 1 purlwise wyif, k1, repeat from * to last 4 sts, sl 1 purlwise wyif, k3.

Row 4 (WS): Purl.

Row 5 (RS): K2, *sl 1 purlwise wyif, k1, repeat from * to last 3 sts, sl 1 purlwise wyif, k2.

Row 6 (WS): Purl.

Repeat these 6 rows 14 (16, 15, 16, 16, 16) more times. There are 67 (71, 75, 79, 83, 85) sts.

Work even, maintaining the stitch pattern, until your sleeve measures 18 inches from turning ridge, or your desired length.

Bind off.

## Creating the shawl collar

The next step involves picking up a lot of stitches (I show you how to pick up vertically and horizontally earlier in this chapter). Grab a cup of coffee, all the size 8 circular needles you've got, and your trusty crochet hook.

Using the circular needle and with the right (public) side facing you, start at the turning ridge on the right front (make sure you're working on the front edge at the tummy rather than on the side edge!) and pick up and knit 357 stitches — that is, pick up 159 stitches along the right front, 39 stitches along the back of the neck, and 159 stitches down the left front, ending at the turning ridge.

I know that 357 is a lot of stitches. Here's a tip to help you manage all of them: Put them on more than one circular needle; maybe two longer ones for the fronts and one shorter one for the back. If you're using more than one needle, just work the stitches on each needle with the ends of that needle, but make sure that you complete all 357 stitches in each row.

After you pick up the stitches, it's time to make the collar itself.

Row 1 (WS): *P3, k3, repeat from * to last 3 sts, p3.

Row 2: *K3, p3, repeat from * to last 3 sts, k3.

Repeat these 2 rows until ribbing measures 6 inches, or your desired length. Bind off loosely in rib (see Chapter 13 for details on this type of binding off).

## Finishing your coat

Measure 9 (9½, 10, 10½, 11, 11¼) inches down from the shoulder seam on the front and place a marker or safety pin on the side edge at this point. Do the same on the back so that you have two markers 18 (19, 20, 21, 22, 22½) inches apart.

Fold one sleeve in half lengthwise to find the center of the upper (bound-off) edge and mark it with a pin. Line up the center of the sleeve with the shoulder seam and the edges of the sleeve with the markers on your coat. Sew the sleeve in place with mattress stitch. Attach the second sleeve the same way. Sew the sleeve seams and side seams of the coat. Sew the hem facings to the wrong side of the coat. Weave in all ends. (See the appendix for information on sewing seams.)

## Variation: A beautiful border

Think of the body of your coat as a backdrop for the collar — it's a lot like a scarf that's attached. You can use any yarn for your collar, regardless of gauge. Choose a hand-spun or hand-dyed yarn that you have a limited quantity of, or any dreamy yarn that you've fallen in love with. Work with your chosen yarn for 2 inches for a subtle border, or go all the way to 8 inches if you want the two sides of the shawl collar to completely overlap.

Simply swatch with the yarn you've chosen to figure out the gauge per inch in your desired stitch pattern (see Chapter 2 for help). Then pick up that number of stitches for every inch along the front edges and back neckline of the coat. If you're working a stitch pattern that requires a certain number of stitches, it's okay to add or subtract a few stitches as needed. Out of the hundreds of stitches that you're picking up, a couple of stitches more or less simply won't make a difference.

# Hooded Coat

This hooded coat (shown in Figure 10-18) has the same shape as the shawl-collared coat, but it's worked in plain stockinette stitch. The hems are worked with a subtle and feminine picot detailing, which works great with the simple lines of the coat. This version of the coat features a hood and a contrasting color-shifting yarn worked in seed stitch for the shawl collar. You can also vary the coat by knitting the collar and hood in feather and fan stitch (see the later variation).

**Figure 10-18:** The hooded coat features contrasting seed stitch on the hood and front panels.

## Materials and vital statistics

- ✔ **Yarn:** You need two yarns for this project:
  - • **Yarn A:** Cascade Eco + (100% Peruvian Highland wool); 478 yards (441 meters) per 250 grams; 3 (3, 3, 3, 4, 4) skeins; color: 7076 Periwinkle
  - • **Yarn B:** Divé Teseo (53% wool, 47% microfiber); 98 yards (90 meters) per 50 grams; 6 skeins (all sizes); color: 44147
- ✔ **Needles:** US 10 (6 mm) needles, or the size needed to match gauge; US 8 (5 mm) needles for collar and hem facings; one long circular needle or two to three shorter ones to work the collar
- ✔ **Other materials:** Stitch holders or spare needles; US H (5 mm) crochet hook; stitch markers or safety pins; yarn needle for finishing

✔ **Size:** Women's XS (S, M, L, 1X, 2X)

- **Finished chest circumference:** 36 (40, 44, 48, 52, 56) inches

- **Finished length:** 30 inches (all sizes)

Figure 10-19 shows the schematic

✔ **Gauge:** 14 stitches and 20 rows per 4 inches in stockinette stitch on US 10 (6 mm) needles with yarn A; 17 stitches and 26 rows per 4 inches in seed stitch on US 8 (5 mm) needles with yarn B

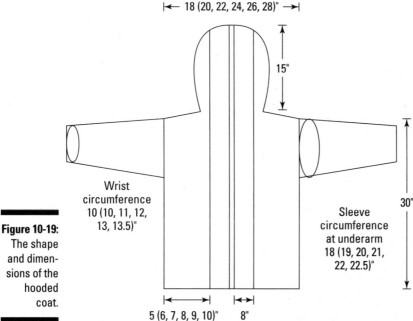

|← 18 (20, 22, 24, 26, 28)" →|

15"

Wrist circumference 10 (10, 11, 12, 13, 13.5)"

Sleeve circumference at underarm 18 (19, 20, 21, 22, 22.5)"

30"

5 (6, 7, 8, 9, 10)"  8"

**Figure 10-19:** The shape and dimensions of the hooded coat.

This coat is simple to knit and easy to wear; it's definitely something you'll love to wrap up in on chilly days. The hood isn't fitted but drapes to form an attractive collar highlighted by the contrasting yarn. Try fastening the coat with a shawl pin or brooch — or even a spare double-pointed knitting needle! This eye-catching coat is knit in three almost rectangles for the back and the two front panels. The sleeves are drop-shouldered, so sewing them in place is straightforward. The contrasting shawl collar and sides of the hood are knit all at once from stitches that you'll pick up from the body.

## Starting with the back

With smaller needles and yarn A, cast on 63 (71, 77, 85, 91, 99) sts.

Work 10 rows in stockinette stitch (knit a row, purl a row) to form the hem facing, ending with a WS row.

Next row (RS): K1, *k2tog, yo, repeat from * to last 2 sts, k2. This row forms a picot edge for the hem when the facing is turned under.

For more information about knit 2 together (k2tog) and yarn over (yo), head to Chapter 6.

Next row (WS): Switch to larger needles and work in stockinette stitch, beginning with a purl row, until the back measures 29.5 inches from picot turning edge, or desired length, ending with a WS row.

### Shoulder shaping

The shoulders of your coat are worked with simple short rows. I didn't wrap the stitches at the turning points, but if you want to wrap them, see Chapter 12 for details.

Next row (RS): Knit to last 8 (10, 12, 14, 15, 17) sts. Turn work, leaving remaining stitches unworked.

Next row (WS): Slip first st, and then purl to last 8 (10, 12, 14, 15, 17) sts. Turn work, leaving remaining sts unworked.

Next row (RS): Slip first st and then knit across to last 17 (21, 25, 29, 31, 35) sts. Turn work, leaving remaining sts unworked.

# Moving to the hood

Next row (WS): Slip first st, p28. Slip the first and last 17 (21, 24, 28, 31, 35) sts to holders or spare needles. 29 sts remain on the needle.

Work these 29 back neck sts in seed stitch for 15 inches (or less for a more fitted hood).

Work each row as *k1, p1, repeat from * to last st, k1.

Bind off.

# Knitting the left front

For this coat, you make two front panels, each of which is only as wide as the shoulder sections of the back. The center portion of the front is worked later along with the sides of the hood.

Cast on 17 (21, 25, 29, 31, 35) sts with smaller needles.

Work 10 rows in stockinette stitch to form the hem facing, ending with a WS row.

Next row (RS): K1, *k2tog, yo, repeat from * to last 2 sts, k2. This row forms a picot turning row for the hem.

Next row (WS): Switch to larger needles and purl.

Switch to larger needles and work in stockinette stitch, beginning with a purl row, until the front measures 29.5 inches, or the same as back to shoulder shaping, ending with a RS row.

Next row (WS): Purl to last 8 (10, 12, 14, 15, 17) sts. Turn work, leaving remaining sts unworked.

Next row (RS): Slip first st, and then knit to end. Do not bind off. Cut the yarn, leaving a tail that's at least 4 feet long. Slip all sts to holders or spare needles for later.

# Knitting the right front

Work the right front the same as the left front to shoulder shaping, ending with a WS row.

### Shoulder shaping

Next row (RS): Knit to last 8 (10, 12, 14, 15, 17) sts. Turn work, leaving these sts unworked.

Next row (WS): Slip first st, and then purl to end. Do not bind off or cut yarn, but leave the sts on the needle, ready for the three-needle bind-off.

# Attaching the front and back panels

Slip the stitches from the right shoulder of the back to the needle so that the right (public) side is facing up, and the needle points toward the neck.

Place the left front, WS up, on top of the back so that the needles are parallel. Use the three-needle bind-off to attach the two pieces. See the earlier section "New skill: The three-needle bind-off" for help if this is a new skill for you.

Attach the right front to the right shoulder of the back in the same way.

# Making the sleeves

Make 2 sleeves that are the same as follows:

With smaller needles, cast on 35 (37, 41, 41, 45, 45) sts.

Work 6 rows in stockinette stitch, ending with a WS row.

For the picot turning edge:

Next row (RS): K1, *k2tog, yo, repeat from * to last 2 sts, k2. This creates the picot edge of the hem.

Switch to larger needles and work 5 rows in stockinette stitch starting and ending with a purl row.

Increase row (RS): Kfb, knit to last 2 sts, kfb, k1.

Kfb stands for "knit into the front and back of the stitch"; see Chapter 11 for information.

Repeat the increase row every 6th row 13 (14, 14, 9, 9, 9) more times and then every 4th row 0 (0, 0, 6, 6, 7) times. There are 63 (67, 71, 73, 77, 79) sts.

Work even until sleeve measures 18 inches, or desired length.

Bind off.

## Working the shawl collar and sides of hood

Now that you've completed the body of the coat, it's time to work the lapels and sides of the hood. It's easiest to work the collar and hood using a couple of appropriately sized circular needles, or several long ones. (I explain how to pick up and knit vertically and horizontally earlier in this chapter.)

Working with the right (public) side of your coat facing you, with your smaller needles and contrasting yarn (yarn B), start picking up stitches at the turning edge of the right front. Pick up and knit 130 stitches up to the shoulder, and then flip the coat around so that you're working on the back — the public side of the hood. Pick up and knit 63 stitches along the right side of the hood, 33 stitches across the top of the hood, and 63 stitches down the left side of the hood. Finally, pick up and knit 130 stitches along the left front of the coat, making sure that you're working with the right (public) side facing you. Not to alarm you, but that's 419 stitches picked up. Don't worry if you don't end up with exactly that number of stitches, but be sure you have an odd number.

Work the collar and sides of the hood in seed stitch continuing with the smaller needles and yarn B as follows:

Row 1: *K1, p1, repeat from * to last st, k1.

Repeat this row until the collar is 8 inches deep (or desired depth).

Bind off.

## Finishing your coat

Measure 9 (9½, 10, 10½, 11, 11¼) inches down from the shoulder seam on the front, and then place a marker or safety pin on the side edge at this point. Do the same on the back so that you have two markers 18 (19, 20, 21, 22, 22½) inches apart.

Fold one sleeve in half lengthwise to find the center of the upper (bound-off) edge, and mark it with a pin. Line this up with the shoulder seam, and line up the edges of the sleeve with the markers on your coat. Sew the sleeve in place. Sew the sleeve seam and side seam. (See the appendix for directions for mattress stitch.)

Attach the other sleeve and work the seams of the remaining side in the same way.

Sew the hem facings loosely to the wrong side of the coat. Weave in all ends.

# Part IV
# Patterns with Circles, Triangles, and More

The 5th Wave    By Rich Tennant

"You're right – I probably will be the only one on the dirt track circuit to own a carburetor cozy."

# In this part . . .

This part of the book is packed with patterns to cover you from head to toe. In Chapter 11, you can practice knitting in the round and develop new skills such as working with circular and double-pointed needles, making cables, and using mosaic patterns. Explore the triangle as you increase, decrease, and short row your way through Chapter 12, making shawls, kerchiefs, and more. Finally, put all the shapes together as you knit your way through Chapters 13 and 14, making great sweaters that fit the whole family. The variations I offer allow you to create many great knits to suit your style.

# Chapter 11

# Knitting in Circles

· · · · · · · · · · · · · · · · · · · · · · · · · · · · · · · · · · · · · · · · · ·

## *In This Chapter*

▶ Creating circles and cylinders with ease

▶ Using circular and double-pointed needles

▶ Making cowls, wrist warmers, hats, and bags

· · · · · · · · · · · · · · · · · · · · · · · · · · · · · · · · · · · · · · · · · ·

Most knitters learn to knit with something flat because they think that it's easier. But aside from the slightly fiddly moment where you have to join your circle after you cast on, knitting in the round is usually easier than knitting flat. Think about it as you doodle a straight line and a circle on paper. If you trace the line over and over again with your finger, your finger has to stop and change direction at each end. But when you trace the circle, your finger is always moving in one direction and never has to stop and go back the other direction. Knitting in the round is like that too; you don't have to turn your work, so you're never working on the wrong side. This means you can knit stockinette stitch without purling. Plus, you do less finishing. You can knit in the round on circular needles or double-pointed needles — this chapter gives you opportunities to try both. (You can head to Chapter 1 for more details about these types of needles.)

This chapter will have you going around in circles as you create all kinds of great accessories. In this chapter, I provide patterns for the following projects:

✔ A cowl that will keep your head and neck warm all winter long. You can also use this pattern to create a poncho.

✔ Two different takes on wrist warmers. The first is an easy fingerless glove and the second is a ruffled muffatee. The muffatee covers the area between your glove and jacket, and does it with great style!

✔ Hat patterns. Hats are the perfect circle project because they're quick to knit and allow you to practice with both circular and double-pointed needles. Try the basic beanie, a cabled beanie variation, or a long-tailed hat.

✔ A wonderful felted purse that's worked in a mosaic pattern. This project is a great way to try your hand at color work.

## Ruffled Cowl

The cowl in Figure 11-1 is fun to knit and is an easy introduction to circular knitting. It features ribbing on one end and a sumptuous ruffle on the other. You might wear the ruffle slouched around your neck or pulled up for an anemone-like head warmer.

It isn't difficult to turn this cowl into a classically styled poncho that's knit in the round — see the later variation for the details.

**Figure 11-1:**
A cowl
makes a
great neck
warmer.

# New skill: Joining your knitting in the round

The one big trick to circular knitting is to "join, being careful not to twist." Nearly every pattern designed to be knit in the round will remind you of this fact. Here's how you do it:

1. **Cast on the number of stitches the pattern calls for.**

2. **Before you start to knit the first round, check to make sure that the stitches aren't spiraling around the circular needle.**

   All the stitches should lay in one direction as they do in Figure 11-2, and the tops of the stitches should be pointing up. Now you're ready to start knitting!

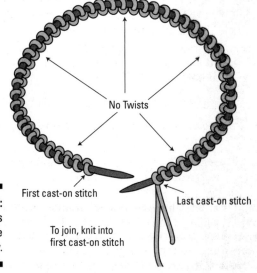

No Twists

First cast-on stitch

Last cast-on stitch

To join, knit into
first cast-on stitch

**Figure 11-2:**
No twists
are in the
cast-on row.

3. **Place a marker on the right needle at the beginning of the round to remind yourself where one round ends and the next one begins.**

   In a pinch, you can use a bit of scrap yarn tied in a loop as your marker.

4. **Hold the needles so that the first cast-on stitch is the first stitch on the left needle and the working yarn is at the right.**

5. **Insert the right needle into the first stitch on the left needle as shown in Figure 11-3 and knit it.**

**Figure 11-3:**
Use a marker when you join your knitting in the round.

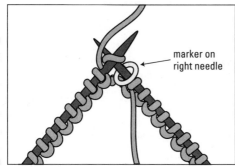

marker on right needle

Take care to snug up the yarn on this first stitch; it tends to be loose. However, don't worry too much about the loose first stitch — it will look better in a couple of rows. Besides, when you weave in the tail at the end you get another chance to tidy it up.

Some knitters like to cast on an extra stitch, transfer it to the left needle, and work a k2tog for the first stitch to make the join less visible — try it if you'd like! (To find out how to knit two stitches together, see Chapter 6.)

## New skill: Increasing with kfb

This cowl pattern uses an increase that's abbreviated as kfb (some knitters abbreviate it k1fb). These abbreviations stand for "knit into the front and back of the stitch." Kfb, which is probably the most common increase, is sometimes called the *bar increase* because it makes a little horizontal bar at the base of the increased stitch.

To knit into the front and back of a stitch and increase 1, follow these steps:

1. **Knit the stitch normally but don't slide the old stitch off the left needle.**

2. **Bring the right needle behind the left needle and insert it into the back of that same stitch as shown in Figure 11-4.**

   Wrap the yarn around the right-hand needle and complete the stitch, and then slide the old stitch off the left needle. You've made 2 stitches from 1.

There are two basic groups of increases: those done *between* stitches (called "make 1"; see Chapter 14 for more details) and those done *in* a stitch, like kfb. They both accomplish the same thing, but because one uses a stitch and one doesn't, you shouldn't substitute one for the other when working from a pattern — you'll end up with the wrong number of stitches between decreases. If a pattern simply says "increase" without specifying a particular increase, stick with kfb.

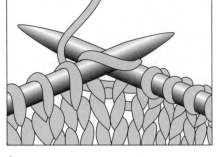
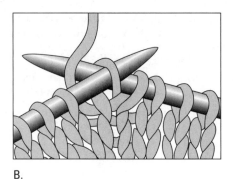

**Figure 11-4:**
Increasing
with kfb.

A.

B.

# Materials and vital statistics

- ✔ **Yarn:** Crystal Palace Yarns Merino Stripes (90% wool, 10% acrylic); 115 yards (105 meters) per 50 grams; 3 skeins; color: 62

- ✔ **Needles:** US 10½ (6.5 mm) circular needle, 16- or 24-inch length

- ✔ **Other materials:** One stitch marker; yarn needle

- ✔ **Size:** 28 inches in circumference and 23 inches long; see the schematic for the cowl in Figure 11-5

- ✔ **Gauge:** 10 stitches and 16 rows per 4 inches in stockinette stitch

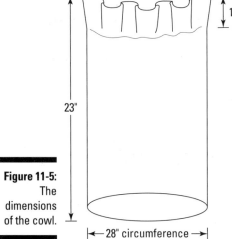

**Figure 11-5:**
The
dimensions
of the cowl.

This cowl is knit in the round in one piece, starting with a bit of ribbing and ending with a playful ruffle. After you get through the first few rounds, you'll discover why people enjoy knitting a project in the round: It's all knit stitches, and with no ends of rows, it's easy to keep knitting away. So, you'll find this neck warmer quick to finish.

# Directions

Cast on 72 sts, place marker, and join in the round, being careful not to twist.

Next round: *K1, p1, repeat from * to end.

Repeat the previous round 3 more times.

Switch to stockinette stitch (knit every round) and continue knitting in the round until your cowl measures 22 inches, and then begin the ruffle.

Next round: Kfb in each st. There are 144 sts.

Next round: Knit.

Next round: Kfb in each st. There are 288 sts.

Next round: Knit.

Bind off and weave in ends.

## Variation: Turning your cowl into a poncho

To make this cowl into a short poncho, you need the same amount of yarn and the same needles, plus four stitch markers. You have to switch to a longer circular needle of the same size (at least 36 inches long) as the poncho grows because there are an awful lot of stitches for the ruffle on the last few rounds!

Both the poncho and the cowl are worked basically the same — from the ribbed end to the ruffle. For the poncho, you increase regularly at four points, but for the cowl, you skip the increasing. Geometrically minded knitters will think of the cowl as a cylinder and the poncho as a truncated cone or four-sided pyramid shape.

This poncho is on the small side: It measures 12 inches from the neck to the hem as shown in Figure 11-6, so it only comes down to about the elbow. If you want to make it bigger, just buy more yarn and keep going!

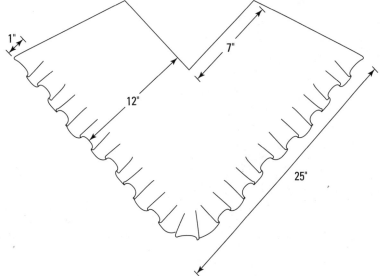

**Figure 11-6:**
The shape and dimensions of the poncho.

Here's how to knit your poncho:

Begin as you would for the cowl: Cast on, place a marker, and join in the round, being careful not to twist. Knit the ribbing as I describe in the basic pattern.

Next round: Slip marker, *kfb, k16, kfb, place marker, repeat from * twice more, kfb, k16, kfb. There are 80 sts.

Next round: Knit, slipping markers as you encounter them.

Next round: *Kfb, knit to last st before next marker, kfb, slip marker, repeat from * to end. 8 sts have been increased.

Repeat the previous 2 rounds 20 more times, switching to a longer circular needle when necessary. There are 248 sts. Your poncho measures about 11 inches.

Knit 1 round.

Work the 4 rounds of the ruffle as I describe in the basic pattern. There are 992 sts (but you don't need to worry about counting them!)

Bind off and weave in ends.

# Wrist Warmers

Wrist warmers, or fingerless gloves, are a great way to get the hang of using double-pointed needles because their shape is simple. If you want to, you can make them longer by knitting a few more inches before making the thumb hole. Try them in a soft, warm, self-striping yarn as shown in Figure 11-7, making both wrist warmers the same or playfully different. They're great under gloves in very cold weather, and perfect on their own indoors, especially as you type on chilly mornings.

**Figure 11-7:**
Wrist warmers are a great project on double-pointed needles.

## New skill: Working with double-pointed needles

Once you get going with double-pointed needles, you'll find that it isn't much different from using a circular needle: You're just going around and around in circles without ever turning. Getting started can feel a bit like juggling chopsticks, though, so give yourself some time to get the hang of it. And know that it gets easier after you have a few rows knit.

To start knitting on four double-pointed needles, follow these steps:

1. **Cast on all your stitches to a single needle.**

   For the wrist warmers, you should be able to fit them all on a single double-pointed needle, but you can also use a longer straight needle if you want.

2. **After all the stitches are cast on, divide them among three of the double-pointed needles as shown in Figure 11-8.**

   For some projects (like socks for instance), it's important to have the stitches divided in a specific way. For the wrist warmers, however, you don't need to have the same number of stitches on each needle; just eyeball it and put about a third of the stitches on each needle.

**Figure 11-8:** Divide your cast-on stitches among three double-pointed needles.

3. **After the stitches are divided, join the stitches in the round just as you do on a circular needle.**

   Make sure the stitches aren't twisted (see the section "New skill: Joining your knitting in the round" earlier in this chapter). Place a marker and knit the first stitch as shown in Figure 11-9 with your remaining empty needle.

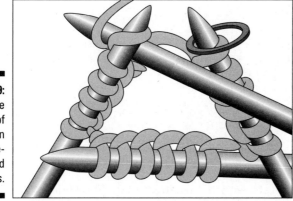

**Figure 11-9:** Knitting the first stitch of the round on double-pointed needles.

4. **Knit all the stitches from the needle in your left hand.**

   The needle that was empty is now full and you have an empty needle in your left hand.

5. **Put the empty needle into your right hand and use it to knit the stitches off the next needle and so on.**

   As you continue with the four needles, remember that you always knit in a circle just as you do on a circular needle, with the four needles "taking turns" being the working needle. If you're having trouble, it may be easier to manage if you keep in mind that you're only knitting with two needles at once. In other words, ignore the rest of them, and just take it one stitch at a time around the circle.

## Materials and vital statistics

✔ **Yarn:** Rowan Tapestry (70% wool, 30% soy); 130 yards (120 meters) per 50 grams; 2 balls; color: Whirlpool

✔ **Needles:** A set of US 4 (3.5 mm) double-pointed needles, or the size needed to match gauge

✔ **Other materials:** One stitch marker; yarn needle to weave in ends

✔ **Size:** Women's S (M, L, 1X)

   • **To fit hand/forearm circumference of:** 6 (7, 8, 9) inches

   • **Length:** 6 (7, 8, 9) inches

✔ **Gauge:** 28 stitches and 32 rows per 4 inches in 2 x 2 rib on US 4 (3.5 mm) needles (if you're looking for a yarn to substitute, you need one that lists its gauge as 22 stitches per 4 inches in stockinette stitch)

After you get started with your double-pointed needles, you'll have these wrist warmers finished in no time. Unlike socks or gloves, you won't have any shaping to worry about; these wrist warmers are simple cylinders with small holes for your thumbs. For more experienced knitters, they're still fun to make and they're a great on-the-go project because they don't take up too much room in your bag — perfect knitting for those few minutes you have on the bus or waiting in the dentist's office.

## Directions

Make 2 wrist warmers that are the same, as follows:

Cast on 40 (48, 56, 64) sts onto 1 double-pointed needle. Divide the sts among 3 double-pointed needles. Place a marker and join in the round, being careful not to twist.

Begin working in rib as follows:

Round 1: *K2, p2, repeat from * to end.

Repeat this round until your wrist warmer measures 5 (6, 7, 8) inches.

Next round: K2, bind off 6 (8, 8, 10) sts, work in rib pattern to the end of the round.

Next round: K2, cast on 6 (8, 8, 10) sts over the bound-off sts, work in rib pattern to the end of the round.

Continue in rib as set for 1 more inch and then bind off all sts. Weave in ends.

# Ruffled Muffatees

Muffatees, a word used by Victorians (and Peter Rabbit's mother, who had to knit them to make ends meet), are simply wrist warmers, but I think of them as being fancier than the more utilitarian Bob Cratchit style. The pair in Figure 11-10, worked in a lovely silk blend, features a belled ruffle that covers the wrist and top of the hand. Unlike the wrist warmers in the previous section, these don't have a thumbhole; these muffatees are really just a knitted tube with a ruffle on the end. They're perfect over gloves on a really icy day or any day under a jacket or coat to add a splash of color and whimsy.

**Figure 11-10:**
Ruffled muffatees warm your wrists with style.

These muffatees are quick to make and the fit only needs to be approximate, so they make a great gift when winter rolls around.

## Materials and vital statistics

- ✔ **Yarn:** Lang Silkdream (50% merino, 50% silk); 100 yards (90 meters) per 50 grams; 2 skeins; color: 0020 Sky Blue

- ✔ **Needles:** US 6 (4 mm) double-pointed needles, or the size needed to match gauge

- ✔ **Other materials:** One stitch marker; yarn needle to weave in ends

- ✔ **Size:** Women's S (M, L)

    - **To fit a forearm circumference of:** 6 (7, 8) inches

    - **Length:** 7 (8, 9) inches, including a 2-inch ruffle

- ✔ **Gauge:** 24 stitches and 28 rows per 4 inches in 2 x 2 rib. (if you're looking for a yarn to substitute, look for one that lists its gauge as 18 stitches per 4 inches in stockinette stitch)

These muffatees, like the wrist warmers in the previous pattern, are a great introduction to using double-pointed needles. The ruffled edges, which you create by increasing rapidly over the last few rows, are fun and feminine. After you get the hang of knitting a ruffle, you'll want to try ruffles on cuffs, hems, or the edges of a scarf.

## Directions

Make 2 muffatees that are the same, as follows:

Cast on 36 (44, 48) sts onto 1 double-pointed needle, and then divide sts among 3 double-pointed needles. Place a marker and join in the round, being careful not to twist.

Round 1: *K2, p2, repeat from * to end of round.

Repeat this round until your muffatee measures 5 (6, 7) inches long.

The ruffle is formed by increasing a lot of stitches over a few rows. The increase I use is the untwisted make 1 (m1), which forms a little decorative hole. If you don't want the holes, twist your m1s. See Chapter 14 for a full explanation of this increase.

Round 1: *M1, k2, m1, p2, repeat from * to end. There are 54 (66, 72) sts.

Rounds 2, 3, and 4: *K4, p2, repeat from * to end.

Round 5: *M1, k4, m1, p2, repeat from * to end. There are 72 (88, 96) sts.

Rounds 6, 7, and 8: *K6, p2, repeat from * to end.

Round 9: *M1, k6, m1, p2, repeat from * to end. There are 90 (110, 120) sts.

Rounds 10, 11, and 12: *K8, p2, repeat from * to end.

Bind off and weave in any loose ends.

# Basic Beanies

A good hat is a must-have in your knitting repertoire, and this basic beanie, sized for babies through adults, fits the bill. Make it plain or cabled. Add in stripes or a color pattern. (Any of the 8-stitch mosaic or Fair Isle patterns given in Chapter 7 can be used with this pattern, but remember to leave out the extra edge stitches since you're working in the round.) After your beanie is knit, top it with a pompom or tassel. The variations are endless. Check out some beanies in Figure 11-11.

**Figure 11-11:**
A basic beanie and its cabled cousin.

## Materials and vital statistics

- ✔ **Yarn:** Berrocco Smart Mohair (41% mohair, 54% acrylic, 5% polyester); 108 yards (100 meters) per 50 grams; 1 (1, 1, 2, 2) balls; color: Pink

- ✔ **Needles:** US 10 (6 mm) circular needle, 16-inch length, or the size needed to match gauge; US 8 (5 mm) circular needle, 16-inch length; US 10 (6 mm) double-pointed needles

- ✔ **Other materials:** Eight stitch markers; yarn needle to weave in ends

- ✔ **Size:** Baby (toddler, child, small adult, large adult); circumference: 14 (16, 18, 20, 22) inches, unstretched

- ✔ **Gauge:** 16 stitches and 20 rows per 4 inches in stockinette stitch on larger needles

This beanie is worked in the round, starting on circular needles and switching to double-pointed needles when you shape the crown of the hat. If you want to include any color patterning, add it to the body of the hat between the ribbing and the decreases. If you'd like to knit cables on your hat, see the variation at the end of the pattern.

## Directions

Cast on 56 (64, 72, 80, 88) sts with the smaller circular needles. Place marker and join in the round, being careful not to twist.

Round 1: *K2, p2, repeat from * to end of round.

Repeat this round for ¾ (1, 1, 1½, 2) inches.

Switch to larger circular needles and begin knitting in stockinette stitch (knit all rounds).

When your hat measures 4½ (5, 5½, 6½, 7) inches, begin the crown shaping as follows:

Next round: *K7 (8, 9, 10, 11), place marker, repeat from * to end.

Next round (Decrease Round): *K2tog, knit to marker, slip marker, repeat from * to end. 8 sts have been decreased.

Next round: Knit.

Repeat these 2 rounds until 8 sts remain, switching to double-pointed needles when you have too few sts to fit comfortably on your circular needle.

Cut yarn, leaving a 12-inch tail.

**Finishing:** Thread the tail of the yarn onto the yarn needle. Slip the stitches from the knitting needle to the yarn needle, making sure that you go through each stitch. Pull the yarn firmly to tighten up the top of the hat, and then run the yarn through the stitches again before weaving in the yarn end on the inside to secure. Weave in any remaining ends.

If you want, you can top your beanie with a pompom, knitted flower, or other adornment for extra flair.

## Variation: Creating a cabled beanie

This cabled hat features straightforward six-stitch cables (see Chapter 6). It is made with the same yarn and needles as the basic beanie, fits a toddler (child, small adult, large adult), and measures 16 (17½, 19, 22) inches around. You need six stitch markers to help keep your decreases lined up.

Using the smaller circular needles, cast on 66 (72, 78, 90) sts. Place a marker and join in the round, being careful not to twist.

Ribbing round: *K1, p1, repeat from * to end.

Repeat this round for 1 (1, 2, 2) inches.

Switch to the larger circular needles and begin the six-stitch right cable pattern as follows, placing markers on the first round as indicated:

Rounds 1, 2, 3, 4, and 5: *K6, p5 (6, 7, 9), place marker, repeat from * to end of round.

Round 6: *Slip 3 sts to the cable needle and hold to back, k3, k3 from cable needle, p5 (6, 7, 9), repeat from * to end of round.

Repeat these 6 rounds until the hat measures 5½ (6, 6½, 7) inches, and then begin decreasing as follows:

Continue the cable pattern as set on the columns of 6 knit sts. In other words, you should cable every 6th round (even though the decreasing is occurring too).

Next round: *K6, p2tog, purl to marker, repeat from * to end of round.

If you're unfamiliar with purling 2 stitches together (p2tog), here's how to do it: Insert the right needle into the next 2 stitches purlwise, wrap the yarn around the right-hand needle, and then purl them to decrease 1 stitch.

Next round: Work even, knitting and purling the sts as they appear.

Repeat the previous 2 rounds 3 (4, 5, 7) more times. There are 42 sts on the needles.

Stop the cable pattern and finish the hat in stockinette stitch (knit all rounds).

Next round: *K5, k2tog, repeat from * to end of round. 36 sts remain.

Next round: Knit.

Next round: *K4, k2tog, repeat from * to end of round. 30 sts remain.

Next round: Knit.

Next round: *K3, k2tog, repeat from * to end of round. 24 sts remain.

Next round: Knit.

Next round *K2, k2tog, repeat from * to end of round. 18 sts remain.

Next round *K1, k2tog, repeat from * to end of round. 12 sts remain.

Next round: *K2tog, repeat from * to end of round. 6 sts remain.

Cut the yarn leaving a 12-inch tail.

**Finishing:** Use the same technique described in the basic pattern to finish your cabled beanie.

# Storybook Hats

Sometimes it's fun to have a silly hat, and the Dr. Seuss meets Waldo chapeau in Figure 11-12 certainly fits the bill. With a thick yarn, this hat is a quick knit and makes a great gift for your favorite snowboarder or snowman maker (or anyone who appreciates the absurd). The later variations show you to how use almost any yarn to make a similar hat. These hats are sure to chase away the winter blues.

**Figure 11-12:** A storybook hat chases away the winter blues.

## Materials and vital statistics

✔ **Yarn:** Cascade Lana Grande (100% Peruvian wool); 87 yards (80 meters) per 50 grams

   • **Color A:** Cream; 1 skein

   • **Color B:** Pink; 1 skein

✔ **Needles:** US 15 (10 mm) circular needle, 16-inch length; US 15 (10 mm) double-pointed needles; US 11 (8 mm) circular needle, 16-inch length

✔ **Other materials:** Two stitch markers; yarn needle

✔ **Size:** Baby (toddler, child, small adult, large adult)

   • **Circumference:** 14 (16, 17½, 19, 21) inches unstretched

   • **Length (without tassel):** 12 (14, 16, 16, 18) inches

✔ **Gauge:** 10 stitches and 12 rows per 4 inches in stockinette stitch

This hat is worked in the round and goes quickly on big needles. You can make it with a single color, but I suggest you try the broad stripes as I have. For information on changing colors look to Chapter 7.

## Directions

With the larger circular needles and color A, cast on 36 (40, 44, 48, 52) sts. Place a marker and join in the round, being careful not to twist.

Round 1: Using the smaller needles, *k1, p1, repeat from * to end.

Continue in rib until your hat measures 2 inches. Cut color A, leaving a 6-inch tail.

As you make this hat, cut and rejoin the yarns each time you switch colors.

Switch to color B and the larger circular needles. Work 6 rounds in stockinette stitch (knit all rounds).

Switch to color A.

Round 1: K9 (10, 11, 12, 13), place marker, k18 (20, 22, 24, 26), place marker, knit to end of round.

Round 2: Knit.

Round 3 (Decrease Round): Knit to 2 sts before marker, k2tog, slip marker, ssk, knit to 2 sts before marker, k2tog, slip marker, ssk, knit to end of round.

Head to Chapter 6 to find out more about the k2tog and ssk decreases if you aren't familiar with them.

Rounds 4, 5, and 6: Knit.

Switch to color B.

Round 7 (Decrease Round): Repeat Round 3.

Rounds 8, 9, and 10: Knit.

Round 11: Repeat Round 3.

Round 12: Knit.

Switch to double-pointed needles when there are too few sts on the needles to knit comfortably.

Continue repeating these 12 rounds until only 8 sts remain. Continue working even on these 8 sts to the end of the 6-round stripe if necessary.

Cut an 8-inch tail and, using a yarn needle, thread it through the remaining sts, pulling gently to gather them in. Run the yarn through the sts once more, and then weave in the tail on the inside. Weave in ends.

To make the tassel, start by wrapping the yarn around a paperback book about 40 times.

Cut the yarn and wrap the tail tightly around all the strands a couple of times. Then tie with a firm knot, leaving the tail to use later to attach the tassel to the hat.

Slip the rounds of yarn off the book and wrap a 1-foot length of yarn around the tassel 1 inch below the knot. Pull firmly before knotting in place. Cut through the loops at the opposite end of the tassel and then trim the ends so that they're even.

Knit a scarf to match any mood or ensemble. Shown here from left to right are a ribbed scarf, a box stitch scarf, and a garter stitch scarf, all found in Chapter 8.

Create these knitted and felted potholders and coasters in colors to match any decor. You'll find the patterns in Chapter 9.

These two tops are surprisingly simple to knit. You'll find the box top, shown on the left, in Chapter 8; the deceptively simple shell, shown on the right, is in Chapter 10.

The longways multiyarn stole in Chapter 8 is an easy project that allows you to combine colors and textures to show off your style.

Knit this modern layette for baby. The one-piece baby sweater featured in Chapter 10 is quick and easy to create. The retro slippers from Chapter 8 can be sized to fit the whole family. A storybook hat adds a whimsical topper to the ensemble; find the pattern in Chapter 11.

This smart felted messenger bag with adjustable linen stitch straps from Chapter 10 holds your books or knitting supplies. You can make this colorful and quick-to-knit journal cover from Chapter 9 for your diary or notebook.

This ruffled cowl is a fun and fashionable alternative to a scarf and can be pulled up over the head to fight off chills. This project, found in Chapter 11, is a great introduction to knitting in the round.

The wrist warmers on the left are fingerless gloves knit in a simple shape. The ruffled muffattees on the right can add a splash of color to any outfit. Find the patterns for both projects in Chapter 11.

Play with color and texture as you create accessories for your home or yourself. Try the short row scarf or harlequin blanket featured in Chapter 12, or knit a variety of throw pillows from Chapter 9.

Consider a knit coat as a perfect addition to your wardrobe. Simple lines and a wide shawl collar make this coat a winning knit. Find the pattern in Chapter 10.

Knit hats from Chapter 11 for the whole family. Shown here are two whimsical storybook hats; you can knit them striped or plain at a variety of gauges. Or try a beanie: The basic pattern is shown in pink, and optional cables adorn the brown hat.

A nested squares baby blanket and a coordinating flat hat make a great gift for baby. Knit the hat in stockinette stitch with duplicate stitch embellishment or in garter stitch with broad stripes. Find the blanket pattern in Chapter 9 and the hat pattern in Chapter 8.

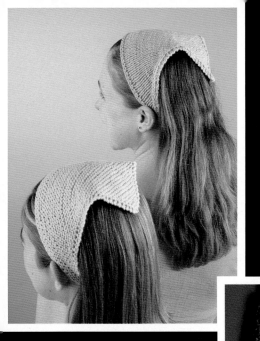

Kerchiefs are a great way to practice increasing and decreasing. The most basic kerchief ever, shown in green, features yarn over increases. The fully fashioned kerchief, shown in blue, uses left- and right-slanting decreases. Find these patterns in Chapter 12.

Add drama to any outfit with the most basic shawl ever. This pattern is a breeze to knit and offers lots of flexibility. Find it in Chapter 12.

These felted mosaic bags from Chapter 11 can be knit in two sizes, with knitted handles as shown on the pinbox mosaic bag at the top or with purchased handles as shown on the woven cord mosaic bag at the bottom.

Try knitting this coat with a generous hood and beautiful seed stitch detailing. Like all the patterns in this book, this coat pattern can be knit in a wide range of sizes from petite to plus. Find this pattern in Chapter 10.

Knit this feather-light lacy shawl in any colors you choose. You'll find the pattern in Chapter 12.

A stretchy halter top, knit in a cotton/Lycra blend, offers careful detailing that bares your back but still provides plenty of coverage; you can find the pattern in Chapter 12. Pair the top with a shrug variation of the loose rib wrap from Chapter 8.

Knit shirts for women and children with two great patterns in Chapter 13. The women's T-shirt can be knit with a V-neck as shown or a crewneck. The kid's top pattern offers options for short or long sleeves and a variation with a horseshoe cable up the front.

This half-ribbed cardigan with raglan sleeves is knit in one piece from the top down. It features ribs on the bottom of the sleeves and body that create a flattering fit and contemporary lines. Find the pattern in Chapter 14.

This pullover features waist shaping, a scoop neck, and clean lines to create a flattering and feminine silhouette. The pattern, featured in Chapter 14, provides options for color work, including the Fair Isle detailing shown here.

Two men's sweater patterns from Chapter 13 cover lots of territory. The rollneck pullover pattern on the left is easygoing and offers a variety of ways to add color. The V-neck sweater on the right is a classic men's knit with a finer-gauged yarn and traditional detailing.

This cardigan from Chapter 14 is knit in one piece and features a zipper closure and seed stitch detailing. The bulky yarn makes it warm, cozy, and quick to knit.

This lacy V-neck top features lace accents at the cuff and hem and a flattering neckline. Knit it cropped, as shown here, or hip length with gentle waist shaping. Find options for both in Chapter 14.

To attach the tassel, thread the tail of yarn from the tassel onto a yarn needle. Insert the needle through the tip of the hat and pull the yarn through. Bring the needle through the base of the tassel. Insert the needle into the tip of the hat, bringing the yarn to the inside and then knot it firmly in place.

## Variation: Changing yarns

If you want to knit this hat with a different weight yarn, use Table 11-1 to figure out your cast-on number, and then follow the directions in the basic pattern. You can use more than one color of yarn (which is a great way to use up your odds and ends!) or try a self-striping yarn.

| Table 11-1 | Cast-On Numbers for Different Yarns and Gauges |
|---|---|
| *Gauge per Inch* | *Cast on Number* |
| 3 | 44 (48, 52, 56, 64) |
| 4 | 56 (64, 72, 76, 84) |
| 4½ | 64 (72, 80, 88, 96) |
| 5 | 68 (80, 88, 96, 104) |
| 5½ | 76 (88, 96, 104, 116) |

Knit the ribbing with needles that are two sizes smaller than the needles you use to get the gauge needed for the body of the hat.

Begin decreasing when the hat measures 4 inches. Place your markers as follows for your gauge:

- ✔ **3 sts per inch:** K11 (12, 13, 14, 16), place marker, k22 (24, 26, 28, 32), place marker, knit to end of round.

- ✔ **4 sts per inch:** K14 (16, 18, 19, 21), place marker, k28, (32, 36, 38, 42), place marker, knit to end of round.

- ✔ **4½ sts per inch:** K16 (18, 20 22, 24), place marker, k32 (36, 40, 44, 48), place marker, knit to end of round.

- ✔ **5 sts per inch:** K17 (20, 22, 24, 26), place marker, k34 (40, 44, 48, 52), place marker, knit to end of round.

- ✔ **5½ sts per inch:** K19 (22, 24, 26, 29), place marker, k38, (44, 48, 52, 58), place marker, knit to end of round.

Follow the 12-round color and decrease pattern outlined in the basic pattern.

# Mosaic Bags

If you're ready for a new challenge, try making a mosaic pattern on the felted purse in Figure 11-13. Even though it looks complicated, if you can knit a stripe and slip a stitch, you're ready to try it. I've included both written directions and a chart for the pinbox mosaic in this pattern (see Chapter 7 for the basics on mosaics and for other mosaic patterns that can be easily substituted in this pattern); both sets of instructions give the same information, but some people find one easier to follow than the other.

The pattern for this bag presents you with lots of options. The featured pattern is for the mosaic purse, but if you want your bag striped or plain, check out the later variations. A plain purse can be stunning if you adorn it with a brooch, knitted flowers, or needle-felted designs. Craft stores and yarn shops carry beautiful ready-made handles that can jazz up any bag. Or you can knit the handle with the bag. This pattern gives you both options.

**Figure 11-13:**
The felted mosaic purse and tote.

You can use colors on this mosaic bag in many ways. I've chosen two shades of the main color (dark brown and lighter brown) and two shades of the contrasting color (yellow and gold) for the pinbox mosaic. You can easily choose to use a single main color and two contrasting colors if you decide on a three-color mosaic pattern. Simpler still is sticking with just two colors. The results are fantastic any way you choose to do it!

## Materials and vital statistics

- ✔ **Yarn:** Cascade 220 (100% Peruvian highland wool); 220 yards (201 meters) per 100 grams
    - **Main color 1 (MC1):** 2403 Dark Brown; 1 skein
    - **Main color 2 (MC2):** 2411 Brown; 1 skein
    - **Contrasting color 1 (CC1):** 7825 Gold; 1 skein
    - **Contrasting color 2 (CC2):** 7827 Yellow; 1 skein
- ✔ **Needles:** US 10½ (6.5 mm) circular needles, 24- or 36-inch length
- ✔ **Other:** One stitch marker; yarn needle to weave in ends
- ✔ **Size:**

    Approximate size before felting for a purse (tote):
    - **Width:** 16 (21) inches
    - **Height:** 18 (21) inches (without handles)
    - **Depth:** 5 inches

    Approximate size after felting for a purse (tote):
    - **Width:** 9½ (12) inches
    - **Height:** 8 (10½) inches (without handles)

• **Depth:** 3 inches

Felting is both art and science. Use the sizes given here as guidelines, but remember that your results may vary.

✔ **Gauge:** 12 stitches and 16 rows per 4 inches in stockinette stitch

This bag is worked in one piece. The bottom is worked back and forth in garter stitch, and from there, you pick up stitches around the rectangle that you've created and work in the round. When the bag is complete, you felt it in the washing machine.

# Directions

With MC1, cast on 48 (64) sts.

Work 32 rows in garter stitch (knit all rows). There will be 16 garter ridges. Don't cut the yarn.

With your 48 (64) sts still on the needles, continue with MC1 and pick up and knit 16 sts down the first short side, 48 (64) sts along the cast-on edge, and 16 sts along the second short side of the base. There will be 128 (160) sts on the needles. Place a marker to indicate the beginning of the round.

Switch to CC1 and knit 2 rounds.

Use the pinbox mosaic pattern presented here or any other 16-stitch mosaic pattern that you like (see Chapter 7 for some choices). I include the pinbox mosaic pattern information in the chart in Figure 11-14, and I also write it out. Use the method that's easiest for you to follow. For each row, the stitches shown in the working color are worked, and the stitches shown in the other color are slipped. Each chart row represents two consecutive pattern rows.

When you're working a mosaic pattern, always slip stitches purlwise.

Rounds 1 and 2: With MC1, *k15, slip 1, repeat from * to end of round.

Rounds 3 and 4: With CC1, *slip 1, k13, slip 1, k1, repeat from * to end of round.

Rounds 5 and 6: With MC1, *k1, slip 1, k11, slip 1, k1, slip 1, repeat from * to end of round.

Rounds 7 and 8: With CC1, *slip 1, k1, slip 1, k9, slip 1, k1, slip 1, k1, repeat from * to end of round.

Rounds 9 and 10: With MC1, *(k1, slip 1) 2 times, k7, (slip 1, k1) 2 times, slip 1, repeat from * to end of round.

Rounds 11 and 12: With CC1, *(slip 1, k1) 2 times, slip 1, k5, (slip 1, k1) 3 times, repeat from * to end of round.

Rounds 13 and 14: With MC1, *(k1, slip 1) 3 times, k3, (slip 1, k1) 3 times, slip 1, repeat from * to end of round.

Rounds 15 and 16: With CC1, *(slip 1, k1) 8 times, repeat from * to end of round.

Rounds 17 and 18: Repeat Rounds 13 and 14.

Rounds 19 and 20: Switch to CC2 and repeat Rounds 11 and 12.

Rounds 21 and 22: Repeat Rounds 9 and 10.

Rounds 23 and 24: With CC2, repeat Rounds 7 and 8.

Rounds 25 and 26: Repeat Rounds 5 and 6.

Rounds 27 and 28: With CC2, repeat Rounds 3 and 4.

Rounds 29 and 30: Repeat Rounds 1 and 2.

Rounds 31 and 32: With CC2, knit.

Rounds 33 and 34: Switch to MC2 and *k7, slip 1, k8, repeat from * to end of round.

Rounds 35 and 36: Switch to CC2 and *k6, slip 1, k1, slip 1, k7, repeat from * to end of round.

Rounds 37 and 38: Switch to MC2 and *k5, (slip 1, k1) 2 times, slip 1, k6, repeat from * to end of round.

Rounds 39 and 40: Switch to CC2 and *k4, (slip 1, k1) 3 times, slip 1, k5, repeat from * to end of round.

Rounds 41 and 42: Switch to MC2 and *k3, (slip 1, k1) 4 times, slip 1, k4, repeat from * to end of round.

Rounds 43 and 44: Switch to CC2 and *k2, (slip 1, k1) 5 times, slip 1, k3, repeat from * to end of round.

Rounds 45 and 46: Switch to MC2 and *(k1, slip 1) 7 times, k2, repeat from * to end of round.

Rounds 47 and 48: Switch to CC2 and *(slip 1, k1) 8 times, repeat from * to end of round.

Rounds 49 and 50: Repeat Rounds 45 and 46.

Rounds 51 and 52: Switch to CC1 and repeat Rounds 43 and 44.

Rounds 53 and 54: Repeat Rounds 41 and 42.

Rounds 55 and 56: With CC1, repeat Rounds 39 and 40.

Rounds 57 and 58: Repeat Rounds 37 and 38.

Rounds 59 and 60: With CC1, repeat Rounds 35 and 36.

Rounds 61 and 62: Repeat Rounds 33 and 34.

Rounds 63 and 64: With CC1, knit.

For the tote only, work Rounds 1–32 again before moving on to the next step.

For both purse and tote, work 4 more rounds with MC in stockinette stitch.

If you want to attach ready-made handles, bind off; you attach the handles after finishing and felting. If you want to knit in your handles, continue with the directions that follow. These knitted handles are made like big buttonholes. (See more on buttonholes in Chapter 10.)

Next round: K16 (22), bind off 16 (20) sts, k47 (59), (there are 48 (60) sts on the right needle after the last set of bound-off sts), bind off 16 (20) sts, knit to end of round.

Next round: Knit, casting on 16 (20) sts over each set of bound-off sts, using the cable cast-on (see Chapter 10). Be sure to turn your work so the WS is facing you as you cast on each set of stitches.

Knit 5 (7) more rounds, and then bind off. Weave in any ends.

Felt your bag in the washing machine. (You can find step by step instructions on felting in the appendix.) You'll know your bag is done when it's firm and you can no longer see the stitches. Your bag should be the approximate finished size that's noted in the "Materials and vital statistics" section.

If you have purchased handles, you can attach them now. Follow any instructions provided with the handles or sew them on with a needle and heavy-duty sewing thread that matches the bag.

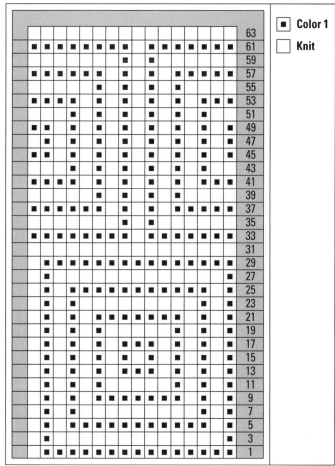

**Figure 11-14:**
The pinbox mosaic pattern repeat presented in a chart.

## Variation: Keeping your bag plain and simple

If you'd rather make a bag in a single color, knit the base and pick up stitches as outlined in the mosaic bag pattern. Begin working in the round and knit for 70 (90) rounds. If you have ready-made handles, bind off. If you want to knit handles, follow the directions given in the main pattern.

Felt your bag by following the instructions in the appendix. After felting, you can attach your handles and embellish your bag if desired.

## Variation: Striping your bag

To work the purse or the tote with a stripe pattern, make the bottom of the bag as I describe in the mosaic pattern with MC1. Pick up stitches for the sides of the bag with MC1 as described in the mosaic pattern, and then knit 1 round. **Note:** This round doesn't count as part of the stripe sequence.

Switch to CC1 (but don't cut MC1) and knit 2 rows.

Knit 2 rows with MC1.

Repeat the previous 4 rounds until you've worked 3 stripes each of MC1 and CC1.

Cut MC1 and join MC2. Work 3 stripes each of CC1 and MC2.

Cut CC1 and join CC2. Work 3 stripes each of CC2 and MC2.

Cut MC2 and join MC1. Work 3 stripes each of CC2 and MC1.

Repeat this stripe sequence until you've knit 72 (96) rounds.

If you're adding ready-made handles, bind off and felt your bag. If you're making the knit-in handle, stop striping and, using MC1 only, follow the directions in the basic pattern. Follow the directions for the mosaic bag on finishing and felting.

When you alternate colors, twist the two yarns around one another at the beginning of each round to keep things tidy and to prevent any gaps. Chapter 8 covers the basics on changing colors as you knit.

# Chapter 12

# Shaping Triangles

• • • • • • • • • • • • • • • • • • • • • • • • • • • • • • • • • • • • • • • • • • • • • • • •

## In This Chapter

▶ Demystifying yarn overs

▶ Discovering fully fashioned decreases

▶ Having a short lesson in short rows

▶ Whipping up kerchiefs, scarves, blankets, and tops

• • • • • • • • • • • • • • • • • • • • • • • • • • • • • • • • • • • • • • • • • • • • • • • •

*I*f you start with a small number of stitches and increase regularly, or start with a large number of stitches and decrease regularly, what do you get? A triangle. These techniques form the basis of kerchiefs and shawls. And most *shaping* (knitting's equivalent of tailoring) relies on triangles. A sleeve cap, for instance, is essentially two triangles and a rectangle. V-necks or raglan sleeves? Triangles. This chapter helps you work all the angles.

The basic kerchief pattern uses yarn overs to create decorative eyelets as you increase your way up from tip to top. Use this same technique with a looser gauge and you've made the basic shawl. If you're ready for something a bit more ambitious, try the lacy shawl. Don't be scared off by the name though — it's just a few more yarn overs and a few more stitches. Making triangles by increasing is perfect for beginners or fretful knitters because you won't have to worry about your gauge much, and you simply stop knitting when your project is the right size.

Making triangles is also a great way to discover decreasing. In knitting, there are lots of ways to decrease. And while all the abbreviations might be confusing at first, remember that all decreases do basically the same thing: get rid of a stitch. Knitting the fully fashioned kerchief in this chapter helps you unlock the alphabet soup mystery of decreases. After you get the hang of decreases, take this technique to the next level and knit a halter top that's made with a cotton-Lycra blend yarn, which gives the top plenty of stretch.

You can also make triangles from the side using short rows. If you've never tried short rows before, they may sound complicated. But, like so many other things in knitting, this technique is surprisingly simple once you understand what you're supposed to do. Use short rows to create a scarf or even a blanket. I show you the steps in this chapter.

## The Most Basic Kerchief Ever

This basic kerchief (see Figure 12-1) is knit from the point to the long edge. This project is a great opportunity to get the hang of increasing stitches using yarn overs (see Chapter 6 for more about yarn overs). Because you start at the point, you can try on your kerchief as you go, which allows you to make it exactly the size you want.

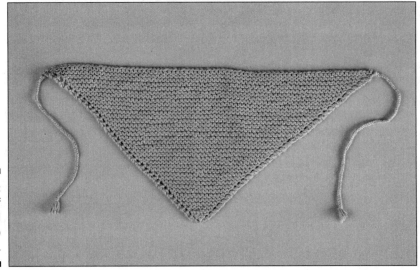

**Figure 12-1:**
A kerchief
worked
from tip to
top.

## Materials and vital statistics

- ✔ **Yarn:** Rowan Calmer (75% cotton, 25% acrylic microfiber); 175 yards (161 meters) per 50 grams; 1 ball; color: Kiwi

- ✔ **Needles:** US 8 (5 mm) needles, or the size needed to match gauge

- ✔ **Other materials:** Yarn needle to weave in ends

- ✔ **Size:** Baby (child, adult)

  - **Finished width:** 12 (15, 17) inches

  - **Finished length:** 5½ (7½, 9½) inches from tip to center of widest edge (without braided ties)

- ✔ **Gauge:** 16 stitches and 32 rows per 4 inches in garter stitch (if you want to substitute yarns, look for one that lists a gauge of approximately 21 stitches and 30 rows per 4 inches in stockinette stitch)

This kerchief is a quick knit and a great way to practice your yarn overs. Find out how to make yarn overs in Chapter 6, and then whip up a kerchief for yourself or the young girl in your life. Or, because it's such a forgiving project, help her knit one for herself! Made in a single color, it's a great backdrop for all kinds of adornments. Consider adding buttons, crocheted designs, or homemade flowers.

## Directions

Cast on 2 sts.

Row 1 (RS): K1, yo, k1.

Row 2: K1, yo, k2.

Row 3: K1, yo, knit to end.

Repeat Row 3 until there are 48 (60, 68) sts.

Bind off loosely and weave in ends.

**Finishing:** Finish your kerchief with 2 braided ties. Cut 6 strands of yarn, each 24 inches long. Thread 3 of the strands halfway through the last yarn over on one side, making 6 tails that are 12 inches long. Divide the tails into 3 pairs, braid them, and then knot the bottom. Repeat with remaining strands on the opposite side.

# The Most Basic Shawl Ever

The simplest shawls are no more difficult to knit than the kerchief pattern in the previous section. In fact, the most basic kerchief ever becomes the most basic shawl ever if you just keep knitting — you simply start at the point of the triangle and keep knitting until the shawl is 60 inches wide.

But, remember, just because it's simple to knit doesn't mean this shawl is ho-hum. I chose a dramatic ribbon yarn and large-gauged needles for a quick shawl with plenty of pizazz. See this beautiful shawl in Figure 12-2.

**Figure 12-2:** A stunning (and stunningly simple) shawl.

## Materials and vital statistics

- **Yarn:** Colinette Giotto (50% cotton, 40% rayon, 10% nylon); 151 yards (140 meters) per 100 grams; 4 hanks; color: Lichen

- **Needles:** US 15 (10 mm) circular needle, 36-inch length or longer, or the size needed to match gauge

- **Other materials:** Crochet hook to attach fringe; yarn needle to weave in ends

- **Size:** 60 inches wide by 40 inches long from tip to center of widest edge (without fringe)

- **Gauge:** 10 stitches and 20 rows per 4 inches in garter stitch

To make this eye-catching wrap, you start with just 2 stitches. From there you increase at the beginning of every row until your shawl is as large as you want it to be. Long, dramatic fringe completes the wrap.

## Directions

Cast on 2 sts.

Row 1 (RS): K1, yo, k1.

Row 2: K1, yo, k2.

Row 3: K1, yo, knit to end.

Repeat Row 3 until there are 150 sts (or more). Every 10 sts you add will increase the width by 4 inches.

Bind off loosely.

**Finishing:** Weave in any ends. Cut 2 20-inch lengths of yarn for each eyelet, and then use these pieces to make fringe. (See Chapter 8 for more information on fringe making.)

## Variation: Changing up your yarn

This basic shawl lends itself well to some variations and substitutions in yarns. For example:

- ✓ Choose any ribbon or tape yarn and a very large needle size to achieve a lacy look. If you're substituting a thicker yarn, use US 17 or larger needles.
- ✓ Consider knitting with one yarn and fringing with a second color or texture to vary the look of your shawl. Or you can leave the fringe off all together for a sleeker look.

## Variation: Making a poncho

If you're more of a poncho person, make two shawls, each with a hypotenuse of about 45 inches (or about 115 stitches, if you're knitting at the same gauge given in the basic pattern). Lay the shawls out so they make a square, as shown in Figure 12-3. Now seam the two hypotenuses together from the points toward the center, leaving a 10-inch wide slit in the center for the neck opening. (To find out how to sew a seam, head to the appendix.)

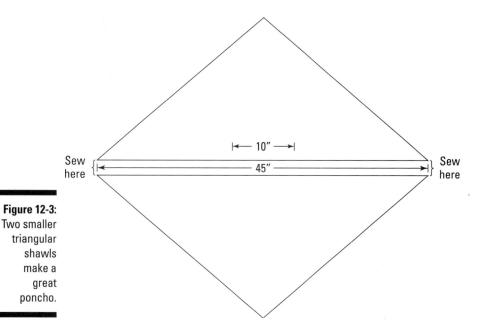

**Figure 12-3:**
Two smaller
triangular
shawls
make a
great
poncho.

# Fully Fashioned Kerchief

This kerchief, shown in Figure 12-4, is quick to make and is a great way to practice different decreases. It's a fun project to make for yourself, or you can make matching ones for little sisters or nieces.

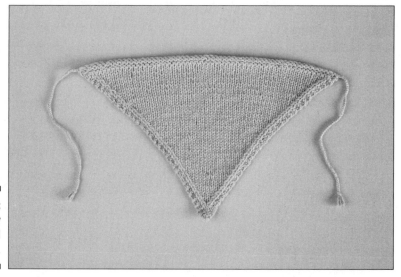

**Figure 12-4:**
A fully
fashioned
kerchief.

## New skill: Additional left-slanting decreases

Here's something you may know about a decrease in knitting: It gets rid of a stitch. On the other hand, here's something you may *not* know about a decrease: It's biased. No, it doesn't have any sort of political view — it simply slants. Knitting 2 stitches together — abbreviated k2tog — leans to the right (see Chapter 6 for more about k2tog). The fact that it slants really doesn't matter much if it's buried in your armpit, but if it shows, it starts to matter.

This slanting matters because decreases tend to be worked in pairs. When you're shaping a garment, you'll often work one decrease near the beginning of a row and one near the end of that same row. If you work all your decreases as k2tog, they'll all slant toward one side of the finished piece. Most knitted pieces are meant to be symmetrical though, and you want the right half and the left half to be mirror images of one another, right down to the way your decreases lean. So your right-leaning k2tog needs to be paired with a left-leaning decrease, just to make things pretty. Decreases that are paired, mirrored, and visible are considered *fully fashioned.*

Figure 12-5 shows both left- and right-slanting decreases. If you've been wondering why someone else's version of the same sweater looks better than yours, especially around the neck, the answer may lie in the slants of her decreases.

When it comes to left-slanting decreases, you have several choices: ssk (which I cover in Chapter 6), K2tog tbl, and skp. You can choose to use any of them to mirror the k2tog and achieve full fashioning. Like anything else, however, trends do come and go — some designers and even some eras seem to prefer one over another. Which do you prefer? Give them all a try and see what suits your fancy.

For many new knitters, the k2tog tbl (knitting 2 stitches together through the back loops) seems to be easiest to work and easiest to remember because it's almost the same as k2tog and doesn't involve multiple steps. But do know that you can choose to substitute one left-slanting decrease for another in just about any pattern.

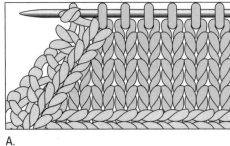

**Figure 12-5:**
Paired right-
and left-
slanting
decreases
add
panache to
a simple
kerchief.

A.                                                                                    B.

Follow these steps and check out Figure 12-6 to decrease with k2tog tbl:

1. **Insert the right needle from right to left through the back loops of the next 2 stitches.**

2. **Wrap the yarn around the right-hand needle and knit the 2 stitches together.**

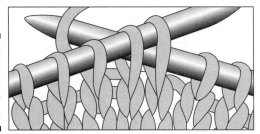

**Figure 12-6:**
The k2tog
tbl stitch
leans to
the left.

You can also decrease with skp (slip 1, knit 1, pass the slipped stitch over). Some pattern designers use the abbreviation sl 1, k1, psso instead of skp. To decrease with skp, follow these steps (and see Figure 12-7):

1. **Slip 1 stitch knitwise.**

2. **Knit 1 stitch.**

3. **Pass the slipped stitch over the stitch that was just knit — just like when you bind off.**

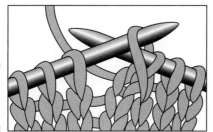

**Figure 12-7:** Decreasing with skp.

Regardless of which decrease you use and how much you think it will show, you should *always* work your decreases in a stitch or two (or 12!) from the edge. Why? Not only will your project look more polished, but decreasing this way will also make things much nicer to seam up later (if you need to). In other words, you'll have a consistent, smooth edge to sew. Knitters always want to know the secret to good finishing, and this is definitely part of the secret. Even if a pattern in another book says to decrease at the beginning and end of the row, knit the first and last stitches plain and simple.

## Materials and vital statistics

- ✔ **Yarn:** Rowan Calmer (75% cotton, 25% acrylic microfiber); 175 yards (161 meters) per 50 grams; 1 ball; color: Refresh

- ✔ **Needles:** US 8 (5 mm) needles, or the size needed to match gauge

- ✔ **Other materials:** Yarn needle to weave in ends

- ✔ **Size:** Baby (child, adult)

   - **Finished width:** 12 (15, 17) inches

   - **Finished length:** 8½ (10½, 12) inches

- ✔ **Gauge:** 20 stitches and 28 rows per 4 inches in stockinette stitch

This kerchief is knit from the long side to the tip. After working a narrow border in garter stitch, you'll work your fully fashioned decreases every right-side row. The ties are made of simple braids added on after the knitting's complete.

## Directions

Cast on 60 (76, 86) sts.

Rows 1, 2, and 3: Knit 3 rows.

Row 4 (RS): K2, k2tog tbl, knit to last 4 sts, k2tog, k2.

Row 5 (WS): K2, purl to last 2 sts, k2.

Repeat Rows 4 and 5 until 6 sts remain.

Next row (RS): K2, k2tog, k2.

Next row (WS): K2, p1, k2.

The next two RS rows use a double decrease to get rid of 2 sts at once. Sk2p or sl 1, k2tog, psso combines skp and k2tog.

Next row (RS): K1, slip 1 knitwise, k2tog, pass the slipped st over, k1.

Next row (WS): K3.

Next row (RS): Sl 1, k2tog, psso.

Cut yarn and pull through remaining st to secure. Weave in ends.

**Finishing:** Cut 6 strands of yarn, each 24 inches long. Thread 3 of the strands halfway through the point on one side of the long edge, making 6 12-inch long tails. Divide the tails into pairs, braid them, and knot at the bottom. Repeat with remaining strands on the opposite point.

## Lacy Shawl

Even though this project is called "lacy," don't be scared away. You simply work stockinette stitch and yarn overs on a needle large enough to let plenty of light shine through. Worked with two strands of a classic mohair blend held together, this light-weight shawl adds warmth and drama to any outfit (see Figure 12-8).

**Figure 12-8:** A lacy shawl is dramatic and flattering.

Loads of yarns now on the market shift from one color to the next on their own (and it's safe to say that I love them all). But you also can create gradual color changes yourself — and control how they change. Changing colors highlights the chevron shape that you create when you knit this shawl.

With this project you use three different colors. So, using two strands of yarn at a time with three colors to choose from means that you can create five different colors — AA, AB, BB, BC, and CC. Choose wild, surprising combinations or colors within the same family. Whatever colors you choose, do think about value as well as hue. In other words, if you want a strong gradient, consider using a very light or very dark color to contrast with two medium-valued colors. (Check out Chapter 8 for the basics of changing colors in a pattern and of using two strands of yarn at once.)

## Materials and vital statistics

- ✔ **Yarn:** Crystal Palace Yarns Kid Merino (28% kid mohair, 28% merino wool, 44% micro nylon); 240 yards (221 meters) per 25 grams
  - **Color A:** Charcoal; 2 balls
  - **Color B:** Misty Blue; 2 balls
  - **Color C:** Pacific Blue; 2 balls
- ✔ **Needles:** US 13 (9 mm) circular needle, 24-inch length or longer, or the size needed to match gauge
- ✔ **Other materials:** Yarn needle to weave in ends
- ✔ **Size:** 34 inches from tip to center of widest edge by 68 inches wide (see the schematic in Figure 12-9)
- ✔ **Gauge:** 10 stitches and 14 rows per 4 inches in stockinette stitch

The lacy shawl starts with just a few stitches at the nape of the neck and grows out in a triangle due to the placement of your increases. You bind off at the two short sides of the triangle. This construction technique means that it's easy to vary the size of your shawl by knitting more or fewer rows.

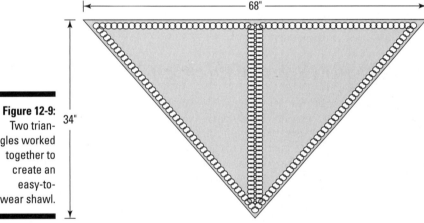

**Figure 12-9:** Two triangles worked together to create an easy-to-wear shawl.

## Directions

With 2 strands of color A held together as if they were 1, cast on 3 sts.

Row 1 (RS): K1, yo, k1, yo, k1. There are 5 sts.

Row 2 and all following WS rows: Purl.

Row 3 (RS): K1, yo, k1, yo, k1, yo, k1, yo, k1. There are 9 sts.

Row 5 (RS): K1, yo, k3, yo, k1, yo, k3, yo, k1. There are 13 sts.

Row 7 (RS): K1, yo, k5, yo, k1, yo, k5, yo, k1. There are 17 sts.

Row 9 (RS): K1, yo, k7, yo, k1, yo, k7, yo, k1. There are 21 sts.

Continue pattern as set, increasing 4 sts every RS row by making yarn overs at each edge and working 2 more sts between each edge and the central pair of yarn overs.

Continue until you've worked 28 rows with 2 strands of color A. There are 57 sts.

Switch to 1 strand of color A and 1 strand of color B held together as 1 yarn and work 24 rows of the pattern. There are 105 sts.

Switch to 2 strands of color B held together and work 20 rows of the pattern. There are 145 sts.

Switch to 1 strand of color B and 1 strand of color C held together and work 16 rows of the pattern. There are 177 sts.

Switch to 2 strands of color C held together and work 8 rows of the pattern, and then work the border as follows:

Next RS row: K1, yo, *k2tog, yo, repeat from * to center 3 sts, k1, yo, k1, yo, k1, **yo, k2tog, repeat from ** to last st, yo, k1. There are 197 sts.

Next row: Purl.

Bind off all sts loosely.

**Finishing:** Weave in ends. Block shawl by wetting it and laying it flat to dry (head to the appendix to find out how to block).

## Variation: Knitting through thick and thin

Because this shawl is a triangle right from the start and grows along its outer edges, it's a great shawl pattern to use with just about any yarn. You can use the yarn I suggest in the original pattern held singly and use smaller needles for a very delicate shawl. Or, you can use a yarn that borders on ridiculously thick and get something interesting — just be sure that the needles you use are large enough to create a shawl that drapes beautifully and lets the light shine though. If you need help choosing the right needles for the job, head to Chapter 1.

# Stretchy Halter Top

A halter top is a fun, summery project to work on. But in creating a pattern for a halter, I wanted to be sure to make one that was both fun *and* functional — a halter should be comfortable, it should stay in place, and it should provide plenty of coverage in the front while still baring the back. Vents at the side, a front that's slightly wider than the back, and Lycra all do their parts to make a fit that's flattering. Figure 12-10 shows this halter.

You've probably noticed that this top isn't a triangle (thank goodness!), but simple triangles worked on the sides of rectangles give this halter its great shape. See the fully fashioned kerchief pattern earlier in this chapter for a full report on fashioning your decreases.

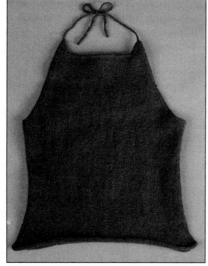

**Figure 12-10:**
A halter top is great on its own or layered with a shawl or jacket.

## Materials and vital statistics

- **Yarn:** Cascade Fixation (98.3% cotton, 1.7 % elastic); 100 yards (92 meters) per 50 grams; 4 (5, 5, 6, 6) balls; color: 3794

- **Needles:** US 7 (4.5 mm) needles, or the size needed to match gauge

- **Other materials:** US H (5 mm) crochet hook; yarn needle to weave in ends

- **Size:** Women's S (M, L, 1X, 2X) or chest circumference of 34 (38, 42, 46, 50) inches

  - **Finished circumference (unstretched):** 26 (29, 32, 35, 38) inches

  - **Finished length:** 19½ (20, 21, 22, 23) inches, not including ties

  See the schematic in Figure 12-11 (the shape and measurements of the front are shown in bold; the back is indicated with dotted lines)

- **Gauge:** 25 stitches and 40 rows per 4 inches in stockinette stitch, unstretched

Because you want this halter to stretch to fit you (and to stay where you want it to), you need to knit it smaller than your actual chest measurement. Choose the size that will fit you based on your chest circumference, and then follow the directions for that size.

## Knitting the front

Cast on 100 (108, 118, 130, 140) sts.

Row 1 (RS): (K1, p1) 2 times, knit to last 4 sts, (p1, k1) 2 times.

Row 2 (WS): (P1, k1) 2 times, purl to last 4 sts, (k1, p1) 2 times.

Row 3 (RS): (K1, p1) 2 times, k2tog tbl, knit to last 6 sts, k2tog, (p1, k1) 2 times.

Row 4: Repeat Row 2.

Repeat these 4 rows 5 more times. 88 (96, 106, 118, 128) sts remain. The front should measure approximately 2½ inches.

Switch to stockinette stitch (knit a row, purl a row), and work even until the piece measures 12 inches, ending with a purl row.

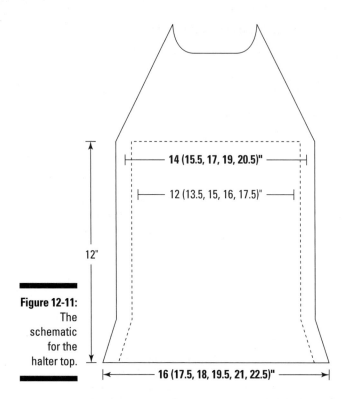

**Figure 12-11:**
The schematic for the halter top.

14 (15.5, 17, 19, 20.5)"

12 (13.5, 15, 16, 17.5)"

12"

16 (17.5, 18, 19.5, 21, 22.5)"

## Underarm shaping

Bind off 4 (4, 5, 6, 6) sts at beginning of the next 2 rows. There are 80 (88, 96, 106, 116) sts. You now shape the angled sides of the top.

Next row (RS): K1, k2tog tbl, knit to last 3 sts, k2tog, k1.

Rows 1, 2, and 3: Work 3 rows in stockinette stitch, starting with a purl row.

Row 4 (Decrease Row) (RS): K1, k2tog tbl, knit to last 3 sts, k2tog, k1.

Repeat the last 4 rows 13 (13, 14, 15, 16) more times. There are 50 (58, 64, 72, 80) sts.

After the last decrease row, purl 1 row. The front measures approximately 6 (6, 6½, 7, 7½) inches from the beginning of the underarm shaping.

## Neck shaping

K10 (11, 13, 16, 17), join a new ball of yarn and bind off center 30 (36, 38, 40, 46) sts, knit to end of row. There are 2 sets of 10 (11, 13, 16, 17) sts on the needle, each with an attached ball of yarn. The 2 sets of sts are worked at the same time, each using its own ball of yarn.

You continue shaping the outside edges of the halter while at the same time shaping the neck. Read through these steps before you continue knitting.

On the outside edges: Continue decreasing every 4th row as set at the outside edge of each piece. (You work the next decrease on the next RS row.)

*At the same time,* shape the neck by decreasing 1 st, 1 st in from neck edge, every RS row. To do so:

On the left side of the neck, end every RS row with k2tog, k1.

On the right side of the neck, start each RS row with k1, k2tog tbl.

Work in this way until 5 sts remain in each set of sts, ending with a purl row.

Work each side of the neck as follows:

Next row (RS): K1, sl 1, k2tog, psso, k1 (3 sts remain).

Next row: Sl 1, k2tog, psso. Cut the yarn and draw it through the last st to secure.

## Making the back

Cast on 88 (96, 106, 112, 122) sts, and then work the back as you did the front starting with Row 1. When all decreases are complete, there will be 76 (84, 94, 100, 110) sts.

Work until the back measures 12 inches, ending with a purl row.

Bind off all sts.

## Finishing your top

Sew together the front and back with mattress stitch (see the appendix for details on this stitch), leaving the lower 2½ inches open at either side to create side vents. Beginning where the front and back meet at the left underarm, work a row of single crochet along the left front, across the neck opening, down the right front, and across the back. At the top of each shoulder, crochet a chain that's 15 inches long. Now cut the yarn and pull it through the last stitch to secure. Weave in any remaining ends. How-to on crochet basics can be found in the appendix.

# Short Row Scarf

You can make triangles without increasing or decreasing. You create the triangles in this scarf one at a time (using just one yarn at a time) with short rows. This unique scarf, shown in Figure 12-12, works with almost any yarn. Choose the same yarn in three colors, or choose yarns in the same color with a variety of textures for a different effect. Note that the width of your scarf will vary depending on the yarns you choose.

**Figure 12-12:** Triangles come together to make a scarf.

# New skill: Working short rows

A *short row* is really nothing mystical. Essentially, when you want to make a short row, you stop knitting somewhere midrow, turn around and knit back in the other direction. This technique was likely first discovered by someone whose knitting group distracted her, causing her to forget which direction she was knitting. Short rows really come in handy when you're turning a sock's heel or shaping the bust of a sweater, but this simple project introduces you to the technique.

When you're knitting short rows, the section with the stitches that are left unknit when you turn around midrow and knit back are two rows shorter than the section with the neighboring stitches the next time you encounter them, which is why we call them short rows! That's also why you get the pesky little holes associated with the short row technique.

Any discussion of short rows soon turns to wrapping, which involves winding the yarn horizontally around the base of the stitch where you turn so that you prevent a hole from forming. Do you need to wrap or don't you? My opinion: I always wrap when I knit stockinette stitch, but I usually don't in garter stitch. How big or visible the holes are depends on the yarn you're using and how many rows per inch there are. It's only a question of aesthetics, though. If you don't like the looks of the little holes formed when you turn your short rows, you should try wrapping.

To wrap a stitch when you work a short row, follow these steps (and see Figure 12-13):

1. **Work the number of stitches that are prescribed in the pattern.**

2. **Slip the next stitch purlwise from the left to the right needle.**

3. **Bring the yarn from back to front between stitches, and slip the stitch back to the left needle, still unworked.**

4. **Turn your work so that you're ready to knit the next row, slip the first stitch purlwise, and start knitting (or purling) back.**

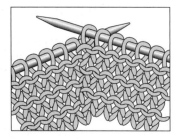

A. Slip the next stitch purlwise.

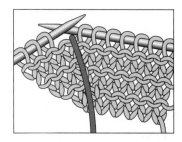

B. Bring the yarn to the front.

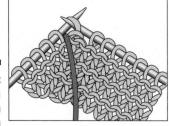

**Figure 12-13:** Wrapping a stitch when working short rows.

C. Slip the stitch back to the left-hand needle.

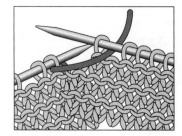

D. Turn the work.

The second step in short row wrapping is to pick up the wrap you made and knit it together with the wrapped stitch to minimize the hole. When you next encounter a wrapped stitch, follow these steps (and check out Figure 12-14):

1. **Slip the wrapped stitch to the right needle without knitting it.**

2. **Stick the left needle into the horizontal wrap at the base of the stitch and then into the slipped (wrapped) stitch.**

3. **Knit these 2 stitches together.**

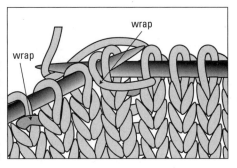

**Figure 12-14:** Picking up and knitting the short row wrap.

# Materials and vital statistics

- **Yarn:** Curious Creek Fibers Etosha (90% kid mohair, 10% nylon); 220 yards (203 meters) per 50 grams

  - **Color A:** Birches in Norway; 1 skein

  - **Color B:** Purple Mountains Majesty; 1 skein

  - **Color C:** Rock Grotto; 1 skein

- **Needles:** US 11 (8 mm) needles, or the size needed to match gauge

- **Size:** 6 inches wide by 60 inches long (see how the scarf is laid out in Figure 12-15)

- **Gauge:** 13 stitches and 24 rows per 4 inches in garter stitch with 2 strands of yarn held together

When you knit this scarf, you only use one color at a time. It's knit conventionally, from one short end to the other, but the short row technique allows you to create the triangles as you knit. The scarf begins and ends with triangles that are half as big as the main triangles to square the corners of the scarf. You always have 20 stitches on the needle, but you only knit a fraction of those stitches on most of the rows.

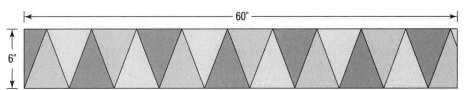

**Figure 12-15:** This scarf is made up of triangles knit one at a time.

60"

6"

## Directions

Always hold together 2 strands of yarn of the same color as you knit this scarf.

With color A, cast on 20 sts for the first triangle.

Rows 1, 3, 5, 7, and 9: Knit to the end of the row.

Row 2: K16, wrap next st and turn.

Row 4: K12, wrap next st and turn.

Row 6: K8, wrap next st and turn.

Row 8: K4, wrap next st and turn.

Row 10: Knit across all 20 sts, picking up wraps and knitting them together with the wrapped sts.

Use color B for the first full triangle (see Chapter 8 if you want more information about changing colors).

Row 1: Change colors, k4, wrap next st and turn.

Rows 2, 4, 6, 8, 10, 12, 14, 16, and 18: Knit to the end of the row.

Row 3: K8, wrap next st and turn.

Row 5: K12, wrap next st and turn.

Row 7: K16, wrap next st and turn.

Row 9: K20.

Row 11: K16, wrap next st and turn.

Row 13: K12, wrap next st and turn.

Row 15: K8, wrap next st and turn.

Row 17: K4, wrap next st and turn.

Row 19: Knit across all 20 sts, picking up wraps and knitting them together with the wrapped sts.

Repeat these 19 rows, alternating between the 3 colors until the scarf reaches approximately 60 inches or your desired length.

Finish with the final triangle as follows:

Row 1: Change colors, k4, wrap next st and turn.

Rows 2, 4, 6, and 8: Knit.

Row 3: K8, wrap next st and turn.

Row 5: K12, wrap next st and turn.

Row 7: K16, wrap next st and turn.

Row 9: K20, picking up wraps and knitting them together with the wrapped sts.

Row 10: Bind off loosely.

**Finishing:** Weave in loose ends and block if necessary (check out the appendix for more on blocking).

# Harlequin Blanket

You can make a beautiful blanket with the same short row technique used in the previous pattern. A full-sized blanket is awe-inspiring, but consider the smaller size for a decorative throw or baby blanket (check it out in Figure 12-16).

**Figure 12-16:**
A beautiful blanket made from triangles.

Sewing together a series of similar scarves or strips is one of my favorite ways to create a blanket. The knitting of each strip is no more cumbersome or daunting than knitting a single scarf, so you can easily take it with you. This method also allows you to divide and conquer a communal knitting project for a shower or special gift. And finally, I'm consoled when I remind myself that if I never manage to finish the blanket, I have several great scarves to give as gifts.

If you're using yarns of different weights, try doubling a finer yarn, as I have with the Etosha. This makes it possible to knit different yarns at the same gauge. If you're having trouble knitting to the same gauge with different yarns, it's okay to use differently sized needles for each yarn.

## Materials and vital statistics

✔ **Yarn:** You need the following three yarns for this project:

- **Yarn A:** Curious Creek Fibers Etosha (90% kid mohair, 10% nylon); 220 yards (203 meters) per 50 grams; 4 (10) skeins; color: Savanna Grasses (*note:* this yarn is held double throughout)

- **Yarn B:** Curious Creek Fibers Kilimanjaro (95% mohair boucle, 5% nylon); 121 yards (111 meters) per 100 grams; 3 (9) skeins; color: Birches in

Norway

- **Yarn C:** Curious Creek Fibers Shira (54% mohair, 23% silk, 18% wool, 5% nylon); 86 yards (79 meters) per 50 grams; 5 (14) skeins; color: Savanna Grasses

✔ **Needles:** US 11 (8 mm) needles, or the size needed to match gauge

✔ **Size:** 36 by 42 (60 by 70 inches); see Figure 12-17 for the blanket layout

✔ **Gauge:** 11 stitches and 20 rows per 4 inches in garter stitch

This blanket pattern works well with almost any yarn combination. A monochromatic palette with a variety of textures is sophisticated, while an easy-care yarn in brightly contrasting colors creates a terrific baby blanket. For the smaller blanket you need about 360 yards of each yarn. For the full-size blanket, get 1,100 yards of each color.

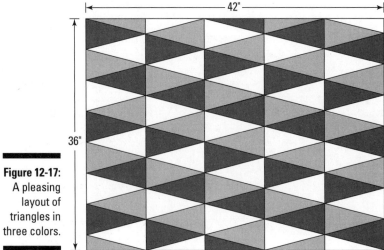

**Figure 12-17:**
A pleasing layout of triangles in three colors.

# Directions

Follow the short row scarf pattern in the previous section to make 6 (10) scarves. Make each strip with 14 (26) full triangles as well as the starting and ending triangles. Each scarf should be approximately 36 (60) inches long.

To create the color arrangement seen in Figure 12-17:

Make 2 (4) scarves with the color sequence A, B, C.

Make 2 (3) scarves with the color sequence B, C, A.

Make 2 (3) scarves with the color sequence C, A, B.

Lay the completed strips next to one another. Using mattress stitch, seam the strips together. Weave in ends. (Get seaming advice in the appendix.)

# Chapter 13

# Putting Together Rectangles and Triangles

• • • • • • • • • • • • • • • • • • • • • • • • • • • • • • • • • • • • • • • • • • • • • • •

## In This Chapter

▶ Picking up neckline stitches

▶ Discovering a new way to set in sleeves

▶ Creating crew necks and V-necks for the whole family

• • • • • • • • • • • • • • • • • • • • • • • • • • • • • • • • • • • • • • • • • • • • • • •

A sweater that's well fitting, comfortable to wear, and attractive to look at is what everyone wants. Some knitters are put off by the idea of knitting a whole sweater, but the truth is that most of the knitting is still just rectangles with a few triangles to create the neckline and sleeve shaping. With this chapter, you can create classically constructed sweaters from patterns that offer lots of flexibility. All of these are wardrobe basics that everyone can wear — and they never go out of style.

✔ A V-neck T-shirt for women (with an option for a crew neck) has easy, everyday wearability.

✔ The kid's top offers short and long-sleeved versions, making it a terrific T-shirt for warm or cool weather. The same pattern makes a classic sweater for boys or girls when knit in superwash wool with a cable up the front.

✔ A casual sweater that's knit in a not-too-bulky yarn with rolled cuffs and collar (and the option of adding zest with broad stripes), is designed with men in mind, but it's suitable for both sexes.

✔ The quintessential manly sweater, which is knit in a finer gauged yarn with simple ribbed edging and a V-neck, is great for any man in your life; it offers an option for a crew neck, too.

My hope is that you'll make these basic patterns your own. To help you do that, I offer lots of suggestions to vary the sweaters to keep them interesting and to allow you to return to the same pattern again and again as your skills improve and your tastes change. Use these patterns to come up with results that you — and those you knit for — will love.

# V-Neck T-Shirt

I call this pattern a T-shirt, but what I mean is that it's short-sleeved and has an easy fit. When knit in a cotton tape yarn, this women's top (see Figure 13-1) definitely has that comfy T-shirt thing going on. But consider knitting it in a yarn with a bit of shimmer or sparkle; when paired with a skirt or slacks, it's suitable for dressier occasions. This basic pattern is for a V-neck T-shirt. If you prefer to make a crew neck, see the later variation.

**Figure 13-1:**
An easygoing short-sleeved shirt for all occasions.

# Materials and vital statistics

- ✔ **Yarn:** Colinette Wigwam (100% cotton tape); 120 yards (130 meters) per 100 grams; 6 (6, 7, 7, 8, 9, 10) skeins; color: Fruit Coulis

- ✔ **Needles:** US 8 (5 mm) needles, or the size needed to match gauge; US 6 (4 mm) needles; US 6 (4 mm) circular needle, 16- or 24-inch length

- ✔ **Other materials:** Two stitch markers or safety pins; 1 stitch holder for V-neck or 2 stitch holders for crew neck; yarn needle for finishing

- ✔ **Size:** Women's XS (S, M, L, 1X, 2X, 3X) or actual chest size of 30 (34, 38, 42, 46, 50, 54) inches

  - **Finished chest circumference:** 34 (38, 42, 46, 52, 56, 60) inches

  - **Finished length:** 23 (23, 23, 24, 24, 25, 25) inches

  Figure 13-2 is a schematic of the finished dimensions

- ✔ **Gauge:** 18 stitches and 23 rows per 4 inches in stockinette stitch

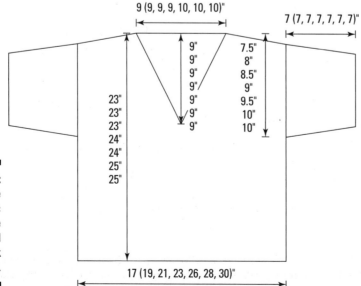

**Figure 13-2:**
The schematic of the finished V-neck T-shirt.

This top is easy to wear and uncomplicated to knit. You knit the seed stitch border as you make the V-neck, so the neckline is done when the sweater's done. Because the sleeves are knit from stitches you'll pick up from the body, the finishing on this shirt involves only sewing the side and underarm seams.

# Starting with the back

Cast on 75 (85, 95, 105, 115, 125, 135) sts with the larger needles.

Switch to smaller needles and work seed stitch as follows:

Row 1: *K1, p1, repeat from * to last st, k1.

Repeat this row 5 more times for the border.

Switch to the larger needles and stockinette stitch (knit a row, purl a row) and work even until the back measures 21½ (21½, 21½, 22½, 22½, 23½, 23½) inches.

### Shoulder shaping

Bind off 4 (5, 6, 7, 8, 10, 11) sts at the beginning of the next 2 rows.

Bind off 4 (5, 7, 7, 9, 10, 11) sts at the beginning of the next 2 rows.

On the next row, begin working the center 41 (41, 41, 45, 45, 45, 45) sts in seed stitch to form the back neckline.

Bind off 4 (6, 7, 8, 9, 10, 11) sts at the beginning of the next 2 rows.

Bind off 5 (6, 7, 8, 9, 10, 12) sts at the beginning of the next 2 rows.

Bind off remaining 41 (41, 41, 45, 45, 45, 45) sts.

# Moving to the front

Cast on 75 (85, 95, 105, 115, 125, 135) sts with the larger needles.

Work 6 rows in seed stitch as for back on smaller needles.

Switch to stockinette stitch and the larger needles, increasing 1 st in the first row. Work even until the front measures 13 (13, 13, 14, 14, 15, 15) inches, ending with a WS row.

### Neck shaping

Next row (RS): K35 (40, 45, 50, 55, 60, 65) sts, k1, p1, k2, p1, k1, knit to end of row. This row establishes the seed stitch neckline border.

Next row (WS): P35 (40, 45, 50, 55, 60, 65) sts, k1, p1, k2, p1, k1, purl to end of row.

Repeat the previous 2 rows 1 more time.

Now divide the sts and work each half of the neck separately.

### Left neck

Next row (RS): K33 (38, 43, 48, 53, 58, 63) sts, k2tog, k1, p1, k1. Turn. (If you're unfamiliar with k2tog, head to Chapter 6.) Place the remaining 38 (43, 48, 53, 58, 63, 68) sts on a stitch holder.

Next row (WS): K1, p1, k1, purl to end of row.

Next row (RS): K32 (37, 42, 47, 52, 57, 62) sts, k2tog, k1, p1, k1. Turn.

Next row (WS): K1, p1, k1, purl to end of row.

Next row (RS): Knit to last 5 sts, k2tog, k1, p1, k1.

Next row (WS): K1, p1, k1, purl to end of row.

Repeat the previous 2 rows until 17 (22, 27, 30, 35, 40, 45) sts remain for left shoulder.

Work even until the front measures 21½ (21½, 21½, 22½, 22½, 23½, 23½) inches, ending with a WS row.

### Left shoulder shaping

Next row (RS): Bind off 4 (5, 6, 7, 8, 10, 11) sts, knit to end of row.

Next row (WS): K1, p1, k1, purl to end of row.

Next row (RS): Bind off 4 (5, 7, 7, 9, 10, 11) sts, knit to last 2 sts, p1, k1.

Next row (WS): K1, p1, k1, purl to end of row.

Next row (RS): Bind off 4, (6, 7, 8, 9, 10, 11) sts, knit last 2 sts, p1, k1.

Next row (WS): K1, p1, k1, purl to end of row.

Next row (RS): Bind off remaining 5 (6, 7, 8, 9, 10, 12) sts.

### Right neck

Replace the held stitches on the needle with the RS facing. Join yarn at neck edge and k1, p1, k1, ssk, knit to end of row. (See Chapter 6 if you're unfamiliar with ssk.)

Next row (WS): Purl to last 3 sts, k1, p1, k1.

Next row (RS): K1, p1, k1, ssk, knit to end of row.

Repeat the previous 2 rows until 17 (22, 27, 30, 35, 40, 45) sts remain for right shoulder. Work even until this side measures 21½ (21½, 21½, 22½, 22½, 23½, 23½) inches, ending with a RS row.

### Right shoulder shaping

Next row (WS): Bind off 4 (5, 6, 7, 8, 10, 11) sts, purl to last 3 sts, k1, p1, k1.

Next row (RS): K1, p1, knit to end of row.

Next row (WS): Bind off 4 (5, 7, 7, 9, 10, 11) sts, purl to last 3 sts, k1, p1, k1.

Next row (RS): K1, p1, knit to end of row.

Next row (WS): Bind off 4 (6, 7, 8, 9, 10, 11) sts, purl to last 3 sts, k1, p1, k1.

Next row (RS): K1, p1, knit to end of row.

Next row (WS): Bind off remaining 5 (6, 7, 8, 9, 10, 12) sts.

## Making the sleeves

Sew together shoulder seams of front and back with mattress stitch (see the appendix for more details). Now work the sleeves from the top down.

Measure 7½ (8, 8½, 9, 9½, 10, 10) inches down from shoulder seam along the side edge of the front and place a marker or safety pin. Repeat on the back so that you have 2 markers 15 (16, 17, 18, 19, 20, 20) inches apart.

Pick up and knit 67 (73, 77, 81, 85, 91, 91) sts between the 2 markers with the larger needles. (See Chapter 10 for pointers on picking up stitches along a straight edge.)

Next row (WS): Purl.

Next row (RS): Knit.

Next row (WS): Purl.

Next row (RS): K1, ssk, knit to last 3 sts, k2tog, k1.

Repeat the previous 4 rows 9 more times. There are 47 (53, 57, 61, 65, 71, 71) sts.

Switch to the smaller needles and work 6 rows in seed stitch.

Bind off remaining sts.

Make the second sleeve the same as the first.

## Finishing your T-shirt

Block the shirt lightly to the measurements given in Figure 13-2. Using mattress stitch, sew the sides and underarms of the shirt together. Weave in all ends. See the appendix for advice on blocking and seaming.

## Variation: Crew neck T-shirt with garter stitch edging

If you favor a crew neck T-shirt over a V-neck, the change is easy to make. This variation uses garter stitch at the edges instead of seed stitch, and the collar edging is worked at the end. The materials, size, and gauge are the same here as they are in the V-neck T-shirt pattern, except that the crew neck is 1 inch narrower than the V-neck for all sizes. In addition, you do need two stitch markers, a crochet hook, and a new skill: picking up neckline stitches. If you're unfamiliar with this skill, I explain what you need to know later in this chapter.

### Back

Cast on 75 (85, 95, 105, 115, 125, 135) sts with the larger needles.

Knit 6 rows to form garter stitch edging.

Switch to stockinette stitch and work even until the back measures 21½ (21½, 21½, 22½, 22½, 23½, 23½) inches.

**Shoulder shaping:** Bind off 4 (5, 6, 7, 8, 10, 11) sts at the beginning of the next 2 rows.

Bind off 4 (5, 7, 7, 9, 10, 11) sts at the beginning of the next 2 rows.

Bind off 4 (6, 7, 8, 9, 10, 11) sts at the beginning of the next 2 rows.

Bind off 5 (6, 7, 8, 9, 10, 12) sts at the beginning of the next 2 rows.

Put remaining 41 (41, 41, 45, 45, 45, 45) sts onto a holder for the back of the neck.

### Front

Cast on 75 (85, 95, 105, 115, 125, 135) sts with the larger needles.

Knit 6 rows to form garter stitch edging.

Switch to stockinette stitch and work even until the front measures 20 (20, 20, 21, 21, 22, 22) inches, or 3 inches less than the desired length, ending with a WS row.

**Neck shaping:** Next row (RS): Knit across 22 (27, 32, 35, 40, 45, 50) sts and slip these sts to a holder for the left shoulder, knit across center 31 (31, 31, 35, 35, 35, 35) sts, and then slip them to a holder for the collar, knit to end of row. There are 22 (27, 32, 35, 40, 45, 50) sts on the needle.

You now work each side of the neck separately.

**Right neck:** Next row (WS): Purl.

Next row (RS): K1, ssk, knit to end of row.

Repeat the previous 2 rows 4 more times. There are 17 (22, 27, 30, 35, 40, 45) sts. The front should measure the same as the back to the beginning of the shoulder shaping.

**Right shoulder shaping:** Next row (WS): Bind off 4 (5, 6, 7, 8, 10, 11) sts, purl to end of row.

Next row (RS): Knit.

Next row (WS): Bind off 4 (5, 7, 7, 9, 10, 11) sts, purl to end of row.

Next row (RS): Knit.

Next row (WS): Bind off 4 (6, 7, 8, 9, 10, 11) sts, purl to end of row.

Next row (RS): Knit.

Next row (WS): Bind off remaining 5 (6, 7, 8, 9, 10, 12) sts.

**Left neck:** Replace the held stitches for the left front on the needle with the WS facing. Rejoin yarn at neck edge, and purl to end of row.

Next row (RS): Knit to last 3 sts, k2tog, k1.

Next row (WS): Purl.

Repeat these 2 rows 4 more times ending with a purl row. There are 17 (22, 27, 30, 35, 40, 45) sts.

**Left shoulder shaping:** Next row (RS): Bind off 4 (5, 6, 7, 8, 10, 11) sts, knit to end of row.

Next row (WS): Purl.

Next row (RS): Bind off 4 (6, 7, 8, 9, 10, 11) sts, knit to end of row.

Next row (WS): Purl.

Next row (RS): Bind off 4 (6, 7, 8, 9, 10, 11) sts, knit to end of row.

Next row (WS): Purl.

Next row (RS): Bind off remaining 5 (6, 7, 8, 9, 10, 12) sts.

### Sleeves

Work the sleeves the same as in the V-neck T-shirt pattern, but work the last 6 rows in garter stitch (knit all rows) instead of seed stitch.

### Collar

The collar is knit in garter stitch in the round (head to Chapter 11 to find out more about knitting in the round). If you need guidance on picking up neckline stitches, check out the later section "New skill: Picking up neckline stitches."

Attach the yarn at the right shoulder. Using the smaller sized 16- or 24-inch length circular needle, with the RS facing out, knit the 41 (41, 41, 45, 45, 45, 45) sts from the back neck holder, pick up and knit 15 sts from the left side of the front neck, knit the 31 (31, 31, 35, 35, 35, 35) sts from the front neck holder, and then pick up and knit 15 sts along the right side of the front neck. There are 102 (102, 102, 110, 110, 110, 110) sts. Place a marker and join in the round.

To knit garter stitch in the round, you knit a round and then purl a round — your pick up round counts as your first knit round.

Purl 1 round.

Knit 1 round.

Repeat the previous 2 rounds 2 more times, and then bind off loosely.

### Finishing

Use the same finishing techniques as described in the basic V-neck pattern.

# Kid's Top

This pattern is for a T-shirt — and so much more! In the beautiful cotton tape yarn recommended for this pattern, this top is great for warmer weather or for an easygoing layer for those in-between days. (Check out the top in Figure 13-3.) Substitute a kid-friendly wool blend and add the optional cable and you can create a great sweater for any youngster. To make your top short-sleeved, see the variations that follow.

Stockinette stitch, by nature, rolls on the edges and knitting it tightly makes a firmer, tidier roll. This pattern takes advantage of stockinette stitch to create rolled edges on the hems, sleeves, and neck. Allow the pieces to roll naturally and take measurements with the edges rolled.

**Figure 13-3:**
A kid's
favorite
hand-knit
top.

# New skill: Picking up neckline stitches

The skill of picking up neckline stitches along a curve comes up in most sweaters, including the men's sweaters later in this chapter. (To find out how to pick up stitches along straight edges, check out Chapter 10.) Some knitters say that they hate this part of finishing. I don't — I actually like it a lot. Picking up a neckline properly is satisfying and it means that you're very close to actually wearing your sweater — and you're 100 percent authorized to go buy more yarn.

To pick up neckline stitches, you need your working yarn, smaller circular needles, and a crochet hook no bigger than your knitting needles (an E, F, or G hook will do nicely here). A crochet hook, you say? Yes! I like to use a crochet hook to bring a loop of yarn through the fabric and make a new stitch. Then I slide it to my knitting needle. Even though I didn't knit anything exactly, it still counts as pick up and knit.

You also need decent light and room enough to work. This project is a bit like one of those old-fashioned pastry recipes that begins with "Choose a clear, dry day." Don't frustrate yourself by attempting something new when you're tired or distracted. Wait until morning when you have good light and a bit of peace.

## Measuring and marking

When you're working along a horizontal edge, you pick up every stitch. That's easy enough. When you're working along a vertical edge, you pick up about 3 stitches for every 4 rows (because that's roughly the ratio of stitches to rows that you get with a stockinette stitch fabric). Also not rocket science. But along a curve you don't have anything nearly so tidy. Instead, you have a ziggurat-like series of bound-off and decreased stitches. Here's what you do when you hit a curve:

1. **When you get to the place where you need to pick up and knit, pause for a moment, put down the needles, pick up your tape measure, and measure along the curved line where you need to pick up stitches.**

   On this kid's sweater, you should have about 3 inches worth of knitted fabric on each side of the front neck.

2. **Place removable stitch markers (or safety pins or bits of string) at regular intervals around the spots where you need to pick up stitches (say every inch or every 2 inches).**

3. **Figure out your gauge per inch so you know how many stitches to pick up between each set of markers.**

The gauge for this pattern, for example, is 18 stitches for every 4 inches of stockinette stitch, or 4½ stitches for 1 inch. If you have 3 spaces between the markers that are each 1 inch long, then 4½ stitches are picked up in each space for this pattern. Because the space is just short of 3 inches and we're stuck with a fraction (4½ x 3 = 13½), pick up 13 stitches in this space. (See Chapter 2 for more information about gauge.)

If you're using a different stitch pattern for your collar, such as ribbing, you need to know your gauge per inch over *that* stitch pattern on the correctly sized needles, and you must pick up *that* number of stitches per inch.

Measuring and marking is worthwhile on almost any knitting project. Often a pattern will say something like "Pick up and knit 70 stitches around the neck." If your neck is 20 inches around, you can figure out that you need to pick up 7 stitches over every 2 inches. This way, you don't end up picking up 40 stitches on the right side and 30 on the left (trust me, that won't look cool). Plus, remember that knitters don't all knit exactly the same. And so you may have done something different from the knitter who wrote the pattern, and maybe 76 stitches is really a better number of stitches for *your* sweater. All I'm saying is that sometimes the number given works perfectly — and sometimes it works poorly. If you measure out your intervals and pick up evenly in each one, you'll end up with a happy result. Just remember that you may need to fudge a little to get, say, a multiple of 4 for 2 x 2 ribbing or whatever stitch pattern you're working with. Patterns may lie, but your sweater speaks the truth.

### Picking up the right stitches

Which stitches should you pick up? Here are some guidelines:

- **Choose whole stitches (they'll likely be further in from the edge than you thought).** You want to be down below any ugliness at the edge because anything that's above where you pick up stitches magically disappears under your collar.

- **Choose stitches that make a nice graceful curve.** The highlighted stitches in Figure 13-4 show which stitches you want to pick up.

- **Choose small stitches.** If you come across a big stitch somewhere, skip over it. By choosing a smaller space to put your needle, you're minimizing holes.

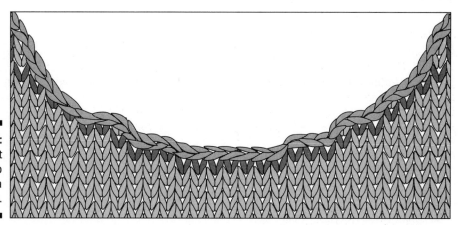

Figure 13-4:
The correct stitches to pick up on a neckline.

Follow these steps to pick up neckline stitches:

1. **With the right side of the sweater facing you and the yarn in back (on the wrong side of the sweater), stick the crochet hook into the center of your chosen stitch, as shown in Figure 13-5.**

   Grab the yarn with the hook and pull the loop through to the front of the work. Slip this stitch to your right-hand needle. This action counts as both picking up and knitting — even though you're using a crochet hook.

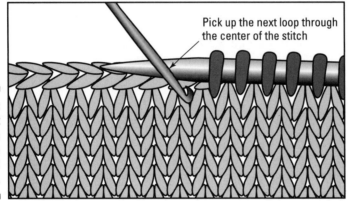

Pick up the next loop through the center of the stitch

**Figure 13-5:** A crochet hook makes it easy to pick up and knit.

2. **Repeat Step 1 until you've picked up all the necessary stitches.**

3. **When you've picked up your stitches, take a moment to even out the tension of the stitches by distributing any slack among the stitches.**

   Picking up stitches, especially around a curve, can mean that your stitches get pulled and tugged. Before you knit the next round, take a minute to even out the tension of the stitches by pulling any slack from stitch to stitch. Look at the body of the sweater, too. If it looks like you have a hole, often you can even it out by moving the slack into the neighboring stitches.

If you're satisfied with how your sweater looks, carry on with the knitting. But remember that do-overs are allowed. Just as carpenters say "Measure twice, cut once," "Pick up twice, knit once" should be the watchword of knitters.

## Materials and vital statistics

- **Yarn:** Colinette Wigwam (100% cotton tape); 120 yards (130 meters) per 100 grams; 4 (4, 5, 5, 6) skeins; color: Earth

- **Needles:** US 8 (5 mm) needles, or the size needed to match gauge; US 6 (4 mm) needles; US 6 (4 mm) circular needle, 16-inch length

- **Other materials:** Two stitch holders; 2 stitch markers; yarn needle; US G (4 mm) crochet hook; 2 removable stitch markers or safety pins

- **Size:** Children's 2 (4, 6, 8, 10) or actual chest size of 21 (23, 25, 26, 28) inches

  - **Finished chest circumference:** 23 (25, 27, 28, 30) inches

  - **Finished length:** 14 (15, 16, 18, 20) inches

  Figure 13-6 is a schematic of the finished dimensions (with an optional cable and short sleeves; see the later variation)

- **Gauge:** 18 stitches and 23 rows per 4 inches in stockinette stitch

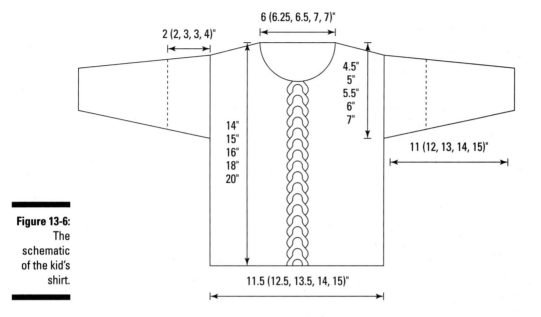

**Figure 13-6:**
The schematic of the kid's shirt.

In this pattern, you knit the front and back, sew them together at the shoulders, and then pick up and knit the sleeves from the top down. Then you pick up and knit the neck to create an easygoing rolled neckline. Finishing is easy because you only have a single seam to sew on each side. If you want to make short sleeves or add a horseshoe cable up the front, see the variation sections.

## Starting with the back

Cast on 52 (56, 60, 64, 68) sts with smaller needles.

Work back and forth in stockinette stitch (knit a row, purl a row) for 1 inch to create a rolled edge.

Switch to larger needles and continue in stockinette stitch until the back measures 13 (14, 15, 17, 19) inches, with the edge rolled, ending with a WS row.

### Neck and shoulder shaping

Bind off 4 (4, 5, 5, 6) sts at the beginning of the next 2 rows.

Bind off 4 (5, 5, 5, 6) sts at the beginning of the next 2 rows.

Bind off 5 (5, 5, 6, 6) sts at the beginning of the next 2 rows.

Slip remaining 26 (28, 30, 32, 32) sts onto a holder for back of the neck.

## Moving to the front

Cast on 52 (56, 60, 64, 68) sts with smaller needles.

Work back and forth in stockinette stitch for 1 inch to create a rolled edge.

Switch to larger needles and continue in stockinette stitch until the piece measures 11 (12, 13, 15, 17) inches, with edges rolled, ending with a WS row.

### Neck shaping

Knit 15 (16, 17, 18, 20) sts and slip them to a holder for the left shoulder, knit across center 22 (24, 26, 28, 28) sts, and then slip them onto a second holder for the front neckline, knit remaining 15 (16, 17, 18, 20) sts.

Now work each side of the neck separately.

### Right neck

Next row (WS): Purl to last 3 sts, p2tog, p1. (If you need help with p2tog — purling 2 stitches together — look to Chapter 6.)

Next row (RS): Knit.

Repeat the previous 2 rows 1 more time. There are 13 (14, 15, 16, 18) sts.

Work even until your piece measures 2 inches from the beginning of neck shaping, or until it's the same length as the back to the beginning of shoulder shaping, ending with a RS row.

### Right shoulder shaping

Next row (WS): Bind off 4 (4, 5, 5, 6) sts, purl to end of row.

Next row (RS): Knit.

Next row (WS): Bind off 4 (5, 5, 5, 6) sts, purl to end of row.

Next row (RS): Knit.

Next row (WS): Bind off remaining 5 (5, 5, 6, 6) sts.

### Left neck

Replace the held stitches of the left shoulder on the needle with the RS facing. Rejoin yarn at side edge.

Next row (RS): Knit to last 3 sts, k2tog tbl, k1. (If you're unfamiliar with k2tog tbl, head to Chapter 12.)

Next row (WS): Purl.

Repeat the previous 2 rows 1 more time. There are 13 (14, 15, 16, 18) sts.

Work even until your piece measures 2 inches from the beginning of neck shaping, or until it's the same length as the back to the beginning of shoulder shaping, ending with a WS row.

### Left shoulder shaping

Next row (RS): Bind off 4 (4, 5, 5, 6) sts, knit to end of row.

Next row (WS): Purl.

Next row (RS): Bind off 4 (5, 5, 5, 6) sts, knit to end of row.

Next row (WS): Purl.

Next row (RS): Bind off remaining 5 (5, 5, 6, 6) sts.

## Making the sleeves

Sew together shoulder seams of front and back with mattress stitch (see the appendix for more info). Place removable markers or safety pins 4½ (5, 5½, 6, 7) inches down from the shoulder seam along 1 side edge of the front and back so that you have 2 markers 9 (10, 11, 12, 14) inches apart.

With larger needles, and a crochet hook if desired, pick up and knit 41 (45, 49, 55, 63) sts between the 2 markers. See Chapter 10 for the details on working this maneuver along straight edges.

Rows 1, 2, 3, 4, and 5: Work 5 rows in stockinette stitch, beginning with a purl row.

Next row (RS): K1, ssk, knit to last 3 sts, k2tog, k1.

Repeat these 6 rows 8 (9, 10, 11, 13) more times. There are 23 (25, 27, 31, 35) sts.

Continue in stockinette stitch without decreasing until the sleeve measures 11 (12, 13, 14, 15) inches.

Switch to smaller needles and work 6 rows in stockinette stitch.

Bind off.

Make the second sleeve the same as the first.

## Knitting the collar

Attach the yarn at the right shoulder, and with the smaller-sized 16-inch circular needle, knit the 26 (28, 30, 32, 32) sts from the back neck holder, pick up and knit 13 sts along the left side of the front neck, knit the 22 (24, 26, 28, 28) sts from the front neck holder, pick up 13 sts along the right side of the front neck. There are 74 (78, 82, 86, 86) sts. (See the earlier section "New skill: Picking up neckline stitches" for more on picking up neckline stitches.)

Place a marker, join in the round, and work in stockinette stitch (knitting all rounds) for 1 inch to create a rolled collar.

Bind off all sts loosely using larger needles. Weave in any loose ends.

You never want a collar to be too tight to go over someone's head, especially if that someone is a kid. Nothing will cause a child to run screaming from your handknits faster than a neck that's too tight (well, except maybe itchy yarn). Binding off with larger needles (2 or 3 sizes up) will give the neck plenty of stretch.

## Finishing your sweater

Block your sweater to the measurements given in Figure 13-7. Sew the side seams and sleeve seams using mattress stitch. (I cover blocking and seaming in the appendix.)

## Variation: Short sleeves

Make this top into your child's favorite easygoing tee by making short sleeves.

The yarn and materials for this variation are all the same as in the basic pattern. But, if you want to change the yarn, you can use any comfy, child-friendly aran weight yarn. Your row gauge isn't significant here as long as you like the fabric of your swatch and you're able to comfortably knit 18 stitches per 4 inches.

Make the front, back, and collar the same as described in the basic pattern.

To make the sleeves: Sew together the shoulder seams of the front and back. Place removable markers or safety pins 4½ (5, 5½, 6, 7) inches down from the shoulder seam on the front and back so that you have 2 markers 9 (10, 11, 12, 14) inches apart.

With larger needles (and a crochet hook), pick up and knit 41 (45, 49, 55, 63) sts between the 2 markers. (See Chapter 10 to find out more about picking up stitches along a straight edge.)

Work 3 rows in stockinette stitch, beginning with a purl row.

Next row (RS): K1, ssk, knit to last 3 sts, k2tog, k1.

Repeat the previous 4 rows 1 (1, 3, 3, 4) more time(s). There are 37 (41, 41, 47, 53) sts. Continue in stockinette stitch without decreasing until your sleeve measures 2 (2, 3, 3, 4) inches.

Switch to smaller needles and work 6 rows in stockinette stitch to form a rolled edge.

Bind off.

Make the second sleeve the same as the first.

# Variation: Cables

Adding a single horseshoe cable up the front of this sweater is a great way to jazz it up. Even though the horseshoe cable looks complex, it's really just a four-stitch left cable and a four-stitch right cable that are worked right next to one another. Make the back and sleeves the same as the basic pattern described earlier, with long or short sleeves. You can find a detailed photo of the horseshoe cable and more information on cabling in Chapter 6. For this variation, you need the same materials as the basic pattern, plus 2 stitch markers and a cable needle.

### Front

With smaller needles, cast on 18 (20, 22, 24, 26) sts, place marker, cast on 16 sts, place marker, and then cast on 18 (20, 22, 24, 26) sts. You have 52 (56, 60, 64, 68) sts, with the center 16 sts marked for an eight-stitch cable with 4 reverse stockinette sts on either side.

Row 1 (RS): Knit to first marker, slip marker, p4, k8, p4, slip marker, knit to end of row.

Row 2 (WS): Purl to first marker, slip marker, k4, p8, k4, slip marker, purl to end of row.

Rows 3 and 4: Repeat Rows 1 and 2.

Row 5 (RS): Knit to first marker, slip marker, p4, sl 2 sts to cable needle and hold to front of work, k2, k2 from cable needle, sl 2 sts to cable needle and hold to back of work, k2, k2 from cable needle, p4, slip marker, knit to end of row.

Row 6 (WS): Purl to first marker, slip marker, k4, p8, k4, slip marker, purl to end of row.

Switch to larger needles and repeat Rows 1–6 until your piece measures 11 (12, 13, 15, 17) inches, with edges rolled, ending with a WS row.

**Neck shaping:** Knit 15 (16, 17, 18, 20) sts and slip them to a holder for the left shoulder, work across center 22 (24, 26, 28, 28) sts, maintaining cable pattern, and then slip them to a holder for the front neck, knit remaining 15 (16, 17, 18, 20) sts.

Work the remaining neck and shoulder shaping the same as in the basic pattern, starting with right neck.

### Collar

Pick up the stitches for the collar and knit it as described in the basic pattern, but maintain the cable pattern over the 16 stitches between the markers until the collar is complete.

# Men's Rollneck Pullover

I think of the pullover in Figure 13-7 as the perfect men's weekend sweater. It has simple lines and a slightly rugged look. It's casual and comfortable like a favorite sweatshirt, but never sloppy. Knit it in his favorite colors or skip the striping altogether if you (or he!) would prefer. See the later variations for more thoughts on colors.

**Figure 13-7:** A casual rollneck sweater for men.

## New skill: Setting in sleeves in a new way

Sleeves, or more specifically the tops of sleeves, are tricky business in knitting. You can shape sleeve caps in several ways. The simplest way has a straight edge at the top of the sleeve, which makes it easy to knit and easy to put together. This sleeve cap shape is called a *drop shoulder* because the top of the sweater is as wide as the chest and therefore extends beyond the shoulder and down the arm. The drop shoulder is a great choice for a T-shirt or a sweatshirt, but it doesn't fit the body as well as a sleeve that has some shape at the armhole, which is usually called a *set-in sleeve*. Setting in the sleeve means that the shoulder of the sweater sits somewhere close to your actual shoulder.

To make a more body-conscious fit, first you shape the armhole on the front and back of the sweater, which isn't very complicated. You simply bind off a few stitches, decrease gradually for a few rows, and then you're done. The only problem with set-in sleeves is that then you have to make a sleeve cap that fits right into the curve you've made at the armhole. You're matching a convex curve and a concave curve, plus the knitting on the sleeve comes in at a different angle than the knitting on the body — and that takes a fair amount of math and know-how. And while I love the Pythagorean theorem, I realize that you may not.

Consider for a moment the architecture of a sleeve cap: It looks a lot like a mountain. Looking at Figure 13-8, you can see a flat part at the bottom on each side — the plain before the start of the slope. You always have exactly the same number of stitches here as the initial bind-off for the armhole because these two parts come together to create the underarm. From there, you have a gradual slope up to the top of the sleeve cap where it levels off, forming the top of the slope — the summit of the sleeve cap mountain, if you will. The summit of a sleeve cap is typically somewhere between 2 and 6 inches across for adults.

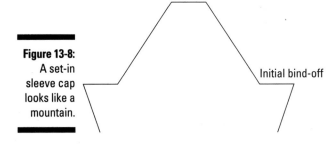

**Figure 13-8:**
A set-in sleeve cap looks like a mountain.

You can knit a set-in sleeve cap from the bottom up, which is the traditional method (I use it in the two women's pullovers in Chapter 14). But this semi-detached, top-down method isn't any more difficult, and the result is nearly foolproof. Have some faith as you walk through the steps. If nothing else, at least try it once before you disagree.

The sleeve you're about to knit is actually knit backwards. That is, you knit it from the top down. You start at the summit, and then you increase to create the gradual slope. Finally, you cast on the final number of stitches on each side for the underarm. From there, it's just what you'd expect: regular gradual decreases to the wrist.

The beauty of this semi-detached sleeve is that it doesn't really matter how you knit the armhole on the sweater. You don't have to do any math. You just have a little conversation with your sweater as you go along, and when the cap fits into the armhole, you stop. Another advantage of this method is that it allows you to try the sweater on and see if you want to make your sleeves shorter or longer than the pattern recommends.

To knit this set-in sleeve, follow these steps:

1. **Sew the front and back of the sweater together at the shoulders.**

2. **Measure down the prescribed amount on each side of the shoulder seam and place a stitch marker.**

   In this pattern, you measure down 3 inches on each side, which gives you a summit measurement of 6 inches.

3. **Pick up and knit your gauge per inch times 6 between the markers.**

   For this sweater, that's 22 stitches because 3¾ stitches per inch times 6 inches is about 22. See Chapter 10 for more information on the pick up and knit technique.

4. **Purl on the first row and on all following wrong-side rows.**

5. **On the next row, and the following right-side rows, increase 1 stitch at each edge.**

6. **Repeat Steps 4 and 5 until the sleeve cap fits into the armhole.**

   To find out if your sleeve cap fits into the armhole, lay your sweater flat on the table so that neither piece is stretched out of shape. Verify that the slope of your sleeve fits into the armhole to the point of the initial armhole decreases, by matching up the two sides, or if you prefer, by measuring each with a measuring tape. If it does, continue to the next step; if it doesn't, take out a few rows or continue repeating the 2 sleeve cap rows until it does. Don't worry if this changes your stitch count.

   Figure 13-9 shows what the sleeve cap should look like when you're ready to move on.

7. **At the beginning of the next 2 rows, cast on the stitches needed to match the initial underarm bind-off.**

   If you're experimenting with this technique in other patterns, you can find the number you need in the first lines in the armhole shaping section. These directions will say something like "Bind off 7 sts at the beginning of the next 2 rows."

8. **Continue knitting the sleeve from the underarm to wrist.**

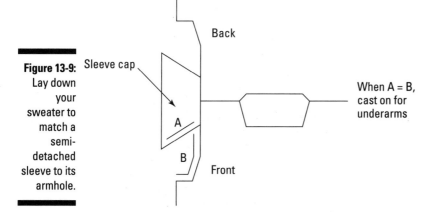

**Figure 13-9:** Lay down your sweater to match a semi-detached sleeve to its armhole.

## Materials and vital statistics

✔ **Yarn:** Cascade Pastaza (50% llama, 50% wool); 132 yards (122 meters) per 50 grams

   • **Main color (MC):** 026 Grey; 6 (7, 7, 8, 8) skeins

   • **Contrasting color 1 (CC1):** 065 Maroon; 2 (3, 3, 3, 4) skeins

   • **Contrasting color 2 (CC2):** 077 Mustard; 1 (1, 1, 1, 1) skein

✔ **Needles:** US 9 (5.5 mm) needles, or the size needed to match gauge; US 7 (4.5 mm) needles; US 7 (4.5 mm) circular needle, 16- or 24-inch length

✔ **Other materials:** Two stitch holders; 2 removable stitch markers or safety pins; crochet hook; yarn needle

✔ **Size:** Men's S (M, L, 1X, 2X) to fit actual chest size of 36 (40, 44, 48, 52) inches

   • **Finished chest circumference:** 40 (44, 48, 52, 56) inches

   • **Finished length:** 26 (27, 28, 29, 30) inches

Figure 13-10 is the schematic of the finished dimensions

✔ **Gauge:** 15 stitches and 20 rows per 4 inches in stockinette stitch on larger needles

The back and front of this sweater are worked separately and then joined at the shoulders. From there, you pick up and knit the sleeves and neck. This means that the finishing on this sweater is straightforward. See my advice on picking colors or making this sweater for women in the variation sections that follows the basic pattern.

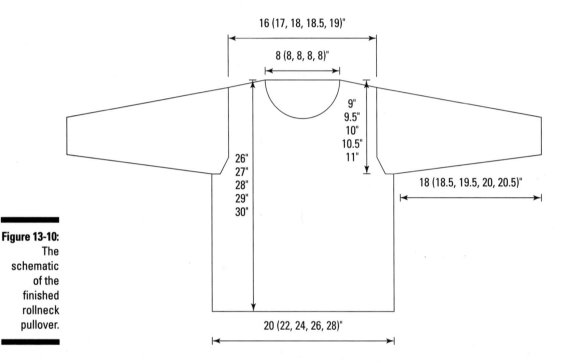

**Figure 13-10:**
The schematic of the finished rollneck pullover.

# Starting with the back

With larger needles and CC2, cast on 74 (82, 90, 98, 106) sts.

Switch to smaller needles and work 6 rows in stockinette stitch (knit a row, purl a row) with CC2 to form a rolled edge. Don't cut CC2.

Switch to larger needles, join CC1, and work 2 rows in CC1 in stockinette stitch.

Don't weave in more ends than you have to! When you're working a two-row stripe, you can simply carry the unused color loosely up the edge of the work. This shortcut saves you yarn — and the hassle of weaving in extra ends. (See Chapter 8 for more info on changing colors.)

Switch back to CC2 and work 2 rows. Cut CC2, leaving a 6-inch tail.

Continue in stockinette stitch using CC1 for 6 inches, ending with a purl row.

Join MC and work 2 rows.

Work 2 rows with CC1. Cut CC1.

Continue in stockinette stitch using MC until sweater measures 16 (16½, 17, 17½, 18) inches, ending with a purl row.

Don't unroll the hem; let it roll naturally and measure from the bottom of the roll.

### Armhole shaping

Bind off 3 (3, 4, 5, 6) sts at the beginning of the next 2 rows.

Next row (RS): K1, ssk, knit to last 3 sts, k2tog, k1. (If you're unfamiliar with k2tog, head to Chapter 6.)

Next row (WS): Purl.

Repeat the previous 2 rows 3 (5, 6, 8, 10) more times. There are 60 (64, 68, 70, 72) sts.

Work even until the sweater measures 9 (9½, 10, 10½, 11) inches from the beginning of the armhole shaping, ending with a purl row.

### Shoulder shaping

Bind off 5 (5, 6, 6, 7) sts at the beginning of the next 2 rows.

Bind off 5 (6, 6, 7, 7) sts at the beginning of the next 2 rows.

Bind off 5 (6, 7, 7, 7) sts at the beginning of the next 2 rows.

Slip remaining 30 sts to a holder to pick up later for the collar.

## Moving to the front

Follow the directions for the back through the armhole shaping. There are 60 (64, 68, 70, 72) sts.

Work even until your piece measures 23 (24, 25, 26, 27) inches, ending with a purl row.

### Neck shaping

Next row (RS): K20 (22, 24, 25, 26) and slip these sts to a holder for the left shoulder, knit center 20 sts (for all sizes), and then put them on a holder for the front neck, k20 (22, 24, 25, 26).

Now work each side of the neck separately.

### Right neck

Next row (WS): Purl.

Next row (RS): K1, ssk, knit to end of row.

Repeat the previous 2 rows 4 more times. There are 15 (17, 19, 20, 21) sts.

Work even until this side measures 9 (9½, 10, 10½, 11) inches from the beginning of the armhole shaping, ending with a knit row.

### Right shoulder shaping

Next row (WS): Bind off 5 (5, 6, 6, 7) sts, purl to end of row.

Next and following RS rows: Knit.

Next row (WS): Bind off 5 (6, 6, 7, 7) sts, purl to end of row.

Next row (RS): Knit.

Next row: Bind off remaining 5 (6, 7, 7, 7) sts.

### Left neck

Replace the held stitches of the left shoulder on the needle with the WS facing. Rejoin yarn at neck edge.

Next row (WS): Purl.

Next row (RS): Knit to last 3 sts, k2tog, k1.

Repeat the previous 2 rows 4 more times. There are 15 (17, 19, 20, 21) sts.

Work even until this side measures 9 (9½, 10, 10½, 11) inches from the beginning of the armhole shaping, ending with a purl row.

### Left shoulder shaping

Next row (RS): Bind off 5 (5, 6, 6, 7) sts, knit to end of row.

Next row (WS): Purl.

Next row (RS): Bind off 5 (6, 6, 7, 7) sts, knit to end of row.

Next row (WS): Purl.

Next row (RS): Bind off remaining 5 (6, 7, 7, 7) sts.

## Making the sleeves

Sew the front and back together at shoulder seams with mattress stitch (see the appendix for more details). Measure 3 inches down from the shoulder seam on the front and back and place markers or safety pins so that you have 2 markers that are 6 inches apart.

With larger needles and MC and with RS facing you, pick up and knit 22 sts between the 2 markers.

Next row (WS): Purl.

Next row (RS): K1, m1, knit to last st, m1, k1.

The abbreviation m1 stands for "make 1." For more details, see Chapter 14.

Repeat these 2 rows 12 (15, 16, 18, 21) more times. There are 48 (54, 56, 60, 66) sts.

Your sleeve cap should reach the underarm at this point. (See the earlier section "New skill: Setting in sleeves in a new way" for guidance.)

Purl 1 more row. Cast on 3 (3, 4, 5, 6) sts at the beginning of the next 2 rows. There are 54 (60, 64, 70, 78) sts.

Work 4 more rows in stockinette stitch, and then begin decreasing as follows:

Next row (Decrease Row) (RS): K1, ssk, knit to last 3 sts, k2tog, k1.

*Note:* Read ahead! You'll switch colors before you complete the upcoming decrease sequence.

Repeat the decrease row every 6th row 11 (13, 9, 7, 7) more times and then every 4th row 0 (0, 5, 9, 12) times. There are 30 (32, 34, 36, 38) sts.

If pattern directions for your size tell you to do something 0 times, you don't do it at all.

Continue decreasing as set, and when the sleeve measures 9 (9½, 10½, 11, 11½) inches from the underarm, switch to CC1.

When decreasing is complete, you'll have 30 (32, 34, 36, 38) sts. Work even until sleeve measures 17 (17½, 18½, 19, 19½) inches from the underarm.

Add CC2 and work 2 rows. Don't cut CC2.

Work 2 rows with CC1. Cut CC1.

Switch to CC2 and smaller needles. Continue in stockinette stitch for 6 rows. Your sleeve should measure 18 (18½, 19½, 20, 20½) inches with cuff rolled.

Bind off loosely, using larger needles.

Work the second sleeve the same way.

## Knitting the collar

If you haven't knit a collar before, check out the section "New skill: Picking up neckline stitches" earlier in this chapter.

Using the circular needle and MC, with the RS facing out, start at the right shoulder and knit the 30 sts from the back neck holder, pick up and knit 12 sts along the left side of the front neck, knit the 20 sts from the front neck holder, and then pick up and knit 12 sts along the right side of the front neck. There are 74 sts on the needle.

Place a marker, join in the round, and begin working in k1, p1 rib as follows:

Round 1: *K1, p1, repeat from * to end of round.

Repeat this round for 1 inch, and then work 8 rounds in stockinette stitch (knit all rounds). Bind off loosely with larger needles.

Cast-on and bound-off edges don't stretch like the rest of your knitting, so binding off with larger needles helps keep the neckband from being too tight.

## Finishing your sweater

Block the sweater to the measurements given in Figure 13-10. Sew the sleeve cap into the armhole, matching the cast-on stitches at the bottom of the sleeve cap to the bound-off edges of the underarm shaping. Sew the sleeve and body seams. Weave in all ends. See the appendix for more information about blocking and seaming.

## Variation: Showing your man's true colors

Some men appreciate some zingy color. Others appreciate colors like taupe. Know who you're knitting for and then knit him something he'll actually wear. I don't believe in the sweater curse — that fable that says if you knit a man a sweater too early in a relationship you're dooming the relationship to fail. But, I do know that I would curse if I poured my love into a sweater that he never wore. When in doubt, ask! Here are some options:

- ✔ **The almost-vanilla option:** Choose a classic guy color for the sweater (for most men that's grey, navy, or taupe) and work only the rolled edges — that is, the first inch of the sweater and the last inch of the sleeves and collar — in a contrasting color. Because these bands will roll, you'll have just a little pop of a stronger color.

- ✔ **The spumoni option:** If you're knitting for someone with bolder tastes you can go for this option. Choose a print yarn or a self-striping yarn and go for it.

- ✔ **The sorbet option:** If your man lives in a warmer climate or finds a wooly sweater too hot or too itchy, choose a cotton or silk blend yarn instead. A yarn that lists its gauge as 15 stitches per 4 inches is what you're looking for.

# Manly Sweater

This pattern helps you create a men's V-neck sweater with classic detailing that will never go out of style (take a look at Figure 13-11). This sweater is knit with a relatively fine-gauged yarn so that it can be worn comfortably indoors and out.

**Figure 13-11:**
A classic V-neck sweater for men.

# New skill: Binding off in rib

When you *bind off in knit,* you create a little chain of stitches that looks a lot like a crochet chain on the side facing you. When you *bind off in purl,* you put this chain on the opposite side. *Binding off in rib* puts this chain in the middle — on the edge — where it's inconspicuous. Usually when you're working ribbing at the edge of a garment, you want to bind the stitches off in rib so that the bound-off edge matches the knitting.

To bind off in rib, work the first 2 stitches as they appear, and then slip the first stitch worked over the most recently completed stitch, just as you do when you bind off in knit (see the appendix for more on binding off in knit). To bind off in 1 x 1 rib, follow these steps:

1. **Knit the first stitch and purl the second stitch.**

   There are 2 stitches on the right needle.

2. **With the yarn still at the front of the work in the purl position, slip the right-most stitch (the knit stitch) over the most recently worked stitch (the purl stitch) and off the needle.**

3. **Bring the yarn to the back of the work and knit the third stitch.**

4. **Slip the rightmost stitch over the stitch just worked.**

5. **Continue binding off in this manner, knitting the knit stitches and purling the purl stitches, until all the stitches are bound off.**

## Materials and vital statistics

- **Yarn:** Rowan Felted Tweed (50% merino wool, 25% alpaca, 25% viscose); 189 yards (175 meters) per 50 grams; 8 (9, 10, 11, 12) skeins; color: Ginger

- **Needles:** US 5 (3.75 mm) needles, or the size needed to match gauge; US 3 (3.25 mm) needles; US 3 (3.25 mm) circular needle, 16- or 24-inch length

- **Other materials:** Two stitch markers; yarn needle; a crochet hook; 2 removable stitch markers or safety pins

- **Size:** Men's S (M, L, 1X, 2X) to fit chest size of 36 (40, 44, 48, 52) inches
  - **Finished chest circumference:** 40 (44, 48, 52, 56) inches
  - **Finished length:** 26 (27, 28, 29, 30) inches

  Figure 13-12 is a schematic of the finished dimensions

- **Gauge:** 24 stitches and 32 rows per 4 inches in stockinette stitch on larger needles

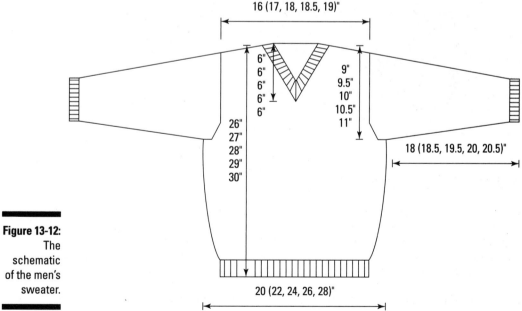

**Figure 13-12:** The schematic of the men's sweater.

This classic men's sweater is created with a slightly unusual technique. You knit the back and front, and then pick up stitches for the sleeve at the shoulder and create a set-in sleeve cap from the top down. Refer to the earlier section "New skill: Setting in sleeves in a new way" if you need help with this technique. After that, you pick up and knit the V-neck collar. If a crew neck is more his style, knit the variation that follows the basic pattern.

# Starting with the back

Cast on 120 (132, 144, 156, 168) sts on smaller needles.

Work in knit 1, purl 1 rib as follows:

Row 1 (RS): K1, *k1, p1, repeat from * to last st, k1.

Row 2 (WS): P1, *k1, p1, repeat from * to last st, p1.

Repeat these 2 rows until the ribbing measures 2 inches.

Switch to stockinette stitch (knit a row, purl a row) and larger needles. Continue in stockinette stitch until the back measures 16 (16½, 17, 17½, 18) inches, ending with a purl row.

## Armhole shaping

Bind off 4 (5, 6, 8, 9) sts at the beginning of the next 2 rows.

Next row (RS): K1, ssk, knit to last 3 sts, k2tog, k1. (Flip to Chapter 6 to learn about ssk and k2tog.)

Next row (WS): Purl.

Repeat the previous 2 rows 7 (9, 11, 13, 16) more times. There are 96 (102, 108, 112, 116) sts.

Continue in stockinette stitch until the armhole measures 9 (9½, 10, 10½, 11) inches and the back measures 25 (26, 27, 28, 29) inches, ending with a purl row, and then begin shoulder shaping.

## Shoulder shaping

Bind off 6 (6, 7, 8, 8) sts at the beginning of the next 2 rows.

Bind off 6 (7, 7, 8, 8) sts at the beginning of the next 2 rows.

Bind off 6 (7, 8, 8, 9) sts at the beginning of the next 2 rows.

Bind off 6 (7, 8, 8, 9) sts at the beginning of the next 2 rows.

Bind off remaining 48 sts.

# Moving to the front

Work the front the same as the back through armhole shaping, until the sweater measures 18 (19, 20, 21, 22) inches.

Note that you'll continue working the armhole decreases as you shape the V-neck. Because you'll be working on the neck and armhole shaping simultaneously, read through all the directions before you start knitting.

When the front measures 18 (19, 20, 21, 22) inches and the armhole measures 2 (2½, 3, 3½, 4) inches, end with a purl row and begin shaping the neck. Count the stitches on the needle and place a marker in the center, evenly dividing the stitches.

Next row (RS): Knit to 3 sts before marker, k2tog, k1, remove the marker and slip all sts just worked to a holder for the left shoulder; k1, ssk, knit to end of row.

Now work each side of the neck separately, continuing with the armhole decreases as you shape the neckline.

### Right neck

Next row (WS): Purl.

Next row (RS): K1, ssk, knit to end of row.

Repeat the previous 2 rows 22 more times. There are 24 (27, 30, 32, 34) sts.

Work even until this side measures 9 (9½, 10, 10½, 11) inches from the beginning of armhole shaping, ending with a RS row, and then shape the shoulder.

### Right shoulder shaping

Row 1 (WS): Bind off 6 (6, 7, 8, 8) sts, purl to end of row.

Row 2 and following RS rows: Knit.

Row 3 (WS): Bind off 6 (7, 7, 8, 8) sts, purl to end of row.

Row 5 (WS): Bind off 6 (7, 8, 8, 9) sts, purl to end of row.

Row 7 (WS): Bind off remaining 6 (7, 8, 8, 9) sts.

### Left neck

Replace the held stitches for the left shoulder on the needle with the WS facing. Join yarn at neck edge and purl to end of row. Don't forget to complete the armhole decreases as you shape the neckline!

Next row (RS): Knit to last 3 sts, k2tog, k1.

Next row (WS): Purl.

Repeat the previous 2 rows 22 more times. There are 24 (27, 30, 32, 34) sts.

Work even until this side measures 9 (9½, 10, 10½, 11) inches from the beginning of armhole shaping, ending with a WS row, and then shape the shoulder.

### Left shoulder shaping

Row 1 (RS): Bind off 6 (6, 7, 8, 8) sts, knit to end of row.

Row 2 and following WS rows: Purl.

Row 3 (RS): Bind off 6 (7, 7, 8, 8) sts, knit to end of row.

Row 5 (RS): Bind off 6 (7, 8, 8, 9) sts, knit to end of row.

Row 7 (RS): Bind off remaining 6 (7, 8, 8, 9) sts.

## Making the sleeves

The sleeves on this sweater are knit semi-detached from the top down. See the earlier section "New skill: Setting in sleeves in a new way" for a detailed explanation on how to do this.

Sew the front and back together at the shoulder seams with mattress stitch (see the appendix for more details). Place a safety pin or removable marker 3 inches down from the shoulder seam along 1 armhole edge of both the front and back so that you have 2 markers that are 6 inches apart. Using larger needles, pick up and knit 36 sts between the 2 markers.

Next row (WS): Purl.

Next row (RS): K1, m1, knit to last st, m1, k1.

Repeat these 2 rows 20 (22, 24, 26, 28) more times. There are 78 (82, 86, 90, 94) sts.

Now is the time to see if your sleeve cap fits in the armhole. Lay your sweater down flat and verify that the slope of your sleeve fits into the armhole to the point of the initial decreases. If it does, continue following the pattern. If it doesn't, rip back or continue repeating the 2 sleeve cap rows until it does — don't worry if this changes your stitch count. When your sleeve cap is the right depth, end with a purl row and shape the underarm as follows:

Cast on 4 (5, 6, 8, 9) sts at the beginning of the next 2 rows. There are 86 (92, 98, 106, 112) sts.

Work 6 more rows in stockinette stitch, and then begin decreasing as follows:

Decrease Row (RS): K1, ssk, knit to last 3 sts, k2tog, k1.

Repeat the decrease row every 6th row 17 (19, 21, 19, 19) more times, and then every 4th row 0 (0, 0, 4, 6) more times. There are 50 (52, 54, 58, 60) sts.

If pattern directions for your size tell you to do something 0 times, you don't do it at all.

Work even until sleeve measures 16 (16½, 17½, 18, 18½) inches, or 2 inches shorter than your desired sleeve length, ending with a purl row.

Switch to smaller needles and work in rib as follows:

Row 1 (RS): K1 *k1, p1, repeat from * to last st, k1.

Row 2 (WS): P1, *k1, p1, repeat from * to last st, p1.

Repeat these 2 rows until the cuff measures 2 inches. Bind off loosely in rib, as I explain earlier in this chapter.

Work the second sleeve the same way.

## Knitting the collar

If you need help picking up stitches for the collar, see the earlier section "New skill: Picking up neckline stitches."

With the smaller circular needle, beginning at the right shoulder, pick up and knit 47 sts along the back of the neck, 48 sts along the left neck to center of the V, place marker, pick up and knit 48 sts along right neck. There are 143 sts. Join and begin working in the round.

Next round: *K1, p1, repeat from * to 3 sts before marker, k1, ssk, slip marker, k2tog, *k1, p1, repeat from * to end of round.

Next round: *K1, p1, repeat from * to 2 sts before marker, ssk, slip marker, k2tog, p1, *k1, p1, repeat from * to end of round.

Repeat these 2 rounds until ribbing measures 1 inch or the desired depth. Bind off loosely in rib.

## Finishing your sweater

Block the sweater to the measurements given in Figure 13-12. Sew the sleeve cap into the armhole, matching the cast-on stitches at the bottom of the sleeve cap to the bound-off edges of the underarm shaping. Sew the sleeve and body seams. Weave in all ends. See the appendix for more information on seaming and blocking.

## Variation: Crafting a crew neck

If you prefer a crew neck to a V-neck, work the back and sleeves the same as written in the basic pattern, and work the front the same through the section on armhole shaping. The materials, size, and gauge are the same here as they are in the V-neck sweater pattern.

### Front

When the front measures 23 (24, 25, 26, 27) inches, end with a WS row and begin shaping the neck.

**Neck shaping:** Next row (RS): K36 (39, 42, 44, 46) and slip these sts to a holder for the left side of the neck, bind off center 24 sts, knit to end of row.

Now work each side of the neck separately.

**Right neck:** Next row (WS): Purl.

Next row (RS): K1, ssk, knit to end of row.

Repeat the previous 2 rows 11 more times. There are 24 (27, 30, 32, 34) sts.

Work even until this side measures 9 (9½, 10, 10½, 11) inches from the beginning of armhole shaping, ending with a RS row, and then shape the shoulder.

**Right shoulder shaping:** Row 1 (WS): Bind off 6 (6, 7, 8, 8) sts, purl to end of row.

Row 2 and following RS rows: Knit.

Row 3 (WS): Bind off 6 (7, 7, 8, 8) sts, purl to end of row.

Row 5 (WS): Bind off 6 (7, 8, 8, 9) sts, purl to end of row.

Row 7 (WS): Bind off remaining 6 (7, 8, 8, 9) sts.

**Left neck:** Replace the held stitches on the needle with the WS facing. Join yarn at neck edge and purl to end of row.

Next row (RS): Knit to last 3 sts, k2tog, k1.

Next row (WS): Purl.

Repeat the previous 2 rows 11 more times. There are 24 (27, 30, 32, 34) sts.

Work even until this side measures 9 (9½, 10, 10½, 11) inches from the beginning of armhole shaping, ending with a WS row, and then shape the shoulder.

**Left shoulder:** Row 1 (RS): Bind off 6 (6, 7, 8, 8) sts, knit to end of row.

Row 2 and following WS rows: Purl.

Row 3 (RS): Bind off 6 (7, 7, 8, 8) sts, knit to end of row.

Row 5 (RS): Bind off 6 (7, 8, 8, 9) sts, knit to end of row.

Row 7 (RS): Bind off remaining 6 (7, 8, 8, 9) sts.

### Collar

You pick up stitches around the neck and complete the ribbed collar knitting in the round on the circular needle. If you need help picking up stitches for the collar, see the earlier section "New skill: Picking up neckline stitches."

With the RS facing out, start at the right shoulder and knit the 48 sts from the back neck holder, pick up and knit 27 sts along the left side of the front neck, knit the 24 sts from the front neck holder, and then pick up and knit 27 sts along the right side of the front neck. You should have 126 sts, but if your neckline is slightly smaller or larger, any even number is fine.

Next round: *K1, p1, repeat from * to end of round.

Repeat this round until ribbing measures 1 inch, or the desired depth. Bind off loosely in rib.

### Finishing

Block the sweater to the measurements given in Figure 13-12. Sew the sleeve caps into the armholes, matching the cast-on stitches at the bottom of the sleeve cap to the bound-off edges of the underarm shaping. Sew the sleeve and body seams. Weave in all ends. See the appendix for more information on seaming and blocking.

# Chapter 14

# Knitting Beyond Geometry Class

## In This Chapter

▶ Knitting raglan sweaters in one piece from the top down

▶ Making shapely pullovers for women

▶ Adding color and complexity with Fair Isle, mosaics, and lace

*E*arlier chapters focus on some pretty basic shapes, but the patterns presented in this final group move beyond the basic rectangle, triangle, or cylinder. While the shapes are more complex, the knitting isn't difficult. But it may demand a little more attention. I firmly believe that even the most complex knitting is only a series of small steps, each of which, on its own, isn't difficult to perform.

In this chapter, I provide two patterns for top-down cardigans — these are great fun to knit because they're worked in one piece and you can try them on as you go. Plus, both of these patterns offer lots of room for your own improvisations. Here are the two raglan cardigan patterns I introduce you to:

   ✔ A lightning fast knit with a zipper closure, which makes for a great outer layer on chilly days.

   ✔ A more refined cardigan with self-facing button bands and ribs on the lower portion.

I also offer two patterns for women's pullovers:

   ✔ The first features a scooped neck, waist shaping, and a wonderful Fair Isle band.

   ✔ The second features a V-neck, lace accents, and a cropped shape.

 You'll notice in examining these last two patterns that they're knit at the same gauge, which means you can easily mix and match between them to choose the features and shaping that you like. Both provide a truly flattering and feminine fit and offer plenty of options for making them your own, whether you want to experiment with mosaic or Fair Isle patterning or dainty lace.

## Bulky Zipped Cardigan

Most cardigans are knit in pieces (two fronts, a back, and the sleeves) and then they're sewn together. This process can be frustrating for some knitters because the pieces have to match up along certain critical seam lines. And, of course, the seams have to be sewn, which isn't every knitter's idea of fun.

Knitting from the top down (as you do in this pattern) is different, however, because the whole thing is worked in one piece. This means that all the pieces of the sweater "match" and you have to do very little finishing. What I like best about top-down raglan knitting, though, is that this technique allows you to try on the sweater at any point and see if you like the fit. If the chest is too small or the sleeve is too long, a quick test fitting tells you so that you can correct the error for a custom fit.

The cardigan in Figure 14-1 features raglan sleeves and a zip-up front as well as seed stitch borders and a collar. It's easy to wear and can easily take the place of a jacket in spring and fall. I've chosen a vibrant pink for mine, but this super-bulky yarn comes in all kinds of great colors.

**Figure 14-1:**
A zipped cardigan chases chills.

# New skill: Trying the make 1 increase

The increase I use in this raglan sweater is called *make 1*, which is usually abbreviated m1. Make 1 refers generically to any increase that's worked *between* stitches. This is in contrast to increases like kfb (see Chapter 11) that are worked *in* a stitch.

To work an m1, follow these steps:

1. **Knit to the spot where you want the increase.**

2. **Stick the left needle from back to front under the horizontal thread between stitches from back to front as shown in Figure 14-2.**

3. **Knit the stitch through the front loop as shown in the figure.**

**Figure 14-2:**
Lift the horizontal thread between stitches and knit it to make one extra stitch.

 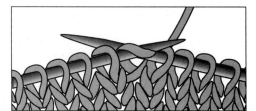

If knitting an m1 feels awkward, you're doing it right! You're twisting the stitch to prevent a hole from forming and making an inconspicuous increase.

If you want, you can skip the twist on all the m1 increases in this project. Doing so will result in paired eyelets along the raglan lines like mini yarn overs — a nice decorative feature (see Chapter 6 for more about yarn overs). Whether you choose to twist or not, be sure to work all the m1 increases the same.

To work an untwisted m1, follow these steps as shown in Figure 14-3:

1. **Stick the left needle under the horizontal bar thread between stitches from front to back.**

2. **Knit the stitch normally through the front loop.**

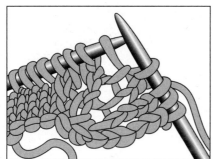

**Figure 14-3:**
Working an untwisted m1.

## *Materials and vital statistics*

- ✔ **Yarn:** Cascade Lana Grande (100% wool); 87 yards (80 meters) per 100 grams; 6 (6, 7, 8, 9) skeins; color: 6033 Magenta

- ✔ **Needles:** US 15 (10 mm) circular needles, 29-inch length or longer; US 15 (10 mm) circular needles, 16-inch length, or double-pointed needles

- ✔ **Other materials:** Ten large stitch markers or scraps of yarn tied in loops (2 should be different from the rest); 2 stitch holders; spare circular needles or lengths of scrap yarn; yarn needle to weave in ends; 1 20-inch separating zipper; straight pins; matching thread; sewing needle

- ✔ **Size:** Women's XS (S, M, L, 1X) or actual chest size of 30 (34, 38, 42, 46) inches

  - • **Finished chest circumference:** 36 (40, 44, 48, 52) inches

  - • **Finished length:** 23 (24, 24, 25, 25) inches

  See Figure 14-4 for detailed measurements

- ✔ **Gauge:** 10 stitches and 12 rows per 4 inches in stockinette stitch

Once you get going, this cardigan is smooth sailing, but there's a lot going on in the first few rows. On the setup row, you place a lot of markers. By doing so, you're accomplishing three things:

- ✔ Designating which stitches are the right front, right sleeve, back, left sleeve, and left front

- ✔ Making it easy to count how many stitches are on the right and left fronts with the 2 A markers (the 2 markers that are different from the rest)

- ✔ Marking off your 4 increase stitches with 1 of the 8 B markers on either side of each one

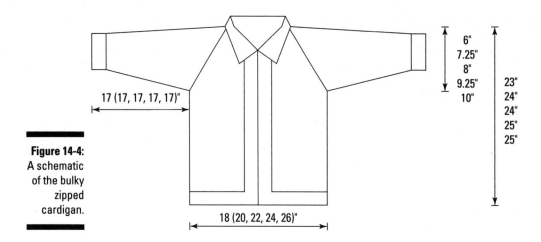

17 (17, 17, 17, 17)"

6"
7.25"
8"
9.25"
10"

23"
24"
24"
25"
25"

18 (20, 22, 24, 26)"

**Figure 14-4:**
A schematic
of the bulky
zipped
cardigan.

From there, you increase regularly at the markers forming the raglan lines between the sleeves and body sections. When the body (the back plus the two fronts) is the correct size, you move the sleeve stitches to holders, join the fronts and back, and complete the body in one piece. Then you go back and knit the sleeves from the underarm to the wrist. Finally, you pick up and knit the collar and finish by sewing in your zipper.

## Starting with the body

The stitches you cast on will form the neck, covering the two sides of the front, the sleeves, and the back. Using the long circular needle, cast on 32 sts. Don't join; the cardigan is worked back and forth in rows.

Setup Row (WS): P2, place marker A, place marker B, p1, place marker B, p4, place marker B, p1, place marker B, p16, place marker B, p1, place marker B, p4, place marker B, p1, place marker B, place marker A, p2.

Row 1 (RS): Kfb, knit to marker A, slip marker A, knit to marker B (there are no sts to knit between markers A and B in Row 1), m1, slip marker B, k1, slip marker B, m1, knit to marker B, m1, slip marker B, k1, slip marker B, m1, knit to marker B, m1, slip marker B, k1, slip marker B, m1, knit to marker B, m1, slip marker B, k1, slip marker B, m1, knit to marker A (there are no sts to knit between markers A and B in Row 1), slip marker A, knit to last 2 sts, kfb, k1. There are 42 sts.

"Kfb" stands for "knit into the front and back of the stitch." See Chapter 11 for more information.

Row 2 (WS): Purl.

Repeat these 2 rows once more. There are 4 sts outside the A marker on each side of the work and 52 sts on the needle.

You now add the final front sts and begin seed stitch bands on the front.

Row 5 (RS): Cast on 5 sts at the beginning of the row, (k1, p1) 3 times, k3, remove the A marker and, increasing with m1 as set before and after each set of B markers, knit to the end of the row. There are 65 sts.

Row 6 (WS): Cast on 5 sts at the beginning of the row, (k1, p1) 3 times, p3, remove A marker, purl to last 6 sts, (p1, k1) 3 times. There are 70 sts.

Row 7 (RS): (K1, p1) 3 times, knit across, increasing as set before and after each set of B markers, knit to last 6 sts, (p1, k1) 3 times. You have increased 8 sts.

Row 8 (WS): (K1, p1) 3 times, purl to last 6 sts, (p1, k1) 3 times.

Repeat the last 2 rows 7 (10, 12, 15, 17) more times, ending with a purl row. There are 38 (44, 48, 54, 58) sts between the markers for the back and 134 (158, 174, 198, 214) sts on the needle.

Now's the time to try your cardigan on! Slip some of the stitches onto a spare circular needle or onto scrap yarn and check the fit. If it's too loose, rip back a few rows and try it on again. If it's too tight, keep knitting. Remember that the body of the sweater will be about 3 inches wider than it is now because you'll be adding a few stitches at each underarm.

On the next row, you move the sleeve stitches to holders and continue on the body only, as follows:

Next row (RS): (K1, p1) 3 times, knit to first marker, remove marker, k1, remove marker; slip the next 26 (32, 36, 42, 46) sts to a spare circular needle or length of scrap yarn for the left sleeve; cast on 4 sts, remove next marker, k1, remove marker, knit across 38 (44, 48, 54, 58) back sts, remove marker, k1, remove marker; slip the next 26 (32, 36, 42, 46) sleeve sts to a spare circular needle or length of scrap yarn for the right sleeve; cast on 4 sts, remove next marker, k1, remove marker, knit to last 6 sts, (p1, k1) 3 times. There are 90 (102, 110, 122, 130) sts on the needle.

Continue working in stockinette stitch, maintaining the first and last 6 sts in seed stitch, until the sweater measures 20 (21, 21, 22, 22) inches, or 3 inches shorter than your desired finished length. Decrease 1 st (k2tog) at the center back when working the last row so that you have an odd number for the seed stitch pattern.

Next row: (K1, p1) to last st, k1.

Repeat this row for 3 inches. Bind off.

## *Moving to the sleeves*

Transfer the 26 (32, 36, 42, 46) sts from the first sleeve to a 16-inch circular needle or double-pointed needles.

Attach the yarn and knit across all the sts. Cast on 4 sts, placing a marker in the middle of these 4 new sts. This marker will now be the beginning of the round. Join and begin knitting in the round. There are 30 (36, 40, 46, 50) sts.

On the 8th (6th, 6th, 4th, 4th) round, work the decrease round as follows:

Decrease Round: K2tog tbl, knit to last 2 sts, k2tog. (To find out more about k2tog tbl, see Chapter 12. For more about k2tog, see Chapter 6.)

Repeat the decrease round every 8th (6th, 6th, 4th, 4th) round, 3 (5, 6, 8, 9) more times to 22 (24, 26, 28, 30) sts. Work even until the sleeve measures 14 inches, or 3 inches shorter than your desired length. Decrease 1 st with k2tog in the last round in preparation for seed stitch pattern.

Switch to seed stitch for cuff as follows:

Round 1: (K1, p1) to last st, k1.

Round 2: (P1, k1) to last st, p1.

Repeat these 2 rounds until cuff measures 3 inches. Bind off.

Make a second sleeve the same way.

## Knitting the collar

Using a US 15 circular needle of any length and working with the RS of the sweater facing you, begin at the right front neckline edge and pick up and knit 47 sts around the neck, ending at the left front neckline edge of the left front seed stitch band. Begin working in seed stitch as follows:

Row 1: (K1, p1) to last st, k1.

Work this row 13 more times, or until collar is the desired depth. Bind off.

## Finishing your cardigan

Weave in any loose ends and block the sweater as desired (see the appendix for blocking tips). Then you're ready to add the zipper to your sweater.

Follow these steps to sew in the zipper (and see Figure 14-5):

1. **Working from the right side (public side) of the sweater with the zipper closed, pin the zipper in place so that the edges of the knit fabric just cover the teeth of the zipper and meet in the center.**

   You may wish to try on the cardigan to make sure the zipper placement is correct.

2. **Baste the zipper in place with the needle and thread and then remove the pins.**

   In case you aren't a seamstress, *basting* is when you sew big, temporary stitches to hold something in place. Try the sweater on again at this point.

3. **Turn the sweater to the wrong side and stitch the zipper to the knitted fabric along the outside edge of the zipper tape on both the left and right sides.**

4. **Turn the sweater back to the right side and sew the zipper in place about ¼ inch in from the edge of the sweater.**

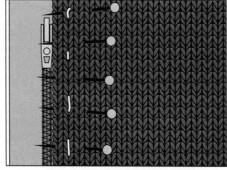
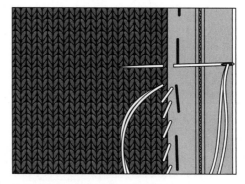

**Figure 14-5:** Attaching a zipper.

A. Pin the zipper in place (working from the right side).

B. Turn the work to the wrong side and whipstitch the zipper in place.

# Half-Ribbed Raglan Cardigan

Many raglan sweater patterns that are knit from the top down begin with a neckline that's sized to your actual neck measurement, which is somewhere between 13 and 16 inches. Considering you add a collar after that, you're dooming yourself to an uncomfortable and unflattering sweater right from the start!

My solution is to simply start with a larger neck measurement — say 20 or 22 inches. This solution gets rid of all that too-close-to-the-neck knitting and reduces the boxiness of the whole sweater.

Figure 14-6 shows the half-ribbed raglan cardigan. The top of the body and sleeves are worked in stockinette stitch. After you divide the sleeves from the body, you begin with the wide ribbed pattern. The ribs create visual interest and a nice clean line. The addition of smooth self-facing buttonbands and a collar make it perfect for the office or casual days about town.

**Figure 14-6:**
A half-ribbed raglan cardigan has an easy-fitting neck.

While the lower portion of the body and sleeves are worked in a rib pattern, you can just as easily work small cables instead — see the variation at the end of the pattern.

## New skill: Fashioning self-facing buttonbands

As you know, a cardigan opens and closes. That's what's so great about it: It's easy to take off and put on, and you can wear it completely opened or closed or halfway in between, so you're never too hot or too cold.

The first cardigan in this chapter features a zipper, which is a great choice for easygoing outerwear to keep out the winter chill. But this cardigan, knit in a cotton and silk blend, is the sort of sweater you might wear all day: walking in the morning, working in your air-conditioned office, and perhaps enjoying a sunny lunch outdoors. Nice buttons dress it up and allow you to fasten it however you like. But because buttons (and buttonholes) need a place to be, you've got to make *buttonbands*.

Buttonbands are a debated topic in knitting because you can make them in lots of different ways. And, unfortunately, they're one of those things that can go wrong and make your sweater look handmade in precisely the way that you don't want it to. Buttonbands can be problematic because often they're knit on lengthwise after the front is done. If a knitter picks up too few stitches or binds off too tightly, the buttonband is too short and cinches the sweater along the front. If she doesn't measure her gauge over rib accurately or picks up too many stitches, the buttonband is too long and looks like a bad ruffle.

To avoid these frustrating situations, I like a pattern that creates a tidy buttonband at the same time as the rest of the sweater. For this sweater, I chose a simple stockinette self-faced buttonband. *Self-facing* means that you essentially line the buttonbands by knitting extra stitches on each front edge separated by a slipped stitch from the rest of the sweater. The slipped stitch creates a nice smooth fold as the extra fabric you've knit is turned under to the wrong side and sewn in place. This sort of buttonband is also extra sturdy because of the double layer, so it stands up to lots of wear. These buttonbands are finished when the sweater's finished — and they always turn out just right.

Here's what you have to do to make your self-facing buttonband:

1. **Determine the desired width of your buttonband.**

   For example, this cardigan has a buttonband that measures 1 inch.

2. **Because the facing needs to be as wide as the buttonband, when you cast on for each side of the front of your sweater, cast on an additional inch worth of stitches plus 1.**

   For example, the gauge for this sweater is 4 stitches per inch, so I cast on 5 extra stitches on each side. Be sure that the extra stitches are placed on the inside edge where the sweater will close.

3. **Knit the buttonband.**

   On right-side rows: Knit the inch of stitches, slip 1, and then carry on with the pattern as described.

   On wrong-side rows: Purl all the extra stitches.

4. **Knit the buttonhole band by making two buttonholes, one for the right side of the buttonband and one for the facing.**

   For example, in this sweater pattern, the buttonhole row is worked like this: K2, yo, k2tog, sl 1, k2tog, yo, k2. The (yo, k2tog) creates the buttonhole in the facing and the (k2tog, yo) creates the buttonhole on the right side of the buttonhole band.

5. **Continue making the facing and the buttonbands as you knit the cardigan. Bind off the extra stitches when you bind off the buttonband.**

6. **When the sweater is done, turn the facings under, folding along the columns of slipped stitches, and then sew them in place on the wrong side.**

## New skill: Decreasing in rib

In this raglan cardigan pattern, you decrease within the rib pattern on the sleeves. This decreasing technique is slightly more complicated than decreasing over stockinette stitch because you need to keep your ribs lined up.

There are a couple of things to keep in mind when decreasing in rib. First, always work the stitches as they appear — you want to knit the knits and purl the purls. This takes care of the part between the decreases and helps keep your ribs in line.

But what about the decreases themselves? Because you're eating into a pattern that's already established, the first 2 stitches (and the last 2 stitches) may sometimes be 2 knit stitches, other times they'll be 2 purl stitches, and sometimes there will be 1 knit and 1 purl. What are you supposed to do?

Ask yourself, "If there were only 1 stitch here, what would it be?" You want to make the 2 stitches into what they should be in the next round. In other words, if it should be a knit stitch, then you should knit the 2 stitches together. If it should be a purl stitch, then you should purl them together. To butcher the mnemonic device you learned in second grade, "When two stitches go walking, the inner one (not the edge one) does the talking."

For this raglan cardigan pattern specifically, here are the guidelines:

> 2 knits = k2tog
>
> 2 purls = p2tog
>
> 1 knit, 1 purl at the beginning of a round = p2tog
>
> 1 knit, 1 purl at the end of a round = k2tog
>
> 1 purl, 1 knit at the beginning of a round = k2tog
>
> 1 purl, 1 knit at the end of a round = p2tog

Head to Chapter 6 for more about k2tog and p2tog.

## Materials and vital statistics

- ✔ **Yarn:** Rowan Summer Tweed (70% silk, 30% cotton); 117 yards (108 meters) per 50 grams; 9 (9, 10, 11, 12, 12) skeins; color: Toast

- ✔ **Needles:** US 8 (5 mm) circular needle, 32-inch length or longer, or the size needed to match gauge after blocking; US 8 (5 mm) circular needle, 16-inch length, or double-pointed needles; US 9 (5.5 mm) needles and US 10 (6 mm) needles for collar

- ✔ **Other materials:** Six stitch markers (2 of these markers should be different from the others); 2 spare circular needles or lengths of scrap yarn; yarn needle; 5 (5, 6, 6, 6, 6) ½-inch buttons

- ✔ **Size:** Women's S (M, L, 1X, 2X, 3X) or actual chest size of 34 (38, 42, 46, 50, 54) inches

  - • **Finished chest circumference (with sweater buttoned):** 37 (41½, 45, 48, 52½, 57) inches

  - • **Finished length:** 24 (24, 25, 25, 26, 26)

  See Figure 14-7 for a detailed schematic

- ✔ **Gauge:** 16 stitches and 24 rows per 4 inches in stockinette stitch

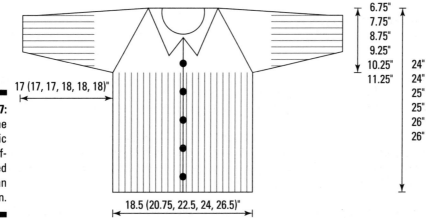

**Figure 14-7:** The schematic of the half-ribbed raglan cardigan.

6.75"
7.75"
8.75"
9.25"
10.25"      24"
11.25"      24"
            25"
17 (17, 17, 18, 18, 18)"      25"
            26"
            26"

18.5 (20.75, 22.5, 24, 26.5)"

This cardigan is worked from the top down, so you cast on for the two fronts, the sleeves, and the back all at once and work downward in stockinette stitch from the neck. After the sleeves and body are wide enough to fit you, you place the sleeve stitches on holders, join the fronts and back, and continue working down in a wide rib until the sweater is the right length. From there you go back to the sleeve stitches, working them in rib down to the wrist. Finally, you pick up and knit the collar.

Note that unlike the bulky zipped cardigan, this cardigan doesn't use m1 increases worked on either side of marked "increase stitches" but rather uses kfb increases on either side of the single markers.

## Starting with the body

Using the long circular needle, cast on 54 (54, 54, 58, 58, 58) sts.

Row 1 (WS): P1, place marker A, p1, place marker B, p10, place marker B, p30 (30, 30, 34, 34, 34), place marker B, p10, place marker B, p1, place marker A, p1.

Row 2 (RS): K1, m1, slip marker A, kfb, slip marker B, kfb, knit to 1 st before next marker, kfb, slip marker B, kfb, knit to 1 st before next marker, kfb, slip marker B, kfb, knit to 1 st before next marker, kfb, slip marker B, kfb, slip marker A, m1, k1. There are 64 (64, 64, 68, 68, 68) sts.

"Kfb" stands for "knit into the front and back of the stitch." See Chapter 11 for more information. Also, you can read more about "m1," which stands for "make 1 increase," in the earlier section "New skill: Trying the make 1 increase."

Row 3 (WS): Purl.

Row 4 (RS): K1, m1, knit to marker A, slip marker A, knit to 1 st before marker B, kfb, slip marker B, kfb, knit to 1 st before next marker, kfb, slip marker B, kfb, knit to 1 st before next marker, kfb, slip marker B, kfb, knit to 1 st before next marker, kfb, slip marker B, kfb, knit to marker A, slip marker A, knit to last st, m1, k1. You have increased 10 sts.

Repeat the last 2 rows 5 (5, 5, 6, 6, 6) more times, until there are 8 (8, 8, 9, 9, 9) sts outside the A marker on each side. There are 124 (124, 124, 138, 138, 138) sts.

You now cast on the remaining sts for the front neck and, at the same time, the self-facing buttonbands.

Next row (WS): Cast on 13 (13, 13, 14, 14, 14) sts at the beginning of the row, and then purl across all sts.

Next row (RS): Cast on 13 (13, 13, 14, 14, 14) sts at the beginning of the row, k4, sl 1, knit to marker A and remove it, knit to last st before marker B, kfb, slip marker, kfb, knit to last st before marker B, kfb, slip marker, kfb, knit to last st before marker B, kfb, slip marker, kfb, knit to last st before marker B, kfb, slip marker, kfb, knit to marker A and remove it, knit to last 5 sts, sl 1, k4. There are 158 (158, 158, 174, 174, 174) sts.

Next row (WS): Purl.

Row 1 (RS): The first and last 9 sts comprise the buttonbands. K4, sl 1, k4, *knit to 1 st before marker, kfb, slip marker, kfb, repeat from * 3 more times; knit to last 9 sts; k4, sl 1, k4. You have increased 8 sts.

Row 2 (WS): Purl.

Buttonhole Row (RS): K2, yo, k2tog, sl 1, k2tog, yo, k2, *knit to 1 st before marker, kfb, slip marker, kfb, repeat from * 3 more times; knit to last 9 sts; k4, sl 1, k4. There are 174 (174, 174, 190, 190, 190) sts.

The abbreviation "yo" stands for "yarn over"; head to Chapter 6 for more about this increase.

Next row (WS): Purl.

Repeat Rows 1 and 2 10 (14, 18, 19, 23, 27) more times, working the buttonhole row every 4 inches. There are 70 (78, 86, 94, 102, 110) sts between the 2 back markers and 254 (286, 318, 342, 374, 406) sts on the needle.

Now is a good time for a test fitting. Slip some of the stitches onto a spare circular needle or length of scrap yarn so that the stitches aren't bunched up and you can make an accurate assessment. If you hold the first 2 markers together at one underarm and the last 2 markers together at the other underarm, you'll get an idea of the fit. The best way to do this is to have a friend hold the markers together while you look in the mirror. Remember that the buttonbands will be folded under and that you'll add 2 inches to the overall width when you join for the underarm. If your cardigan is too wide, decide how many rows to unravel for a perfect fit, mark that spot with a safety pin, and rip back. Or, if the cardigan is still too tight, knit another few rows and try again.

Divide the sleeve stitches from the body and put them on holders as follows:

Next row (RS): K4, sl 1, knit to first marker; slip sleeve sts (the sts between the first and second markers) to a holder or length of scrap yarn; to join the front and back, cast on 4 sts for underarm, and then knit the 70 (78, 86, 94, 102, 110) back sts; slip the second set of sleeve sts to a holder or length of scrap yarn, cast on 4 sts for the second underarm, and then knit to the last 5 sts, sl 1, k4. There are 162 (178, 194, 210, 226, 242) sts on the needle and 50 (58, 66, 70, 78, 86) sts on each sleeve holder.

Next row (WS): Purl.

In order for the rib pattern to work out evenly, you need to decrease a couple of stitches for some sizes.

If you've altered your sweater for a custom fit and have a different number of stitches on the needle, you need to do a bit of math at this point. Follow these steps:

1. **Count the number of stitches on the needle and write that number here:** \_\_\_\_\_

2. **Subtract 18 for the buttonbands:** \_\_\_\_\_ – 18 = \_\_\_\_\_

3. **Subtract 2:** \_\_\_\_\_ – 2 = \_\_\_\_\_

4. **Divide by 6:** \_\_\_\_\_ ÷ 6 = \_\_\_\_\_

If, in Step 4, you come up with a whole number, you don't need to increase or decrease; follow the pattern as written. But if you come up with a fraction, such as 34.33, round down to the nearest whole number (in this case, 34) and follow these steps:

1. **Multiply the whole number by 6:** \_\_\_\_\_ × 6 = \_\_\_\_\_

2. **Add 2:** \_\_\_\_\_ + 2 = \_\_\_\_\_

3. **Add 18 for the buttonbands:** \_\_\_\_\_ + 18 = \_\_\_\_\_

The result of Step 3 is the number of stitches that you need to have on the needle. On the next row, decrease evenly across the row to get to this number.

Next row (RS): K4, sl 1, k4, decrease 4 (2, 0, 4, 2, 0) sts evenly across the row, end k4, sl 1, k4. There are 158 (176, 194, 206, 224, 242) sts.

If the pattern says to do something 0 times, don't do it at all.

Next row (WS): Purl.

From now on, you work the body back and forth without any increasing or decreasing. Continue working the first and last 9 sts as the buttonbands and continue making buttonholes every 4 inches as set.

Next row (RS): K4, sl 1, k4, *p2, k4, repeat from * to last 11 sts, p2, k4, sl 1, k4.

Next row (WS): P9, *k2, p4, repeat from * to last 11 sts, k2, p9.

Repeat the previous 2 rows until your sweater measures 24 (24, 25, 25, 26, 26) inches from shoulder, or your desired length.

Now it's time to try on your sweater to see if you like the length. If it's too short, continue in the rib pattern as set until you like the length. If it's too long, rip it back to the right length. When you're happy with the length, bind off loosely.

## Moving to the sleeves

To make the sleeves, you can use double-pointed needles rather than a single short circular needle.

Slip the held sts for one sleeve to the 16-inch circular needle. Rejoin yarn and pick up and knit 4 sts from the cast-on underarm sts, and then knit across the 50 (58, 66, 70, 78, 86) sleeve sts. There are now 54 (62, 70, 74, 82, 90) sts on the needle. Join in the round, k2 (to center of underarm sts) and place a marker to indicate the beginning of the round.

Knit 4 rounds.

Begin ribbing as follows: K2 (0, 4, 0, 1, 2), p2 *k4, p2, repeat from * to last 2 (0, 4, 0, 1, 2) sts, knit to end.

Next round (Decrease Round): Work first 2 sts together, p2 (0, 1, 0, 1, 2) *k4, p2, repeat from * to last 8 (6, 7, 6, 7, 8) sts, k4, p2 (0, 1, 0, 1, 2), work last 2 sts together.

When I say "work 2 stitches together," knit or purl them together depending on which sort of stitches you're looking at. See the earlier section "New skill: Decreasing in rib" for more info.

Work 2 sts together at the beginning and end of the round every 10th (8th, 6th, 6th, 4th, 4th) round 7 (10, 12, 14, 18, 19) more times, maintaining rib pattern. There are 38 (40, 44, 44, 44, 50) sts.

Continue in rib pattern as set until your sleeve measures 17 (17, 17, 18, 18, 18) inches from the underarm, or your desired length. Remember, you can try it on any time and see what length is right for you!

Make a second sleeve the same as the first.

## Crafting the collar

Because this polo collar folds over, you want to pick up stitches from the inside (the wrong side) of the sweater. Doing so hides any untidiness of picking up stitches under the collar and keeps the visible side smooth.

When a pattern says "the left side" or "the left armhole" which one does it mean? It means that when you're wearing it, that will be the one on the left. It may help you to imagine you're trying it on if you're still flummoxed.

With the WS facing you, start at the center of the buttonband on the left side and, with the longer circular needle, pick up and knit 6 sts before the neck shaping starts, 10 (10, 10, 14, 14, 14) sts along the left front neckline, pick up and knit the 54 (54, 54, 58, 58, 58) cast-on sts, 10 (10, 10, 14, 14, 14) sts along the right front neckline, and 6 sts along the horizontal edge of the right front neck, ending at the center of the buttonband. There are 86 (86, 86, 98, 98, 98) sts. (Head to Chapter 13 for details on picking up neckline stitches.)

Row 1: K2, *k4, p2, repeat from * to last 6 sts, k6.

Row 2: K2, *p4, k2, repeat from * to last 6 sts, p4, k2.

It's nice to have a polo collar that gradually increases so that the collar can fold over and lie gracefully around your neck. One way to do this is to increase a bit as you go. But with a rib pattern this technique can be fiddly and more complicated than it needs to be. My solution is to switch to larger- and larger-gauged needles as you go so that the outside edge of the collar is larger and has more drape (but the pattern remains uninterrupted).

Repeat Rows 1 and 2 until your collar measures 2 inches. Switch to needles that are one size larger than the ones you used to knit the sweater and continue in rib pattern for 2 more inches. Then move up one more needle size (to a needle that's two sizes larger than the one you used for the body of the sweater) and continue in rib until your collar measures 5 inches. Bind off loosely.

## Finishing your cardigan

Fold the buttonbands over to the inside of the sweater, using the column of slipped stitches as your fold line. Use a yarn needle to sew the edge of the buttonband to the inside of the sweater. Be sure to keep your buttonholes lined up!

Weave in any loose ends and block your sweater to the measurements given in Figure 14-7. See the appendix for blocking advice. Sew on buttons opposite the buttonholes.

## Variation: Using the perfect buttons

You've put a lot of effort into making your sweater, so be sure to put some effort into choosing the perfect buttons. Buttons can really make or break a cardigan. My advice on buttons is to wait until the sweater is done to choose them. Doing so assures you that you've chosen the proper size to fit into the buttonholes that you've created — and it's a heck of a lot easier to find buttons to fit your buttonholes than it is to make buttonholes that fit your buttons! Plus, the button that looks great next to your yarn in its on-the-skein form may not actually be the button that suits your finished sweater best.

There are millions of beautiful buttons out there. And your buttons don't all have to be the same — choose a variety of buttons of the same color or shape to add zest to something a little ho-hum. And don't forget that vintage stores or thrift shops are great places to look for unusual buttons.

# Women's Scoop-Neck Pullover

Turned under hems, waist shaping, and a scooped neck combine to give you the attractive and flattering top in Figure 14-8. Add in Fair Isle detailing at the hem and cuffs and you have a handknit that's sure to turn heads. (I give you the full scoop on Fair Isle color work in Chapter 7.) If Fair Isle isn't your cup of tea, try a mosaic motif — directions are given in the variation after the basic pattern. But because this top has such a great shape, it'll look great plain, too.

The pattern for the lacy V-neck top later in this chapter is knit at the same gauge as this one, so if you prefer a V-neck sweater, you can follow the neck shaping directions from that pattern.

**Figure 14-8:** The scoop-neck pullover with Fair Isle borders.

## Materials and vital statistics

- ✔ **Yarn:** Crystal Palace Yarns Creme (60% wool, 40% silk); 124 yards (114 meters) per 50 grams
  - **Main color (MC):** 2005 Buttercup; 9 (10, 11, 12, 14, 15) skeins
  - **Contrasting color 1 (CC1):** 2015 Henna; 1 skein
  - **Contrasting color 2 (CC2):** 2014 Russet; 1 skein
  - **Contrasting color 3 (CC3):** 2031 Vine Green; 1 skein
  - **Contrasting color 4 (CC4):** 2032 Royal Purple; 1 skein
- ✔ **Needles:** US 7 (4.5 mm) circular needle, 24-inch length, or the size needed to match gauge; US 6 (4 mm) circular needle, 24-inch length; US 5 (3.75 mm) circular needle, 24-inch length
- ✔ **Other materials:** Yarn needle; stitch markers or safety pins; stitch holder
- ✔ **Size:** S (M, L, 1X, 2X, 3X) or actual chest size of 34 (38, 42, 46, 50, 54) inches

- **Finished chest circumference:** 36½ (39½, 43, 49, 55½, 59) inches
- **Finished length:** 24½ (24½, 25, 25, 26, 26)

See the schematic in Figure 14-9 for detailed measurements of this sweater

✔ **Gauge:** 20 stitches and 24 rows per 4 inches in stockinette stitch and in Fair Isle pattern

This sweater has simple, clean lines that make it a classic, but the subtle detailing makes it flattering. You start by knitting a hem facing; it's just a couple of inches of stockinette stitch that's turned under and sewn in place when the sweater's done. The hem facing does away with the need for a border or ribs, so the line and the pattern of the sweater flows uninterrupted.

After that you add some color. You can follow the multicolor Fair Isle pattern that I use in the basic pattern, or, if you like, you can substitute one of the other Fair Isle or mosaic motifs given in Chapter 7; they've been specifically tailored to work for this top. Another option is to work the pullover in a single color. The shape of the sweater, combined with a butter-soft silk and wool yarn, will make it a wardrobe favorite no matter how you decide to color it.

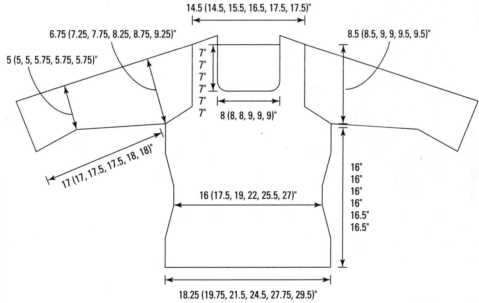

**Figure 14-9:** The measurements of the scoop-neck pullover.

After the color work is complete, you add a bit of waist shaping. A few decreases from the hip to the waist and a few increases from the waist to the chest make the fit on this sweater feminine. The front is worked the same as the back, but with a deep scoop neck. The sleeves, like the body, feature a turned-under hem facing and a repeat of the color work done on the body.

Many knitters knit stranded patterns, like Fair Isle, tighter than single-color stockinette. To avoid an inconsistent gauge, take time to swatch over both patterns. And, if necessary, work the Fair Isle portion with larger needles to keep your gauge consistent.

## Starting with the back

Using US 6 needles (or one size smaller than needed to match gauge), cast on 91 (99, 107, 123, 139, 147) sts with MC.

Work in stockinette stitch (knit a row, purl a row) for 10 rows, ending with a WS row.

Purl 1 RS row to create a turning ridge for the hem.

Switch to US 7 needles (or the size needed to match gauge) and continue in stockinette stitch for 1 inch, ending with a WS row.

### Fair Isle border

Begin the Fair Isle pattern, following the chart shown in Figure 14-10. To begin the color pattern, work the right selvedge stitch outside the dark line, work across the 8-stitch pattern between the dark lines 11 (12, 13, 15, 17, 18) times, and then work the 2 left selvedge stitches. Working these 3 selvedge (or edge) stitches keeps your pattern centered and gives you a stitch on each side for your seams.

When you're working a WS row, the 2 selvedge stitches at the left side of the chart are worked first, and then the chart repeat is worked 11 (12, 13, 15, 17, 18) times. Finally you work the selvedge stitch at the right side of the chart.

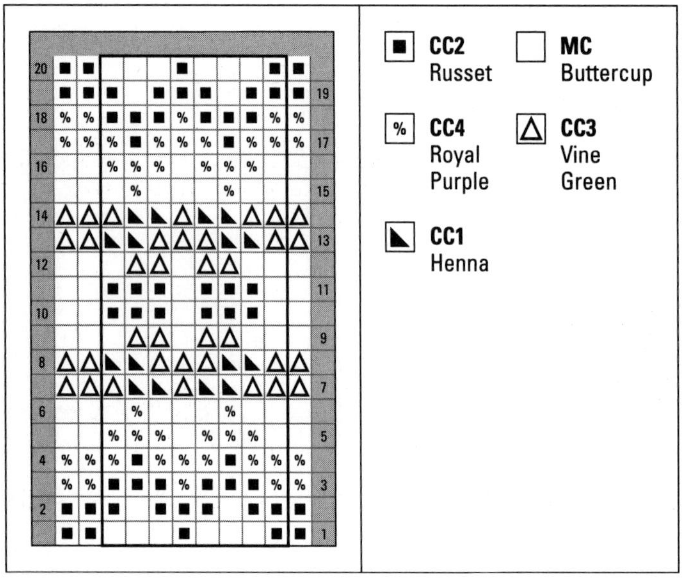

**Figure 14-10:** The 8-stitch Fair Isle chart, with three selvedge stitches.

| | |
|---|---|
| ■ CC2 Russet | □ MC Buttercup |
| % CC4 Royal Purple | △ CC3 Vine Green |
| ◣ CC1 Henna | |

Work through all 20 rows of the chart, and then continue in stockinette stitch with the main color only. The pullover will measure about 4½ inches from the turning ridge.

### Waist shaping

Next RS row (Decrease Row): K2, ssk, knit to last 4 sts, k2tog, k2. (See Chapter 6 for more about ssk and k2tog.)

Repeat the decrease row every 4th row 4 more times. There are 81 (89, 97, 113, 129, 137) sts.

Work even until the sweater measures 9 inches from the turning ridge, ending with a WS row, and then begin increasing as follows:

Next RS row (Increase Row): K2, m1, knit to last 2 sts, m1, k2. (I show you how to do the m1 increase earlier in this chapter.)

Continue in stockinette stitch and repeat the increase row every 6th row 4 more times. There are 91 (99, 107, 123, 139, 147) sts.

Work even until the front measures 16 (16, 16, 16, 16½, 16½) inches from the turning ridge.

### Armhole shaping

Bind off 5 (6, 7, 8, 11, 12) sts at the beginning of the next 2 rows.

Bind off 3 (5, 5, 8, 10, 12) sts at the beginning of the next 2 rows.

Decrease 1 st at each side of every RS row 1 (2, 3, 4, 5, 6) times, as follows:

Next row (RS): K2, ssk, knit to last 4 sts, k2tog, k2.

When all decreases have been worked, 73 (73, 77, 83, 87, 87) sts remain.

Work even until the back measures 5½ (5½, 6, 6, 6½, 6½) inches from the beginning of the armhole shaping, ending with a WS row.

### Neck shaping

You now work each side of the neck separately.

Next row (RS): K22 (22, 24, 24, 26, 26) and slip these sts to a holder for the left shoulder, bind off 29 (29, 29, 35, 35, 35) sts, knit to end of row. There are 22 (22, 24, 24, 26, 26) sts.

### Right neck

Next row (WS): Purl.

Next row (RS): K1, ssk, knit to end of row.

Repeat the previous 2 rows 5 more times. There are 16 (16, 18, 18, 20, 20) sts on this shoulder.

Work even until the armhole measures 8½ (8½, 9, 9, 9½, 9½) inches, ending with a RS row.

### Right shoulder

Bind off 8 (8, 9, 9, 10, 10) sts at the beginning of the next 2 WS rows.

### Left neck

Replace the held stitches on the needle with the WS facing and rejoin the yarn.

Next row (WS): Purl.

Next row (RS): Knit to last 3 sts, k2tog, k1.

Repeat the previous 2 rows 5 more times. There are 16 (16, 18, 18, 20, 20) sts on this shoulder.

Work even until the armhole measures 8½ (8½, 9, 9, 9½, 9½) inches, ending with a WS row.

### Left shoulder

Bind off 8 (8, 9, 9, 10, 10) sts at the beginning of the next 2 RS rows.

## Moving to the front

Work the front the same as the back through the end of the armhole shaping. There are 73 (73, 77, 83, 87, 87) sts.

Work in stockinette stitch for 1 inch, and then work the neck and shoulder shaping in the same way as for the back, beginning with the "Neck shaping" section. Note that the front neckline is deeper than the back, so there will be more rows worked between the end of the neckline decreases and the beginning of the shoulder shaping.

## Making the sleeves

Using the US 6 needles (or one size smaller than the size needed to match gauge), cast on 51 (51, 51, 59, 59, 59) sts. Work in stockinette stitch for 6 rows, ending with a purl row.

Purl 1 RS row to create a turning ridge.

Switch to the US 7 needles (or the size needed to match gauge) and continue in stockinette stitch until the sleeve measures 1 inch from the turning ridge.

Begin working the Fair Isle border, if desired. To do so, work the right selvedge stitch outside the dark line, work across the 8-stitch pattern between the dark lines 6 (6, 6, 7, 7, 7) times, and then work the 2 left selvedge stitches. Working these 3 extra stitches keeps your pattern centered and gives you a stitch on each side for your seams. Remember that when you're working a WS row, the 2 selvedge stitches at the left side of the chart are worked first, and then the chart repeat is worked 6 (6, 6, 7, 7, 7) times. Finally the selvedge stitch at the right side of the chart is worked.

Work through all 20 rows of the chart.

When the Fair Isle border is complete, work 3 rows in stockinette stitch with MC.

Next RS row (Increase Row): K2, m1, knit to last 2 sts, m1, k2.

Continue in stockinette stitch with MC and repeat increase row every 8th row 7 (0, 0, 0, 0, 0) times; every 6th row 0 (10, 12, 11, 8, 4) times; then every 4th row 0 (0, 0, 0, 5, 12) times. There are 67 (73, 77, 83, 87, 93) sts.

If the pattern tells you to do something 0 times, don't do it at all!

Work even until the sleeve measures 17 (17, 17½, 17½, 18, 18) inches from the turning ridge, ending with a WS row.

Now shape the sleeve cap as follows:

Bind off 5 (6, 7, 8, 11, 12) sts at the beginning of the next 2 rows.

Bind off 3 (5, 5, 8, 10, 12) sts at the beginning of the next 2 rows.

Decrease 1 st at each side of the work every RS row 17 (17, 18, 17, 15, 15) times as follows:

Next row (RS): K2, ssk, knit to last 4 sts, k2tog, k2.

Bind off remaining 17 (17, 17, 17, 15, 15) sts.

Make a second sleeve the same way.

## Finishing your pullover

Block all of the pieces to the measurements given on the schematic (see Figure 14-13). Using mattress stitch, sew shoulder seams together. (See the appendix for more about blocking and mattress stitch.)

Place a marker or safety pin every 2 inches around the neck. Starting at the right shoulder, use the smallest needles to pick up and knit 9 sts between every 2 markers all the way around the neck. (See Chapter 13 for guidelines on picking up neckline stitches, if you need help.)

Place a marker and join to work in the round. Switch to the largest needles and purl 1 round to begin garter stitch.

Switch to needles one size smaller and work 2 more rounds in garter stitch (knit 1 round, purl 1 round).

Go down one more needle size, work 2 more rounds in garter stitch, and then bind off.

Sew sleeve caps into place, and then sew sleeve seams and side seams.

Turn under hems at the turning ridges and then sew them in place, keeping these seams loose enough so that you aren't causing any puckering. Weave in remaining ends and block again if desired.

## Variation: Making a mosaic border

To make a mosaic border in place of the Fair Isle, you need the same amount of the main color yarn specified for your size in the basic pattern and one ball of yarn in a contrasting color. Remember that stronger contrasts give the best results.

Follow the directions for the basic version of the sweater but instead of the Fair Isle border, work one of the 8-stitch mosaic patterns presented in Chapter 7. Like the Fair Isle pattern, these patterns have 3 selvedge stitches. Depending on the height of your mosaic, you may need to work several rows in the main color before your sweater measures 4½ inches from the turning ridge and you're ready to begin the waist shaping.

# Lacy V-Neck Top

This lace-trimmed top can be knit hip length like the previous scoop-neck pullover or cropped as you see in Figure 14-11. But don't slam the book shut at the thought of a cropped top! I'm not suggesting that anyone bare her midriff, but over a slim shirt or an empire waist dress, a shorter sweater like the one in Figure 14-11 can look really great, especially on your favorite teen. This top features a deep, wide V-neck that's great for layering. Coupled with the lace, it's feminine and flattering. Besides, it's a lot less knitting than the full-length sweater. This pattern gives you more than this one trendy top, though! You can find directions for a full-length version with gentle waist shaping to flatter your form in a later variation.

The yarn I've chosen for this pattern has wonderful drape and is a delight to wear, but the gauge makes it easy to substitute, so you can use this pattern for ages. And remember, the critical numbers for this top and the scoop-neck pullover in the previous pattern are the same, which means that you can knit this one with the rounded neckline if you prefer — simply follow the directions for the scoop-neck pullover when you get to the armhole shaping.

**Figure 14-11:**
This lacy V-neck can be knit cropped or hip length.

# Materials and vital statistics

- **Yarn:** Berocco Softwist (41% wool, 59% rayon); 100 yards (92 meters) per 50 grams; 8 (9, 10, 11, 13, 15) skeins; color: 9437 Green

- **Needles:** US 7 (4.5 mm) needles; 16-inch or 24-inch circular needle, or the size needed to match gauge

- **Other:** Yarn needle; 1 stitch marker; stitch holder

- **Size:** S (M, L, 1X, 2X, 3X) or actual chest size of 34 (38, 42, 46, 50, 54) inches

  - **Finished chest circumference:** 36½ (39½, 43, 49, 55½, 59) inches

  - **Finished length:** 14½ (14½, 15½, 15½, 16½, 16½) inches

  See the schematic in Figure 14-12 for detailed measurements of this sweater

- **Gauge:** 20 stitches and 28 rows per 4 inches in stockinette stitch

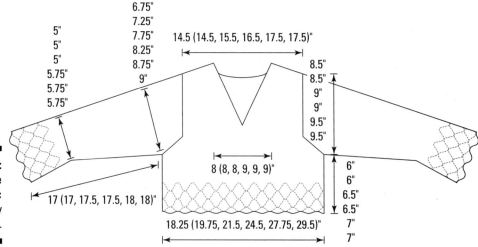

**Figure 14-12:**
The schematic of the lacy V-neck top.

The back, front, and sleeves of this sweater begin with a straightforward lace pattern. (If you're new to lace knitting, head to Chapter 6, where you can also find a couple of different lace patterns to use as substitutes.) For the cropped version, you begin the armhole decreases shortly after you finish the lace. If you want to make this into a more traditional sweater, see the variation at the end of the pattern. The finished top will have the same silhouette as the scoop-neck pullover, but with the same lace detailing as the cropped top.

## *Starting with the back*

Using a straight or circular US 7 needle (or the size you need to match gauge), cast on 91 (99, 107, 123, 139, 147) sts.

Next row (WS): Purl.

Begin lace pattern as follows:

Row 1: K2 *yo, k2, sl 1, k2tog, psso, k2, yo, k1, repeat from * to last st, k1. (See Chapter 6 if you're unfamiliar with yo, k2tog, or psso.)

Row 2: Purl.

Row 3: K3, *yo, k1, sl 1, k2tog, psso, k1, yo, k3, repeat from * to end.

Row 4: Purl.

Row 5: K4, *yo, sl 1, k2tog, psso, yo, k5, repeat from * to last 7 sts, yo, sl 1, k2tog, psso, yo, k4.

Row 6: Purl.

Repeat these 6 rows 3 more times — your sweater will measure approximately 4 inches.

Work even in stockinette stitch (knit a row, purl a row) until the back measures 6 (6, 6½, 6½, 7, 7) inches, ending with a WS row.

### Armhole shaping

Bind off 5 (6, 7, 8, 11, 12) sts at the beginning of the next 2 rows.

Bind off 3 (5, 5, 8, 10, 12) sts at the beginning of the next 2 rows. There are 75 (77, 83, 91, 97, 99) sts.

Decrease 1 st at each side of every RS row 1 (2, 3, 4, 5, 6) times, as follows:

Next row (RS): K2, ssk, knit to last 4 sts, k2tog, k2.

When all decreases have been worked, 73 (73, 77, 83, 87, 87) sts remain.

Work even until the back measures 6½ (6½, 7, 7, 7½, 7½) inches from the beginning of armhole shaping, ending with a WS row.

### Neck shaping

You now work each side of the neck separately.

Next row (RS): K22 (22, 24, 24, 26, 26) and slip these stitches to a holder for the left shoulder, bind off 29 (29, 29, 35, 35, 35) sts, knit to end of row. There are 22 (22, 24, 24, 26, 26) sts.

### Right neck

Next row (WS): Purl.

Next row (RS): K1, ssk, knit to end of row.

Repeat the previous 2 rows 5 more times. There are 16 (16, 18, 18, 20, 20) sts on this shoulder.

Work even until the armhole measures 8½ (8½, 9, 9, 9½, 9½) inches, ending with a RS row.

### Right shoulder

Bind off 8 (8, 9, 9, 10, 10) sts at the beginning of the next 2 WS rows.

### Left neck

Replace the held stitches on the needle with the WS facing and rejoin the yarn.

Next row (WS): Purl.

Next row (RS): Knit to last 3 sts, k2tog, k1.

Repeat the previous 2 rows 5 more times. There are 16 (16, 18, 18, 20, 20) sts on this shoulder.

Work even until the armhole measures 8½ (8½, 9, 9, 9½, 9½) inches, ending with a WS row.

### Left shoulder

Bind off 8 (8, 9, 9, 10, 10) sts at the beginning of the next 2 RS rows.

## Moving to the front

Work the front the same as the back to the beginning of the armhole shaping. There are 91 (99, 107, 123, 139, 147) sts, and the front measures 6 (6, 6½, 6½, 7, 7) inches from the cast-on edge.

### Armhole shaping

Bind off 5 (6, 7, 8, 11, 12) sts at the beginning of the next 2 rows.

Bind off 3 (5, 5, 8, 10, 12) sts at the beginning of the next 2 rows. There are 75 (77, 83, 91, 97, 99) sts.

You'll be shaping the neck and the armhole at the same time, so read through the whole section before continuing to knit.

### Neck shaping

You'll decrease at each armhole edge and make the first neckline decreases, dividing the left and right neck, which you then work separately as follows:

Next row (RS): K1, ssk, k31 (32, 35, 39, 42, 43), k2tog, k1, slip all sts just worked to a holder for the left shoulder; bind off the center st, ssk, k31 (32, 35, 39, 42, 43), k2tog, k1. There are 35 (36, 39, 43, 46, 47) sts. (I show you how to do the ssk decrease in Chapter 6.)

### Right neck and shoulder

Continue decreasing 1 st at the armhole edge every RS row 0 (1, 2, 3, 4, 5) more times.

If the pattern tells you to do something 0 times, don't do it at all.

At the same time, shape the neck.

Next row (RS): K1, ssk, knit to end of row. Remember to work the armhole decrease if needed for your size.

Next row (WS): Purl.

Repeat these 2 rows 19 (19, 19, 22, 22, 22) more times. There are 16 (16, 18, 18, 20, 20) sts on the right shoulder.

Work even until the armhole measures 8½ (8½, 9, 9, 9½, 9½) inches, ending with a RS row.

Bind off 8 (8, 9, 9, 10, 10) sts at the beginning of the next 2 WS rows.

### Left neck and shoulder

Replace the held stitches on the needle with the WS facing, and then rejoin the yarn.

Continue decreasing 1 st at the armhole edge every RS row 0 (1, 2, 3, 4, 5) more times.

At the same time, shape the neck, as follows:

Next row (WS): Purl.

Next row (RS): Remember to work the armhole decrease if needed for your size, and then knit to the last 3 sts, k2tog, k1.

Repeat the previous 2 rows 19 (19, 19, 22, 22, 22) more times. There are 16 (16, 18, 18, 20, 20) sts on the left shoulder.

Work even until the armhole measures 8½ (8½, 9, 9, 9½, 9½) inches, ending with a WS row.

Bind off 8 (8, 9, 9, 10, 10) sts at the beginning of the next 2 RS rows.

## Making the sleeves

The sleeves are slightly belled and use the same lace detailing as the body.

Cast on 51 (51, 51, 59, 59, 59) sts.

Next row (WS): Purl.

Begin the lace pattern as follows:

Row 1: K2 *yo, k2, sl 1, k2tog, psso, k2, yo, k1, repeat from * to last st, k1.

Row 2: Purl.

Row 3: K3, *yo, k1, sl 1, k2tog, psso, k1, yo, k3, repeat from * to end.

Row 4: Purl.

Row 5: K4, *yo, sl 1, k2tog, psso, yo, k5, repeat from * to last 7 sts, yo, sl 1, k2tog, psso, yo, k4.

Row 6: Purl.

Work the 6 rows of the lace pattern 4 more times.

Switch to stockinette stitch and begin the sleeve increases:

Next RS row (Increase Row): K2, m1, knit to last 2 sts, m1, k2.

Repeat increase row every 8th row 7 (0, 0, 0, 0, 0) times, every 6th row 0 (10, 12, 11, 8, 4) times, and then every 4th row 0 (0, 0, 0, 5, 12) times. There are 67 (73, 77, 83, 87, 93) sts.

Work even until the sleeve measures 17 (17, 17½, 17½, 18, 18) inches or desired length, ending with a WS row.

Now shape the sleeve cap as follows:

Bind off 5 (6, 7, 8, 11, 12) sts at the beginning of the next 2 rows.

Bind off 3 (5, 5, 8, 10, 12) sts at the beginning of the next 2 rows.

Decrease 1 st at each side of every RS row 17 (17, 18, 17, 15, 15) times as follows:

Decrease Row (RS): K1, ssk, knit to last 3 sts, k2tog, k1.

Bind off remaining 17 (17, 17, 17, 15, 15) sts.

Make a second sleeve the same way.

## Creating the collar

I've chosen to finish the collar with a repeat of the lace pattern. If this seems daunting to you, leave it as it is or finish it with a simple crochet edging.

Start by sewing the shoulder seams together with mattress stitch. (See the appendix for hints on crochet and mattress stitch.)

With the RS facing, use a US 7 circular needle (and a crochet hook if desired) to pick up and knit 152 sts, as follows:

Beginning at the right shoulder seam, pick up and knit 56 sts along the back neckline, 48 sts from left shoulder seam to bottom of left front neck shaping, place marker, pick up and knit 1 st in bound-off st at center, place marker, pick up and knit 47 sts up right front neck.

You can find out about picking up neckline stitches in Chapter 13.

Place a marker and join in the round.

Round 1: *K1, yo, k2, sl 1, k2tog, psso, k2, yo, repeat from * to 8 sts before the marked center st, k1, yo, k2, sl 1, k2tog, psso, k2, slip marker, knit center st, slip marker, k2, sl 1, k2tog, psso, k2, yo, resume lace pattern from * to end of round. There are 150 sts.

Round 2: Knit.

Round 3: *K2, yo, k1, sl 1, k2tog, psso, k1, yo, k1, repeat from * to 7 sts before marked center st, k2, yo, k1, sl 1, k2tog, psso, k1, slip marker, knit the center st, slip marker, k1, sl 1, k2tog, psso, k1, yo, k1, resume lace pattern from * to end of round. There are 148 sts.

Round 4: Knit.

Round 5: *K3, yo, sl 1, k2tog, psso, yo, k2, repeat from * to 6 sts before marked center st, k3, yo, sl 1, k2tog, psso, slip marker, knit the center st, slip marker, sl 1, k2tog, psso, yo, k2, resume lace pattern from * to end of rounds. There are 146 sts.

Round 6: Bind off.

## Finishing your top

Block all pieces to the measurements given on the schematic (see Figure 14-12). Sew the sleeve caps in place, and then sew the side seams and sleeve seams. Weave in your ends. (See the appendix for more about blocking and mattress stitch).

## Variation: Lengthening your top

The cropped top is fun, but it isn't right for everyone. This longer version, shown in Figure 14-13, is just as lovely; the same lace detailing and flattering neckline combined with waist shaping will give you a very feminine result. It's so fabulous you'll want to make more than one! The sleeves and collar are the same as the basic pattern — only the front and back are different. You need 3 (3, 4, 4, 5, 6) more skeins of Softwist to make this longer version.

### Back

Cast on and work the lace pattern as directed in the basic pattern.

Continue in stockinette stitch (knit a row, purl a row) until the back measures about 4½ inches, ending with a WS row, and then begin the waist shaping.

**Waist shaping:** Next row (Decrease Row) (RS): K2, ssk, knit to last 4 sts, k2tog, k2.

Repeat the decrease row every 4th row 4 more times. There are 81 (89, 97, 113, 129, 137) sts.

Work even until the sweater measures 9 inches from the cast-on edge, ending with a WS row, and then begin increasing as follows:

Next row (Increase Row) (RS): K2, m1, knit to last 2 sts, m1, k2.

Repeat the increase row every 6th row 4 more times. There are 91 (99, 107, 123, 139, 147) sts.

Work even until the back measures 16 (16, 16, 16, 16½, 16½) inches from the cast-on edge.

Work the armhole and neckline shaping as described in the basic pattern.

### Front

Work the front the same as the back to the beginning of the armhole shaping. There are 91 (99, 107, 123, 139, 147) sts, and the front measures 16 (16, 16, 16, 16½, 16½) inches from the cast-on edge.

Work the armhole and neckline shaping as described in the basic pattern.

### Finishing

Follow the directions in the basic pattern for the sleeves and collar as well as for the finishing of the sweater.

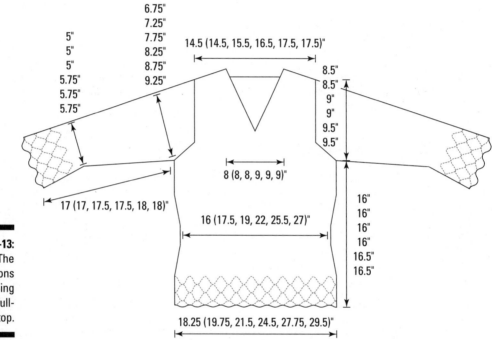

**Figure 14-13:**
The dimensions and shaping of the full-length top.

6.75"
7.25"
7.75"
8.25"
8.75"
9.25"

5"
5"
5"
5.75"
5.75"
5.75"

14.5 (14.5, 15.5, 16.5, 17.5, 17.5)"

8.5"
8.5"
9"
9"
9.5"
9.5"

8 (8, 8, 9, 9, 9)"

17 (17, 17.5, 17.5, 18, 18)"

16 (17.5, 19, 22, 25.5, 27)"

16"
16"
16"
16"
16.5"
16.5"

18.25 (19.75, 21.5, 24.5, 27.75, 29.5)"

# Part V

# The Part of Tens

The 5th Wave       By Rich Tennant

"Don't even think about it."

# In this part . . .

And now for something completely different! This part
has bits and pieces that are meant to be informative
and fun. Flip through this part to find out about caring for
your handknits. You can also have some fun thinking
about things to do with all those swatches. Stuck in a knitting jam? Check out the tips on MacGyvering your knitting.
Or if you're stuck without needles or yarn, this part shows
you some surprising things that you can knit with.

# Chapter 15

# Ten Things You Can Knit with that Aren't Yarn or Needles

● ● ● ● ● ● ● ● ● ● ● ● ● ● ● ● ● ● ● ● ● ● ● ● ● ● ● ● ● ● ● ● ● ● ● ● ● ● ● ● ● ● ●

## In This Chapter

▶ Finding something to knit when you have nothing to knit with

▶ Getting your knitting groove back with unusual supplies

● ● ● ● ● ● ● ● ● ● ● ● ● ● ● ● ● ● ● ● ● ● ● ● ● ● ● ● ● ● ● ● ● ● ● ● ● ● ● ● ● ● ●

Sometimes you're stuck with nothing to knit, or worse, nothing to knit with! Other times, you may have something to knit but you're bored with it or you've misplaced your knitting mojo. At times like these, knitting something absolutely absurd is just what you need to renew your enthusiasm for your project.

This chapter lists ten things you can knit with that aren't standard equipment. Only the most stalwart will follow through with a whole project with these substitutes, but just playing with them for a while can remind you how cool knitting is.

## Raffia or Ribbon

Real or fake raffia or the curling ribbon that you use when wrapping gifts is easy to knit. You can use raffia or ribbon to knit things like hand bags or totes, but also consider using them to knit a whimsical gift bag. Raffia and ribbon are sturdy and can be economical if you pick them up on sale.

## Kite String

Kite string knits up well and is sturdier than any conventional knitting yarn. Try using it for something rugged, such as a mesh market bag or even a lace seat bottom for that old patio chair! Kite string (and other sorts of twine) can be found at hobby shops or the hardware store, often in a rainbow of colors.

## Plastic Bags

Those plastic bags that you get at the supermarket are one of those things that seem to breed behind your back. Here's a way to use them up: Cut the bags into strips or loops, join them together, and then wind them into a giant ball of plastic yarn. You're then ready to knit away. You'll never run out of "yarn," because your friends will always be eager to help you get more. I've seen purses, raincoats, and even a wedding dress knit from plastic bags, so give this method of recycling a try!

# Old T-Shirts

Like plastic bags, old T-shirts are a dime a dozen. To recycle your stash of T-shirts, use sharp scissors or a blade to cut the shirts into long strips less than 1 inch wide. Join the strips together by tying, looping, or sewing, and then wind the "yarn" into a nice big ball. Depending on how you cut them, you probably need three or four shirts to make a scarf. This homemade yarn is soft and comfy, like, well, an old T-shirt!

# Cassette Tapes

Okay, it's sort of difficult to knit with the tape from a cassette, but it's shiny and inarguably cool. Because cassette tape is a bit fragile and can't get wet, stick to scarves or big swatchy art pieces to hang on the wall.

# Licorice Ropes

Believe it or not, long licorice ropes can be used as yarn. Indeed, famously so. A pattern published in the free online magazine, Knitty.com, that was knit with licorice got lots of attention. Your licorice knit won't last long, but a quick knit snack is fun to make.

# Pencils

Chances are, even if you're stuck someplace without your knitting supplies, you can somehow get your hands on a couple of pencils to knit with. An added bonus: Pencils measure up at that elusive 7 mm size, midway between a US 10½ and a US 11.

# Chopsticks

Try using chopsticks as needles. I've met more than one knitter who learned to knit on chopsticks! The rounder variety is easier to knit with than the squared kind because they have a nice, tapered point. Bonus points will be awarded if you manage to knit your noodles with chopsticks! Because chopsticks are tapered, their gauge is variable.

# Skewers or Toothpicks

Bamboo skewers, which you can find at just about any grocery store, measure somewhere between a US 2 and a US 3 needle. Toothpicks weigh in at a diminutive US 0 and are double-pointed, making them perfect for knitting the world's tiniest socks.

# Tinkertoys

Sharpen the Tinkertoy tips in a pencil sharpener (the kind that works on fat kindergarten pencils), sand them down a bit to create a point you like, and then glue the end caps onto the other end. A set of these makeshift needles is wonderful for teaching your kids to knit!

# Chapter 16

# Almost Ten Things You Can Do with Your Swatches

*In This Chapter*

▶ Encouraging reasons to swatch

▶ Using your swatches for something productive

*I*f you've heard it once, you've heard it a million times: Swatching before you knit is important. Why? Knowing what gauge you're knitting at is vital to having a finished product that you like. (See Chapter 2 for more on gauge and swatching.) In this chapter are some useful (though sometimes more silly than useful) things that you can do with your swatches. After you read this chapter, you'll definitely want to swatch!

## Knit a Set of Coasters

Consider turning a set of swatches into coasters. Felted swatches are a great choice for coasters because they'll insulate your table best. But any square swatch will do the job and add a touch of whimsy to your tabletop. Flip to the appendix for the lowdown on felting.

## Sew Some Cozies

Chances are you have something rattling around in your purse or knitting bag that deserves a little cushioning. Fold your swatch in half and sew up two sides. This instant cozy can be used as a case for your glasses, cellphone, camera, or music player. If you have larger items that need cozies, you can use multiple swatches.

## Create Cat Toys

Cats love all things made from yarn. Fold your swatch into a rectangle or triangle and sew up all but a couple of inches. Add stuffing or catnip, and then finish the seam. Your cat will be very happy.

## Whip Up Washcloths and Soap Sacks

If your swatch is cotton or a cotton blend, consider pressing it into service as a washcloth or dishrag. Slightly more glamorous: Make a sack to hold a bar of soap.

To make the soap sack, knit 5 inches in whatever stitch pattern you need to swatch, and then work this eyelet row: K2, *yo, k2tog, repeat from * to last 1 or 2 sts, and then k1 or k2 as needed. Work the last inch of the swatch to finish your soap sack, fold the swatch in half and sew up the bottom and side, leaving the eyelet end open. Insert a nice bar of soap and run a length of yarn though the eyelets and tie it. It's better than soap on a rope!

# Make Slippers

If you look at Chapter 8, you'll notice that the retro slippers are really just squares. They're worked in garter stitch, but you can use almost any stitch or color pattern. Make the swatch the size that you need to fit your foot, but work the last inch (or two if you're working on a large slipper) in rib before gathering the swatch up and finishing it as described in the slipper pattern. And, of course, don't forget that you need to make a second one if you want a pair!

# Stitch a Crazy Quilt

If you take it upon yourself to always knit standardized swatches (say 4 inches square with a 1 inch garter stitch border all the way around) and stockpile them, sooner or later you'll have enough to stitch together into a baby blanket or even a larger afghan. Imagine yourself decades from now wrapped in a blanket made of swatches from a lifetime of knitting projects. Doesn't that make you want to swatch?

# Keep a Knitting Journal

If you want to be a wise and organized knitter, consider keeping your swatch in a knitting journal. Include the yarn's label, the needle size you used, the pattern information, and any changes or corrections you made. That way, if you ever want to re-create a garment, you have all the information that you need.

# Stash Away Swatches for Later Mending

If you save your swatches long enough, you can use them for later repairs. Ten years from now when your cardigan seam starts to go or a moth chews through the elbow of your mate's favorite sweater, you'll be darned glad that you kept the swatch.

# Store Swatches as Emergency Yarn

Whatever you choose to do with your swatch, be sure to keep it around at least until your project is done. That way, if you run out of yarn just as you're about to bind off, you can unravel your swatch and use the yarn.

# Chapter 17

# Ten Ways to MacGyver Your Knitting

*In This Chapter*

▶ Getting yourself out of a knitting bind

▶ Knitting with unconventional supplies

**S**ome knitters always have what they need. They have a cute box or bag that they carry all their supplies in. They always have a tape measure and a matching set of stitch markers. Most of the time I just make do. I enjoy the duct-tape-and-chewing-gum approach that got MacGyver out of so many tight spots on late-80s TV. If you're ever stuck on a desert island without your tools (or it's Saturday night and the knitting shop won't be open again until Tuesday morning), this chapter shows you how to make do with the stuff you have.

## Winding Your Yarn with Power

If you buy your yarn in a hank, you have to wind it into a ball before you start knitting. You can always accomplish this task as our foremothers did, but who can resist the lure of power tools? To wind yarn into a ball in a flash, put a toilet paper tube over the beater on your hand mixer, attach one end of the yarn to it and let 'er rip — "stir" is probably a smarter speed than "whip" if you don't want to court disaster. You need a swift or an assistant to hold the yarn on their outstretched hands, of course. Oh, and don't try this with delicate or wildly expensive yarns . . . or those likely to tangle.

## Crafting Your Own Knitting Needles

True, it's difficult to knit without knitting needles, but check out the tips offered in Chapter 15 for some workable substitutes. Or, if your desert island has a hardware store, you can make your own needles using wooden dowels. Dowels come in a variety of standard widths. A ³⁄₁₆-inch dowel is about the same as a US 7 needle; a ¼-inch dowel is almost a US 10½; and a ⁵⁄₁₆-inch dowel is a US 11 needle. Cut the dowel to your desired needle length using a saw, a kitchen knife, or a pair of pruning shears. Then sharpen one tip of the dowel in a pencil sharpener and glue a bead or glob of clay to the other end. Sanding, staining, or polishing can be nice ways to finish your needles, but those are optional steps. The hardcore adventurer may attempt to make circular needles using dowels and line stolen from the weed whacker as the connecting cable.

## Using Makeshift Cable Needles

If I decide to throw a cable into a project and find myself without a cable needle (which I invariably do), I use a spare double-pointed needle. With thicker yarns, a pencil does the trick. With skinny yarns, an unbent paperclip works just fine.

# Measuring Your Knitting with Handy Items

The tool that I'm always wishing that I had handy is a tape measure. I have a bunch, but they never seem to be where I want them to be! So what are the alternatives? Instead of holding up my knitting until I can measure the piece, I commit to memory the measurements of things that I can count on having handy. For instance, my index finger from the tip to the first knuckle is exactly 1 inch, and my hand is 7 inches long. A dollar bill is just a tad larger than 2½ inches by 6½ inches. And an 8½- by-11-inch piece of paper obviously measures exactly that. Fold the dollar bill or the piece of paper in half to come up with smaller measurements.

# Substituting for Stitch Markers

Stitch markers are cheap and plentiful, which is good because they always get lost! In lieu of stitch markers, I have used safety pins, ponytail holders, O-rings from the bead box, washers from the hardware store, and bits of pipe cleaner formed into loops (to name just a few). Usually, though, I just grab a piece of scrap yarn, and tie it into a small loop.

# Storing Your Notions

As a knitter you've probably found that you have a few little notions that you always want to have on hand, such as stitch markers, yarn needles, and the like. Since these things are so tiny, they often go missing in the bottom of your bag. Try keeping them in little metal tins (for example, the ones that gum or mints come in). These little containers have lids that stay put, they're nice and sturdy, and they're just the right size for storing these little items.

# Smoothing Out Your Rough Edges

An imperfection on a wooden needle or a broken fingernail can stop your knitting cold. Your yarn will catch on any rough edge, and sometimes even on ones that you can't see. Keep an emery board with your knitting supplies and you'll always be able to smooth out these rough edges and keep your knitting on track.

# Putting Your Stitches on Hold

A stitch holder can come in quite handy, but here are a few options on what to do when you don't have one: any spare needle, straight or circular (use a cork as a stopper on the pointy end); a length of scrap yarn (use a yarn needle to slip the stitches onto the yarn and tie the ends together so you don't lose any stitches); a pipe cleaner; or a safety pin for a small number of stitches.

# Counting Stitches and Rows the Low-Tech Way

A stitch counter is another tool that can come in handy. However, almost always, you can simply count your stitches or rows to figure out where you are in your knitting. Or you can make tally marks on a scrap of paper, provided that you actually remember to make the mark each time you finish a row. That is my trouble with counters — I never remember to advance them when I finish a row!

If you're working a pattern like cable or lace, you may find that you're having trouble remembering which row of the pattern you're on. My solution for you is to make what I call a "Kate" (after the person who showed it to me). Double a length of scrap yarn and then tie a series of knots making a chain of little loops. Make one chain link for each row of your pattern repeat. If I have a cable that turns every 4th row, for instance, I make four loops. I stick the knotted scrap yarn on my needle with the needle through the first loop and then knit the first row. Each time I finish a row, I move the needle up to the next hole in the chain. When you get to the last hole, you know that it's cable time! A Kate is a delightfully low-tech solution.

# Cutting Yarn without Scissors

Lots of yarns don't need to be cut. Instead, you can just break them if you pull hard enough. Try holding your hands farther apart as you pull to make breaking the yarn easier. For other yarns, you need to find something sharp. Those who carry dental floss in their purses or bags may try the floss cutter on the box. Others may try to surreptitiously bite through the yarn. Or you can try sawing yarn with your keys or a nail file in a pinch.

# Chapter 18

# Ten Smart Ways to Care for Your Knits

## In This Chapter

▶ Washing your knits carefully

▶ Storing your knits the right way

▶ Giving away your knits

Despite what many people think, handknits aren't all that difficult to take care of. If you don't believe me, just take a look through this chapter, which explains how to tend to your handknits so they look their best and hold up for a long time. And because many knits are given as gifts, I tell you about some smart things to do before you wrap them up.

## Read the Label

The following recommendation seems like it should almost go without saying, but I'm going to say it anyway: Read your yarn labels! Those little paper bands give you lots of useful information, including fiber content, yardage, dye lot, needle and gauge recommendations, and washing instructions. If, in your eagerness to get to the yarn, you tend to fling these labels aside like yesterday's candy wrappers, break yourself of the habit.

If this caution comes too late, consult the Web site of your yarn's manufacturer. Or ask the yarn shop where you purchased the yarn — they'll be happy to clue you in.

Some yarn labels give instructions in plain English, such as "Hand wash in cool water." Others instead offer inscrutable pictographs that tell you how to care for the knits that you make from the yarn (these symbols are actually the same ones used for clothing). Because yarns are marketed around the world, manufacturers want to be sure that the information can be understood without requiring you to speak Italian or Japanese. Figure 18-1 is a handy guide. Copy it and attach it to the laundry room door, and then you won't be stuck staring at the washer muttering, "Circle in a box with two lines under it, what do I do?"

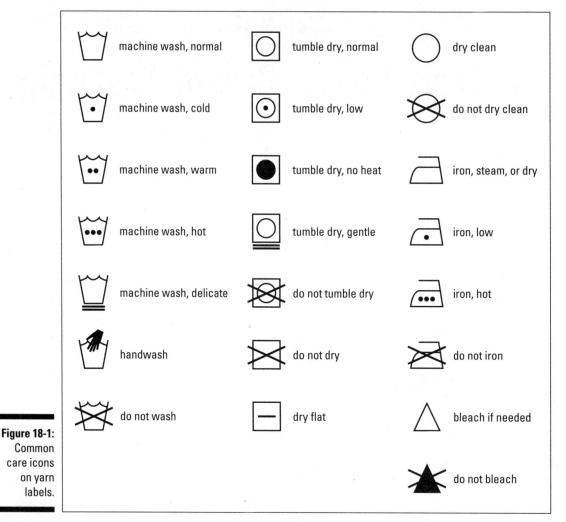

| | | |
|---|---|---|
| machine wash, normal | tumble dry, normal | dry clean |
| machine wash, cold | tumble dry, low | do not dry clean |
| machine wash, warm | tumble dry, no heat | iron, steam, or dry |
| machine wash, hot | tumble dry, gentle | iron, low |
| machine wash, delicate | do not tumble dry | iron, hot |
| handwash | do not dry | do not iron |
| do not wash | dry flat | bleach if needed |
| | | do not bleach |

# *Wash Wisely*

There are some general washing guidelines for knit items, some of which may surprise you. Very few items *must* be dry cleaned, and more knits than you would expect can survive the washing machine on the gentle cycle. There are exceptions though!

Whatever washing technique you're going to use, it's a good idea to use your swatch as a pilot test (you did swatch, didn't you?). Subject your swatch to a fairly thorough version of whatever washing technique you're planning to use based on the label information and see how the swatch fares. Chances are you won't weep over a felted or matted swatch. Measure your gauge before and after washing to see whether your swatch shrinks or grows. Honestly, you should really wash your swatch and wait for it to dry before you even knit your garment, because you want to account for any gauge change that comes about after you've washed it. It can be difficult to wait, but a day's delay is well worth it in the end. (Chapter 2 has all the details on gauge and swatches.)

The least finicky pieces to wash are usually those that are made with synthetics or synthetic blends. And if your piece is a single color and it's cotton, you can probably stick it in the washer. Likewise, superwash wools have been treated so they won't felt, which means they're safe for the washing machine. Yarns that are marketed particularly for children's clothing usually are washing machine safe. However, you should always use the gentle cycle.

Don't machine wash anything that's 100 percent wool unless the label says it's okay to do so (this warning also includes other animal fibers, such as alpaca, mohair, or cashmere). It's better to err on the side of caution.

The only things that you *must* leave to the cleaners are pieces that are knit with the most novel of novelty fibers, such as those that contain bits of paper, metal, or other things that may not respond well to water. In addition, if you've used several colors, the colors sometimes can bleed with a wet washing technique (they shouldn't, but they do!), so test your swatch if you're unsure. Some people like to dry clean everything and that's fine, but not necessarily better because dry-cleaning chemicals can actually be damaging to some fibers. Read the label and see if it specifies that your item *must* be dry-cleaned.

Most knits fall in the middle between machine washing and dry cleaning. You wash these knits by hand. To wash a knitted piece by hand, follow these steps:

1. **Fill the sink with cool water and add some soap.**

   Any mild soap is fine. Some people use a specially-designed wool wash that requires no rinsing. Me, I usually use a lavender-scented shampoo. Wool is the hair of a sheep, right? And honestly, soap is soap. Just add a little squirt of whatever is handy.

   Soap is soap, but detergent and bacteria-killing hand wash aren't soap, so don't use them!

2. **Gently put your knitted object into the sink and push it down into the water so that the entire piece is wet.**

   You can swish gently, but for the most part you should just let it soak for 10 minutes.

3. **Drain the water from the sink and then rinse with water of the same temperature.**

   Rinse until all the soap is out.

4. **Let any excess water drain out of your knitting as you support it from underneath.**

   Don't pick it up by one corner and let it stretch out! And don't squeeze or wring it aggressively.

5. **Place the garment on a towel and roll it up like sushi.**

   You can apply a bit of pressure to your roll to get some water out. Repeat with dry towels until the towels are no longer getting soaked.

# Avoid Hot Water and Agitation

If you've ever done any felting (accidentally or on purpose), you know what happens: Your knitting shrinks substantially and turns into a dense, thick fabric. But do you know what makes something felt? Very hot water, shifting temperatures, and agitation. So, whether you're washing by hand or by machine, avoid these things for all handknits, especially wool and other animal fibers. What should you do instead? Follow these guidelines:

✔ It's fine to use cold, cool, or even warmish water, but *do not* change temperatures. So, if your washing machine always rinses with cold water, set the wash for cold water too. Likewise, if you're hand-washing, don't change temperatures as you wash and rinse.

✔ Most machines offer a "gentle" or "delicate" wash cycle. In these cycles, the agitator should move slowly. A gentle stirring sort of action is fine, but whether in the machine or the sink, what your knit wants is a relaxing bath, not a trip through a water park. No wringing, shaking, or washboard-style rubbing, please!

# Always Air-Dry

Unless you're 100 percent sure it's okay, don't put any handknits in the dryer! Dryers are a pretty tough ride. In fact, they put more wear and tear on your clothes than the washer. Cottons may shrink, and wools may shrink or, worse, felt, so approach the dryer with extreme caution. If you must stick something in the dryer, use a cool or air-dry setting and keep your eye on it.

Your knits shouldn't stay wet longer than they need to, so get as much water out of your knits as you can by wrapping them in dry towels before you lay them out on a towel or screen, particularly if you have damp weather. A handknit that stays damp or gets put away damp can mildew. After removing excess water, pat your knits gently into shape and allow them to dry completely. With bulkier things, you may want to flip them over, or turn them inside out to make sure that they're dry all the way through before you put them away. How long a handknit will take to dry depends a lot on your climate (or your climate control), how thick the piece is, and what it's made of. In warm, dry conditions, a piece may dry in less than a day. But it may be 48 hours before that piece is dry enough to fold and store.

By patting your sweater into shape while it's damp, you're actually *blocking*. Blocking is your chance to make your knits fit just right. You can make your ribbing relax, make a sleeve a bit wider, or line up something that seems a tad off. You won't be able to work miracles, but blocking can make a big difference to the overall look of your piece. Break out a tape measure and keep things even so that, for example, one sleeve isn't longer than the other. Refer to the measurements given in a pattern schematic and gently pull everything into line, and then let your piece dry thoroughly. You can find out more about blocking in the appendix.

# Clean Your Knits Regularly

Each time you wear or use your knits, take a moment to inspect them before you put them away. If you've dipped your cuff into your dinner plate, it's reasonable to spot clean that area in the sink or with a gentle sponging before you go to bed. Always blot things rather than rub them. Rubbing breaks down and weakens the fibers in the yarn, which can lead to pilling or felting. If you act on spills and stains promptly, you can prolong the life of your sweater or other knitted garment.

Regardless of how often you wear and wash your knits, be sure to give them a good cleaning at the end of the season. Stains will become more difficult to remove if they sit. And any traces of food or perspiration can lead to deterioration or mildew and can attract moths if your knits sit undisturbed for several months of warmer weather.

# Store Your Knits Flat or Folded

Knits should always be stored flat or folded. Don't hang them or they may stretch out of shape and put too much strain on the stitches that are resting on the hanger. Wetting and blocking your knits can undo the damage at first, but eventually you'll ruin them. Fold and store them in a drawer or on a shelf. Tuck pieces of cedar or sachets of lavender in with your knits — they'll smell nice and you'll deter moths.

For longer-term storage, it's okay to put your knits in sealed plastic bins, but really they do best where there's some air circulation, so don't store them in the dry cleaner's plastic bags and don't leave them in the garage forever. At the very least, take them out, check them for damage, and refold them on different lines at least once a year.

# Save Some Yarn for Later (Just in Case)

Saving some extra yarn from a project is never a bad idea. To do so, simply tuck the yarn label into a baggie with some leftover yarn and any spare buttons or other tidbits and toss it in the bottom of your drawer. That way, if you ever need to make a repair to your knitted item, or if you need to remember whether you have to send the garment to the dry cleaner, you have what you need!

You also can tape your label and leftover yarn into a knitter's notebook along with any notes that you took while making the item (like what needles you used or whether you made any changes to the pattern). Some knitters attach their swatch and a photo of the finished item and have a great resource to look back on (it's a bit like a scrapbook). My aunt kept a knitter's notebook, and it's a wonderful memento of her life as a knitter.

# Knit Like You Care

If you still act like a teenager whose clothes end up all over the floor, if you *are* a teenager with clothes all over the floor, or if you're knitting *for* a teenager with clothes all over the floor, you're wise to take care into account when choosing your yarn. Washing your knits by hand really isn't a big deal, and it takes maybe 20 minutes of your time and a bit of your patience, but don't knit something that requires more care than it will get. There are plenty of easy-care yarns available, and you should choose them when they're appropriate. For instance, it's a lovely idea to knit a new mother a baby sweater in cashmere, but perhaps the more generous gift is the one that she can heedlessly toss into the washing machine.

# Give Care Instructions with a Gift

A hand-knit gift is always a special one. But before you tie on that ribbon, consider these few suggestions:

- ✔ If you knit a lot of gifts, you might consider investing in some of those tags that say "Handknit by Ethel," "Made with love by Grandma," or whatever sentiment you hope to express. You can get these tags made to order for not very much money, and they'll remind people, perhaps for generations, who made the gift.

- Extra yards of yarn and spare buttons are smart things to include with a gift. (Or simply keep them on hand yourself if you're prepared to make any necessary repairs in years to come.)

- Make care tags for the knits that you give. I like to make tags from index or business cards. On them I write the care instructions. For example, I might write, "100% superwash wool. Machine wash, air dry." Choose a tone and set of instructions that suits the mood of the gift. After the tag is completed, I punch a hole in the corner and tie it to the gift with a bit of yarn.

# Remember that Not Everything You Knit Is an Heirloom

Some pieces that you knit are destined to become heirlooms. That beautiful lace layette, for instance, or that marvelously cabled aran that took you two years to complete. It's good to treat these pieces with the reverence they deserve. That way they really can last for generations. However, not everything you knit needs to be handled with kid gloves.

If you knit things for people, expect them to get worn (and even worn out). Surely it's a greater compliment that the sweater you knit for your granddaughter is stretched out and grayish on the cuffs and has a big splotch of blue paint on the elbow (because she simply won't take it off) than if it's lying there pristine on the shelf. Be honest with yourself, and if you mean for something to be treated as an heirloom, maybe keep it and care for it yourself and knit something less ambitious (or less delicate) to give away.

# Appendix

# Basic Knitting Skills

*E*ven when you've been knitting for a while, you may find yourself needing a refresher on how to accomplish basic tasks, such as casting on, knitting, purling, and binding off. This appendix gives you guidance on these fundamentals (organized in alphabetical order for easy reference) as well as on a few tasks to finish your knitting in style.

## Binding Off

*Binding off,* or *casting off* as some knitters call it, is what you do when you're done with your knitting. You usually bind off at the end of a piece, but sometimes you bind off in the middle of a piece when you need to get rid of some stitches. To bind off (abbreviated as "BO" in some patterns), follow these steps:

1. **Knit the first 2 stitches on the left-hand needle.**

   There are 2 stitches on the right needle.

2. **Insert the tip of the left-hand needle into the first stitch (the stitch on the right) on the right-hand needle, as shown in Figure A-1a.**

3. **Bring this stitch up and over the second stitch on the right-hand needle and off the needle, leaving 1 stitch on the right needle as shown in Figure A-1b.**

4. **Knit the next stitch so that there are again 2 stitches on the right-hand needle.**

5. **Repeat Steps 2–4 until the necessary number of stitches are bound off.**

   If you're at the end of a piece, cut the yarn, leaving a tail at least 6 inches long. Bring this tail through the last stitch, pulling it to secure the last stitch.

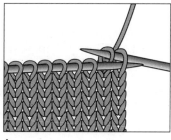 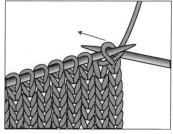

**Figure A-1:**
Binding off.

A.                     B.

## Blocking

*Blocking* sounds fancier than it really is, which either scares people off or sends them running to pricy dry cleaners to have them do the job. In plain terms, blocking involves some water (spritzing, steaming, or soaking) and more or less prodding and pinning things into shape. Then you allow the knitted piece to dry. Sounds pretty easy, right? After reading the directions for light and serious blocking in the following sections, you'll see why blocking is something you can (and should!) do yourself.

Before you block anything, keep these guidelines in mind:

- ✔ **Don't expect miracles.** Someone may tell you that you can block a garment to fit or that you can block rolled edges. This is only a little true. You can make things smoother and you can even out some irregularities. And, depending on the type of yarn, you can make the garment a bit bigger in some spots and a bit smaller in others. Things look better blocked, it's true. But don't expect blocking to make up for the fact that the back is 4 inches longer than the front or that you knit something two sizes too small. You also can't force stockinette stitch edges not to roll with blocking.

- ✔ **Avoid blocking with heat.** Some people block garments by steaming them with an iron (not actually touching the knitting) or a steamer. This method dries faster than wet blocking, but I'm too squeamish most of the time to get a hot iron so close to my hard work. Wool, cotton, and some blends can take the heat, but anything fuzzy (mohair), synthetic (any novelty yarn), or highly textured (cables) is best served by wet blocking. Any damage you do with water can usually be undone. Damage you do with heat, however, may be permanent. Let your degree of risk aversion guide you in deciding.

- ✔ **Find out whether your yarn is colorfast.** A few yarns out there aren't colorfast. If you've done color work (see Chapter 7), test the colorfastness of the yarn before getting the completed garment wet. I guarantee you that it's better to spare yourself the agony of finding out the hard way! Take lengths of the yarn you used (in all of the colors), wet them, and then wrap them in a white cloth or paper towel and let them dry. Check for any signs of bleeding. If you think the yarns aren't colorfast, you'll have to send the piece to the dry cleaner.

- ✔ **Always read the yarn label.** Not only does the label provide important info about the yarn's gauge and yardage, but it also serves as your knit's care tag. (See Chapter 18 for more on caring for your knits.)

- ✔ **It's up to you to decide when to block your piece.** Blocking the components (sleeves, front, back) separately can make them easier to sew up, but this is strictly dealer's choice. You can also block a piece when it's complete or any time you wash it.

## Light blocking

If your finished piece looks pretty good and just has some hints of unevenness, such as a scarf or shawl with edges that aren't quite straight, you'll probably be happy with *light blocking,* which is the quicker approach. To block a piece lightly, follow these steps:

1. **While the piece is still dry, gently pull it in all directions; this stretching helps even out the stitches.**

   You don't want to be rough, but it's definitely okay to tug. Be judicious with fragile yarns, though.

2. **Lay a couple of towels on any surface large enough to hold the finished piece.**

   This surface may be your ironing board, your kitchen table, your guest bed, or even the floor. If you have a *blocking board* (a special board with a measured grid on it), use it.

3. **Put the knitted piece on top of the towels (any stockinette stitch should be right side down, and anything textured should be right side up).**

4. **Using a spray bottle filled with plain water, spritz the knit liberally, particularly in any problem areas.**

5.  **Use your hands to mold the piece into shape as needed — neatening cables, opening lace, and making things nice and smooth.**

    As with wet blocking (see the next section), you can use rustproof pins or blocking wires to hold your piece in place while it dries. But for many pieces you can simply pat them into place and move on to the next step.

6.  **Leave your piece there to dry.**

    The amount of drying time is extremely variable. Synthetics dry quicker than natural fibers, and thinner pieces dry faster than thicker ones. Assume that it will take most of a day for your knit to dry completely, but it can take even longer in damp weather. Resist temptation and leave the piece flat until it's completely dry.

## *Wet blocking*

*Wet blocking* is a bit more serious than a little spritzing and patting. Any garment that's made of several pieces will surely benefit from wet blocking (as will any piece that features lace, color work, or cables). Okay, pretty much everything looks better and fits better after wet blocking. But, if you just can't stand waiting three days for your new knit to dry, you can skip blocking and wear it for a while. Just be sure to wash and block your knit using the following steps before you put it away for the winter:

1.  **While the piece is dry, tug it gently into shape, pulling it lengthwise and widthwise.**

    If the piece is finished, try it on and note any problem areas. If the neckline seems wonky or the sleeves are an inch too short, you may be able to correct these as you block.

2.  **Fill the sink with water.**

    Use water that's lukewarm or room temperature, and more important, don't change water temperature when you rinse. Doing so can cause wool to felt.

3.  **If you want, give your sweater a wash.**

    Even a new sweater may benefit from a wash if it's been dragged around in your knitting bag for several months! You can read all about washing your knits in Chapter 18.

4.  **Let your knit soak for 10 to 20 minutes.**

5.  **Drain the water from the sink, but leave the knit in, allowing the water to drain from it.**

    Pressing gently on your knit is okay, but don't wring or squeeze it. Don't let any part of your knit get pulled into the drain!

6.  **Pick the piece up from the bottom and place it on a large towel.**

    Don't pick the garment up by one sleeve; instead, support the whole thing from the bottom. A wet knit is very heavy, and the wet yarn can be more susceptible to damage. You risk stretching (or worse) if you don't support the weight of the garment as you remove it from the sink.

7.  **Roll up the towel and then gently squeeze to remove some of the extra water.**

    At this point, you aren't trying to dry the sweater; you're simply getting it to the no-longer-dripping stage.

8.  **Put the piece onto a blocking board or more dry towels.**

9.  **Looking at the pattern schematic, gently stretch and pat the piece to the correct measurements (be sure to grab a tape measure!).**

You'll be surprised at how malleable your wet knit is! Start with the width at the chest, and then work on the length. Don't stretch any ribbing out too much if you want it to remain elastic. Finish with the neckline and collar, neatening the edges and moving things into place. If you want, use waterproof pins or blocking wires to help the garment hold its shape.

10. **Let the knit dry.**

    Drying can take a while, particularly if you live someplace damp. When planning to block, try to choose a dry day if possible. Placing a fan nearby can help also. You can dry pieces outside, weather permitting, but don't leave your knits out in direct sunlight. Cover the piece with another towel or a sheet to prevent it from fading. It can take a day or two for your piece to dry. Don't be tempted to skimp on drying time; wait until the knit has dried completely! Check the seams to assess whether the piece is truly dry as these spots take longest to dry.

# Casting On

There are a number of ways to get stitches onto the needle, called *casting on* (abbreviated "CO"). Most knitters use the *long-tail cast-on* (or *Continental cast-on*) at the beginning of a piece. It's attractive and elastic. It's worked using an extra yarn tail in addition to the working yarn (the yarn coming from the ball), which leads to two disadvantages:

✔ It can be tricky to correctly judge the length of yarn tail needed.

✔ It can't be used in the middle of a piece.

To use the long-tail method, follow these steps:

1. **From the end of the yarn, measure off a length of yarn for your tail.**

    There are two rules of thumb to figure out how much of a tail you need. These general rules don't always agree with one another, however. Err on the side of too much yarn, because the only thing to do if you run out of tail is start over!

    • Calculate about 1 inch per stitch (or more with bulky yarns or big needles).

      For example, 100 stitches = about 100 inches of yarn

    • Calculate a length 4 times the width of the piece you're making.

      For example, 20 inches wide × 4 = 80 inches of yarn

2. **At the end of that length, make a slip knot.**

    Insert one needle into the slip knot, and hold it in your right hand.

3. **Grasp the two tails with the last two fingers of your left hand, with the tail on the left and the working yarn on the right.**

    Put your thumb and index finger between the two strands of yarn, and then bring the needle down between your thumb and index finger as shown in Figure A-2a.

4. **Bring the needle up through the loop of yarn on your thumb as shown in Figure A-2b.**

5. **Bring the needle down through the loop on the front of your index finger, pulling the strand of yarn forward and down through the loop on the thumb, as shown in Figure A-2c.**

6. **Drop the loop off your thumb, leaving a new stitch on the needle.**

7. **Put your thumb back into position under the yarn in front as shown in Figure A-2d, tightening the stitch slightly and preparing to cast on the next stitch.**

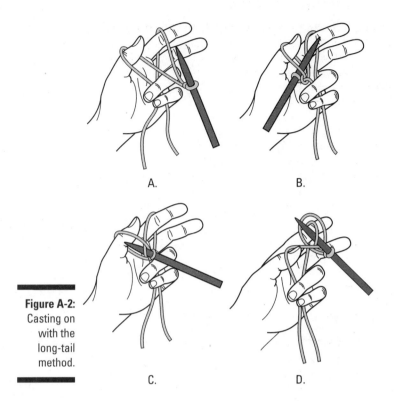

A.

B.

**Figure A-2:**
Casting on with the long-tail method.

C.

D.

8. **Repeat Steps 4–7 until the required number of stitches are cast on.**

If you want to try the cable cast-on, see Chapter 10.

# Crocheted Edging

Knitting and crocheting are different, but they do have a lot in common. And sometimes a bit of crochet is just what your knit needs. If the edge of a piece looks unfinished to you, you can neaten it up with a row of single crochet as an edging. A crocheted edging around a neck or an armhole keeps it from stretching out over time. You also can try a contrasting colored edge of single crochet on a blanket to protect the edges from wear and tear.

To crochet a simple single crochet edging, use the same yarn as you used for the project (or a contrasting yarn if you prefer) and a crochet hook that's the same diameter as the knitting needles you used for the project.

Just as the needle size you use affects your knitting gauge, the hook size you use affects your crochet gauge. If your crochet stitches seem too big and the edging is too loose, try a smaller hook; if the crochet stitches are too small and the edging pulls in too much, try a larger hook.

Follow these directions:

1. **Make a slip knot with the yarn you're using for the edging and slip it onto your crochet hook.**

2. **Stick your hook through the knitted fabric between stitches working from the right side (the public side) to the wrong side.**

3. **Grab the working yarn with the hook and pull a loop back through to the front as shown in Figure A-3.**

   There are 2 loops of yarn on the hook.

4. **Reach the hook over the edge of the piece and grab the yarn again, and then pull this loop through both loops on the hook.**

   You now have 1 loop on the hook.

5. **Repeat Steps 2–4 around the edge of your piece.**

   If you're working on a piece that has corners, like a blanket, make 3 crocheted stitches in each knitted stitch at the outside corners. You also may want to skip a knitted stitch here and there when you're working on an inside curve.

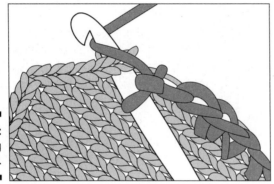

**Figure A-3:**
Crocheting
an edge.

# Crocheting a Chain

A *crochet chain* can be used to make simple straps, ties, or loops. To work a crochet chain, follow these steps:

1. **Make a slip knot with the working yarn and place it on your crochet hook.**

   If you're crocheting a chain onto a finished piece, skip the slip knot and instead follow Steps 2–3 in the previous directions for crocheted edging.

2. **Wrap the yarn around the hook and pull this new loop through the old loop (this is your slip knot for the first stitch) as shown in Figure A-4.**

   You have chained 1 stitch.

3. **Repeat Step 2 until the chain reaches your desired length.**

   Cut the yarn and pull the tail through the last loop to secure it.

**Figure A-4:**
Crocheting
a chain.

# Felting

*Felting* is a way of transforming your knitting into a dense, sturdy fabric. If you've ever (accidentally or purposefully) run a wool sweater through the washing machine, you've experimented already with felting. When you do it on purpose, you can make lots of great pieces, including bags and slippers.

To knit something that you're going to felt, use pure wool or another animal fiber, and knit it at a looser than normal gauge. When the knitting is done and your seams are sewn, here's how to felt your piece:

1. **Place the item in a zippered pillowcase or mesh lingerie bag to protect your washer's pump from the excess fuzz.**

   Trust me on this one; I'm the owner of a $300 felted bag.

2. **Put the item in the washing machine with a pair of old jeans (the jeans improve the agitation; towels may leave terry-cloth fuzz on your felted item).**

   Set the washer for a small, hot load and add a small amount of soap. If possible, leave the lid up to stop the cycle before it rinses; this saves on the amount of hot water you use, but isn't strictly necessary.

3. **At the end of the cycle, check on the progress of the felting.**

   If you can still see the stitches, add a kettle of boiling water and start the wash cycle again (at the same setting as in Step 2). Very hot water makes your item felt faster.

4. **When the fabric looks very firm, you can no longer see the stitches, or the item is the correct size, remove it from the washer and rinse it in the sink with water.**

   The spin cycle of the washer may leave your felted item with permanent creases, so it's safer to remove the piece before the spin cycle begins.

5. **Pull the item into the desired shape and size, using empty cereal boxes wrapped in plastic or something else of the correct size.**

6. **Allow the item to dry completely before using it.**

   Keep the item out of direct sunlight. Drying may take a couple of days; placing your felted item near a fan to dry may speed the drying process.

# Knit Stitch

The *knit stitch* is the most basic building block of knitting. It's the very first thing you learn and the thing that you do most in just about any knitting project.

To knit a stitch, follow these steps:

1. **Insert the right-hand needle into the first stitch on the left-hand needle from front to back and from left to right.**

   The right-hand needle should sit perpendicular to and under the left-hand needle as shown in Figure A-5.

2. **Wrap the yarn counterclockwise around the back (right-hand) needle, coming up on the left, over the top, and down on the right as shown in Figure A-6a.**

   This creates the new stitch.

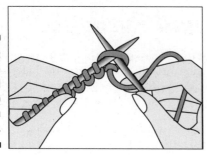

**Figure A-5:**
Inserting the
right-hand
needle into
the stitch
to knit.

3. **Keeping some tension on the working yarn held in your right hand, bring the right-hand needle and the newly formed stitch through the old stitch on the left needle, as shown in Figure A-6b.**

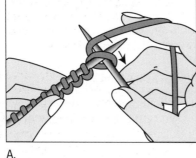
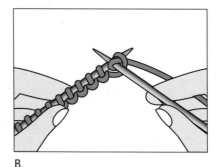

**Figure A-6:**
Making a
new knit
stitch.

A.                                        B.

4. **Slide the right-hand needle to the right until the old stitch drops off the needle.**

5. **Repeat Steps 1–4 to knit.**

To get the hang of the knit stitch, you may want to consider repeating the mnemonic phrase used to teach children to knit, "In through the front door, around the back, out through the window, and off jumps Jack."

# Knitting into the Back of a Stitch

*Knitting through the back loop* (abbreviated as k tbl) twists the stitch. Sometimes this stitch is used decoratively; other times it's knit as a part of more complex stitches.

To knit through the back loop, follow these steps:

1. **Stick the right-hand needle into the next stitch from the center through the back of the stitch, from right to left.**

2. **Wrap the yarn around the needle counterclockwise and complete the stitch as you would a normal knit stitch.**

# Making Stitches Knitwise and Purlwise

If a pattern tells you to do something *knitwise,* it means that you should do it as if you were going to make a knit stitch. So, slipping a stitch knitwise, for example, means that you put the needle into the stitch as though you were going to knit it (from front to back, from left to right), and then you slip it over to the right needle without knitting it.

Doing something *purlwise* means that you should do it as though you were purling. So, you stick the needle into a stitch from right to left.

# Mattress Stitch

I've never sewn a mattress, and I have no idea how mattresses relate to knitting, but the tidiest method of sewing a seam in knitting is called *mattress stitch.* If you're a seamstress, some elements of this stitch will seem counterintuitive. You work from the right side (public side) with the two pieces next to one another rather than sandwiched together with right sides facing as you would when sewing fabric.

When learning to use mattress stitch, it's helpful to make a couple of swatches to practice on. Use yarn that's smooth enough and big enough for you to easily see the stitches. I teach people this technique using a contrasting yarn to sew with. The contrasting color allows you to see what's going on, and you'll be impressed with just how invisible the seam is when you're finished. After you get the hang of the mattress stitch with the swatches and contrasting yarn, you'll be ready to sew up any project.

Depending on whether you're sewing together the sides or the ends (where you cast on and bind off), the technique is slightly different, as you find out in the following sections.

Here are a few general principles of sewing up your knitting project:

- Don't be tempted to overdo your seams. Look at the knitted stitches for a moment. The stitches you sew don't need to be smaller, tighter, or tougher than the stitches you knit.

- You can sew things together like a seamstress, with a straight stitch or a whip stitch worked on the wrong side. But knitters usually prefer to work from the right side with the pieces next to one another rather than on top of one another.

- Sewing a seam isn't difficult. The bald truth is that you can sew up your knitting any old way you want as long as you're satisfied with the way it looks. Sacrilege? Perhaps, but if it makes you sleep better at night, I'm all for it.

## Stockinette stitch, side to side

Before you get started, have a close look at your knitting. Gently pull at the edge of your knitted swatch and look between the edge stitch and the next stitch. You should see a ladder of horizontal threads as shown in Figure A-7. The rungs of the ladder on each of the two pieces are where the mattress stitch action happens.

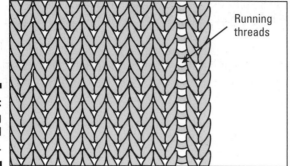

Running
threads

**Figure A-7:**
Identifying
horizontal
threads.

To sew a side seam using mattress stitch, follow these steps:

1. **Lay out your two pieces with the right sides up and the two edges to be sewn next to one another (the bottom edges should be nearest you).**

2. **Thread some of the yarn from the project onto your yarn needle.**

When sewing up, some people like to use the yarn tail from the cast-on. Others, including me, start with a fresh length of yarn, and then use the tail at the end to tidy up the seam. Either way is fine; you'll discover which method you prefer as you gain more experience with it.

3. **Insert the yarn needle under the bottom rung of the ladder on the left piece, with the needle running parallel to the edge of the knitted piece.**

4. **Draw the yarn through and insert the needle under the first rung on the right piece, with the needle parallel to the edge.**

You don't need to pull anything tightly. It's fine to have an inch or so between the two pieces so you can see what you're doing. You'll tighten it up later.

5. **Go back to the left piece and insert the needle into the ladder at the point where you came out at the beginning of Step 4. Run the needle under two rungs and draw the yarn through.**

6. **Move to the right piece and insert the needle into the ladder where you came out before. Run the needle under two rungs and draw the yarn as shown in Figure A-8.**

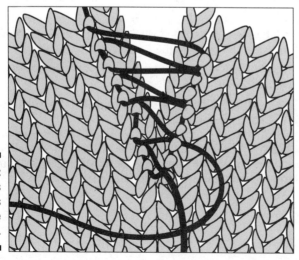

**Figure A-8:**
A mattress
stitch forms
an invisible
seam.

7. **Repeat Steps 5 and 6 until your seam is a couple of inches long.**

   Pull gently on the two ends of your sewing yarn until the seam closes up and the mattress stitches disappear.

8. **Continue in this manner until your seam is finished.**

   When you're satisfied with your seam, take the cast-on tail and join the edge with a figure eight as shown in Figure A-9. Weave in any remaining loose ends.

**Figure A-9:**
Tidying up the cast-on edge.

# Garter stitch, side to side

To start sewing two garter stitch sides together, place the two pieces side by side with the right sides up. Match the pieces so that the top and bottom edges are aligned; for a long seam, consider pins or clips to keep things lined up.

Look closely at your garter stitch piece and you'll see that each stitch is composed of a top bump and a bottom bump. You'll use these bumps to create your seams:

1. **Thread a length of yarn onto a yarn needle.**

2. **With the two pieces next to one another, put the yarn needle through the bottom bump of the edge stitch in the first row of the left piece and pull the yarn through, leaving a 6-inch tail.**

3. **Bring the yarn over to the right piece and put the yarn needle through the top bump on the edge stitch in the first row and pull the yarn through as shown in Figure A-10.**

   There's no need to pull the yarn tight; it's easier to work with the stitches slack. You can tighten them up later.

4. **Bring the needle back to the left piece, go through the bottom bump of the edge stitch of the next row, and pull the yarn through.**

5. **Bring the needle to the right piece, go through the top bump of the edge stitch of the next row, and pull the yarn through.**

6. **Repeat Steps 4 and 5 until the seam is complete.**

   Gently pull on the two ends of the yarn you sewed the seam with until the seam closes up, and then weave in the ends (which I cover later in this chapter).

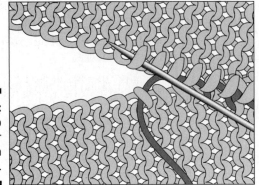

**Figure A-10:**
Seaming up
two garter
stitch
pieces.

# End to end

When you're joining pieces end to end you can often use the three-needle bind-off and skip the sewing all together. See Chapter 10 for more on this technique.

But sometimes you want to sew two ends together using mattress stitch. To do so, place the two pieces next to each other, right sides (public sides) up. You'll be working on whole stitches below the bound-off edge. Why? Bound-off edges can often be jagged or untidy, so it's better to work a row or so down to be sure that you're hiding these uneven stitches in the seam. Follow these steps to sew two pieces together end to end:

1. **Thread the yarn needle and begin at one edge (or use a convenient yarn tail if you prefer).**

2. **On the first piece, go under 1 stitch (both legs of the V) with your yarn needle.**

3. **Bring the needle to the second piece and go under 1 stitch.**

4. **Come back to the first piece, go in with the needle where you came out last time (where you can see the working yarn).**

5. **Repeat Steps 2–4 until your seam is complete.**

    Pull the yarn gently to tighten the seam; it shouldn't be tighter (or looser) than the knitted stitches around it.

# End to side

Sewing a bound-off edge to a side seam, as when you're attaching a sleeve to the body of a sweater, is slightly different from joining two sides or two ends. When both pieces are the same, the stitches match up exactly, and you're always joining 1 stitch to 1 stitch. (Okay, that's only in theory.)

When you're joining an end to a side, however, you need to pay attention to the fact that there are more rows than stitches per inch. See Figure A-11 for an example.

To join an end to a side, follow these steps and see Figure A-11:

1. **Thread your needle and place your pieces flat with right sides up and the edges to be seamed next to one another.**

    If the seam is long, consider pinning or clipping it to help keep you on track.

2. **Beginning at the edge of the seam, go under both legs of the first stitch on the top of the first piece with the yarn needle and pull the yarn through, leaving a 6-inch tail.**

3. **Bring the needle to the other piece and go under one ladder rung between the first and second stitches, and then pull the yarn through.**

4. **Go back to the first piece and put the needle in where it came out and then under both legs of the next stitch, and pull the yarn through.**

5. **Repeat Steps 3 and 4, but on every 4th stitch, bring the needle under two ladder rungs rather than just one to make up for the difference between the number of stitches and the number of rows in an inch.**

Picking up an extra rung every 4th row works as a general rule because 3 to 4 is roughly the ratio of stitches to rows in stockinette stitch at most gauges. If you want to be precise, think of it this way: If your gauge is 5 stitches and 7 rows per inch, you need to use seven ladder rungs for every 5 stitches. And remember that there's as much art as there is science to this. Don't stick to the ratio slavishly; instead, work on keeping your two pieces lined up and your seam relatively even.

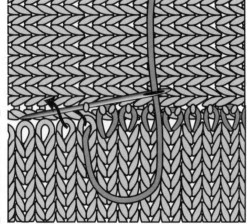

**Figure A-11:** Joining a side and an end with mattress stitch.

# Purl Stitch

A purl stitch is one of the basic building blocks of knitting. Follow these steps to purl:

1. **With the yarn held to the front of the work, put the right-hand needle into the stitch from back to front and from right to left, as shown in Figure A-12a.**

2. **Wrap the yarn around the right-hand needle counterclockwise, as shown in Figure A-12b.**

This loop will form the new stitch.

**Figure A-12:** The first steps in purling.

A.                                                     B.

3. **Keeping some tension on the working yarn, bring the right-hand needle and the new stitch down and through the old stitch on the left-hand needle, as shown in Figure A-13a.**

4. **Slide the right-hand needle to the right until the old stitch drops off the needle, as shown in Figure A-13b.**

A.

B.

**Figure A-13:**
Finishing a
purl stitch.

5. **Repeat Steps 1–4 to purl.**

# Ripping Back Stitches

Mistakes happen. If you catch your mistake sooner than later, the easiest way to rectify the problem is to unknit (or rip back) the stitches one by one until you get to the problem. Sometimes knitters call this *tinking* because *tink* is *knit* backwards.

To unknit stitch by stitch to an error in the row that you're working on, follow these steps:

1. **With the knit or purl side facing you, insert the left-hand needle from front to back into the stitch below the one on the right-hand needle, as shown in Figure A-14.**

2. **Remove the right-hand needle from the stitch and gently pull on the yarn.**

3. **Repeat Steps 1 and 2 until you come to your error.**

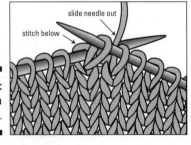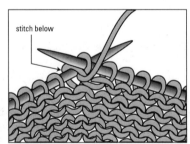

**Figure A-14:**
Unknitting a
stitch.

If your mistake happened several rows back, decide whether it's something you can live with or whether you need to rip all the way back to the mistake. This is another time to remind yourself that you enjoy the process of knitting and that doing the section over is not really a bad thing.

Take a deep breath and then follow these steps:

1. **Pull the needle out of the work and begin unraveling the rows by pulling gently on the working yarn.**

   Continue until you've taken out the mistake and the row with the mistake.

2. **To put the stitches back on the needle, hold your work with the working yarn on the right, and put the needle into the first stitch in the second row from back to front as indicated by the arrow in Figure A-15.**

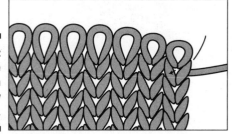

**Figure A-15:** Inserting the needle in the row below.

3. **Gently pull on the yarn to remove the stitch.**

4. **Repeat Steps 2 and 3 (see Figure A-16) until you've got all the stitches back on the needle, and then carry on with your knitting.**

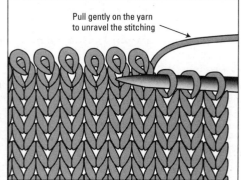

Pull gently on the yarn to unravel the stitching

**Figure A-16:** Putting your stitches back on the needle.

# Slipping Stitches

Slipped stitches (abbreviated "sl") can be part of decreases (which I cover in Chapters 6 and 12) or can be used as part of stitch patterns, such as linen stitch (see Chapter 10) or mosaics (see Chapter 7). To slip a stitch, simply slide it from the left-hand needle to the right-hand needle without wrapping it or knitting it. The yarn will trail or "float" across the work over (or behind) the slipped stitch. Remember that this float should be 1 stitch wide. Don't try to pull tight to make it disappear!

When you slip a stitch, you can do it knitwise (putting the right-hand needle into the stitch from left to right) or purlwise (putting the right-hand needle into the stitch from right to left). The rule of thumb on slipping knitwise or purlwise is this: Slip the stitch purlwise unless you're told otherwise. Slipping purlwise leaves the stitch untwisted. The only times you'll slip knitwise in this book are in the ssk and skp decreases. Find out about ssk in Chapter 6 and skp in Chapter 12.

# Weaving in Ends

Weaving in your ends is one of the last steps you'll take with a project. When you finish knitting, you'll have at least a couple of yarn tails hanging off the work. Don't be tempted to just cut them off; they can work themselves loose and your knitting will unravel. Instead, weave them in.

There are several approaches to weaving in ends; whichever approach you use, your goal is to hide the tails in the knitted fabric and secure them so they don't come out. Here are some general guidelines:

- ✔ Before you weave in your ends, take a look at the knitting around the tails. By gently tugging on the tails, you may be able to even out loose stitches.

- ✔ Thread your yarn tail onto a yarn needle and work on the wrong side of the piece.

- ✔ If your piece has seams, you can simply run the needle in and out of the seam a few times to hide the end.

- ✔ If you don't have any seams to hide your ends in, a tidy way to weave in your tails is to follow the path that the yarn takes over several stitches as shown in Figure A-17. This is very similar to the embellishment technique known as duplicate stitch (see Chapter 7).

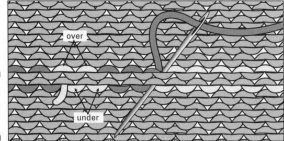

**Figure A-17:**
Weaving in
your ends.

After you weave in 2 to 3 inches of your tail, cut off the remaining yarn close to the work.

# Index

• *T* •

tools
  finishing, 20
  gauge measurement, 28
  measuring, 18
  organizational, 19
toothpicks, 258
top (kid's) pattern, 207–215
top (women's) pattern, 247–254
total length, measuring guidelines, 34
true rib, 56
2 x 2 rib knitting, 57–58
two-row stripes, 77
two-stitch rib knitting, 59–60
two-stitch twist knitting, 61–62

## • V •

V-neck T-shirt pattern, 201–205
value, 76
vegetable fiber yarn, 12

## • W •

w&t, 39
waist, measuring guidelines, 34
washcloths, 259
washing
  knitted pieces by hand, 267
  tips, 266–268
wave cable knitting, 65–67
weaving in ends, 286
Web sites, sizing standards, 33
weight
  classifications, 12–13
  yarn label overview, 11
wet blocking, 273–274
work even, 39
woven cord mosaic, 86–87
wrist warmers pattern, 168–170
WS, 39
wyib, 39, 126
wyif, 39, 126

## • X •

x, 39

## • Y •

yarn
  alternates, 257–258
  changing, 177
  estimating quantity, 14–15
  label components, 10–11, 265–266
  packaging, 9–10
  saving, 269
  selection, 11–13
  substituting, 13–14, 134, 186
  swatches as emergency, 260
  tips, 261, 263
yarn needles, 20
yarn over
  defined, 56, 67
  making, 67–68
  overview, 67
yarn weight, 12
yd(s), 39
yo, 39

## • Z •

zipped cardigan pattern, 229–23

# Notes

## BUSINESS, CAREERS & PERSONAL FINANCE

0-7645-9847-3

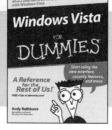

0-7645-2431-3

**Also available:**
- Business Plans Kit For Dummies
  0-7645-9794-9
- Economics For Dummies
  0-7645-5726-2
- Grant Writing For Dummies
  0-7645-8416-2
- Home Buying For Dummies
  0-7645-5331-3
- Managing For Dummies
  0-7645-1771-6
- Marketing For Dummies
  0-7645-5600-2

- Personal Finance For Dummies
  0-7645-2590-5*
- Resumes For Dummies
  0-7645-5471-9
- Selling For Dummies
  0-7645-5363-1
- Six Sigma For Dummies
  0-7645-6798-5
- Small Business Kit For Dummies
  0-7645-5984-2
- Starting an eBay Business For Dummies
  0-7645-6924-4
- Your Dream Career For Dummies
  0-7645-9795-7

## HOME & BUSINESS COMPUTER BASICS

0-470-05432-8

0-471-75421-8

**Also available:**
- Cleaning Windows Vista For Dummies
  0-471-78293-9
- Excel 2007 For Dummies
  0-470-03737-7
- Mac OS X Tiger For Dummies
  0-7645-7675-5
- MacBook For Dummies
  0-470-04859-X
- Macs For Dummies
  0-470-04849-2
- Office 2007 For Dummies
  0-470-00923-3

- Outlook 2007 For Dummies
  0-470-03830-6
- PCs For Dummies
  0-7645-8958-X
- Salesforce.com For Dummies
  0-470-04893-X
- Upgrading & Fixing Laptops For Dummies
  0-7645-8959-8
- Word 2007 For Dummies
  0-470-03658-3
- Quicken 2007 For Dummies
  0-470-04600-7

## FOOD, HOME, GARDEN, HOBBIES, MUSIC & PETS

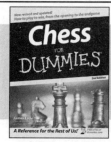

0-7645-8404-9

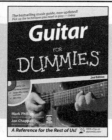

0-7645-9904-6

**Also available:**
- Candy Making For Dummies
  0-7645-9734-5
- Card Games For Dummies
  0-7645-9910-0
- Crocheting For Dummies
  0-7645-4151-X
- Dog Training For Dummies
  0-7645-8418-9
- Healthy Carb Cookbook For Dummies
  0-7645-8476-6
- Home Maintenance For Dummies
  0-7645-5215-5

- Horses For Dummies
  0-7645-9797-3
- Jewelry Making & Beading For Dummies
  0-7645-2571-9
- Orchids For Dummies
  0-7645-6759-4
- Puppies For Dummies
  0-7645-5255-4
- Rock Guitar For Dummies
  0-7645-5356-9
- Sewing For Dummies
  0-7645-6847-7
- Singing For Dummies
  0-7645-2475-5

## INTERNET & DIGITAL MEDIA

0-470-04529-9

0-470-04894-8

**Also available:**
- Blogging For Dummies
  0-471-77084-1
- Digital Photography For Dummies
  0-7645-9802-3
- Digital Photography All-in-One Desk Reference For Dummies
  0-470-03743-1
- Digital SLR Cameras and Photography For Dummies
  0-7645-9803-1
- eBay Business All-in-One Desk Reference For Dummies
  0-7645-8438-3
- HDTV For Dummies
  0-470-09673-X

- Home Entertainment PCs For Dummies
  0-470-05523-5
- MySpace For Dummies
  0-470-09529-6
- Search Engine Optimization For Dummies
  0-471-97998-8
- Skype For Dummies
  0-470-04891-3
- The Internet For Dummies
  0-7645-8996-2
- Wiring Your Digital Home For Dummies
  0-471-91830-X

\* Separate Canadian edition also available
† Separate U.K. edition also available

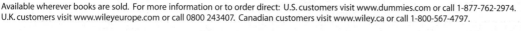

Available wherever books are sold. For more information or to order direct: U.S. customers visit www.dummies.com or call 1-877-762-2974.
U.K. customers visit www.wileyeurope.com or call 0800 243407. Canadian customers visit www.wiley.ca or call 1-800-567-4797.

## SPORTS, FITNESS, PARENTING, RELIGION & SPIRITUALITY

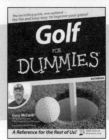
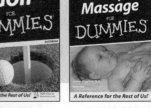

0-471-76871-5          0-7645-7841-3

**Also available:**
- ✔Catholicism For Dummies
  0-7645-5391-7
- ✔Exercise Balls For Dummies
  0-7645-5623-1
- ✔Fitness For Dummies
  0-7645-7851-0
- ✔Football For Dummies
  0-7645-3936-1
- ✔Judaism For Dummies
  0-7645-5299-6
- ✔Potty Training For Dummies
  0-7645-5417-4
- ✔Buddhism For Dummies
  0-7645-5359-3

- ✔Pregnancy For Dummies
  0-7645-4483-7 †
- ✔Ten Minute Tone-Ups For Dummies
  0-7645-7207-5
- ✔NASCAR For Dummies
  0-7645-7681-X
- ✔Religion For Dummies
  0-7645-5264-3
- ✔Soccer For Dummies
  0-7645-5229-5
- ✔Women in the Bible For Dummies
  0-7645-8475-8

## TRAVEL

0-7645-7749-2          0-7645-6945-7

**Also available:**
- ✔Alaska For Dummies
  0-7645-7746-8
- ✔Cruise Vacations For Dummies
  0-7645-6941-4
- ✔England For Dummies
  0-7645-4276-1
- ✔Europe For Dummies
  0-7645-7529-5
- ✔Germany For Dummies
  0-7645-7823-5
- ✔Hawaii For Dummies
  0-7645-7402-7

- ✔Italy For Dummies
  0-7645-7386-1
- ✔Las Vegas For Dummies
  0-7645-7382-9
- ✔London For Dummies
  0-7645-4277-X
- ✔Paris For Dummies
  0-7645-7630-5
- ✔RV Vacations For Dummies
  0-7645-4442-X
- ✔Walt Disney World & Orlando
  For Dummies
  0-7645-9660-8

## GRAPHICS, DESIGN & WEB DEVELOPMENT

0-7645-8815-X          0-7645-9571-7

**Also available:**
- ✔3D Game Animation For Dummies
  0-7645-8789-7
- ✔AutoCAD 2006 For Dummies
  0-7645-8925-3
- ✔Building a Web Site For Dummies
  0-7645-7144-3
- ✔Creating Web Pages For Dummies
  0-470-08030-2
- ✔Creating Web Pages All-in-One Desk
  Reference For Dummies
  0-7645-4345-8
- ✔Dreamweaver 8 For Dummies
  0-7645-9649-7

- ✔InDesign CS2 For Dummies
  0-7645-9572-5
- ✔Macromedia Flash 8 For Dummies
  0-7645-9691-8
- ✔Photoshop CS2 and Digital
  Photography For Dummies
  0-7645-9580-6
- ✔Photoshop Elements 4 For Dummies
  0-471-77483-9
- ✔Syndicating Web Sites with RSS Feeds
  For Dummies
  0-7645-8848-6
- ✔Yahoo! SiteBuilder For Dummies
  0-7645-9800-7

## NETWORKING, SECURITY, PROGRAMMING & DATABASES

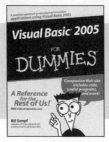

0-7645-7728-X          0-471-74940-0

**Also available:**
- ✔Access 2007 For Dummies
  0-470-04612-0
- ✔ASP.NET 2 For Dummies
  0-7645-7907-X
- ✔C# 2005 For Dummies
  0-7645-9704-3
- ✔Hacking For Dummies
  0-470-05235-X
- ✔Hacking Wireless Networks
  For Dummies
  0-7645-9730-2
- ✔Java For Dummies
  0-470-08716-1

- ✔Microsoft SQL Server 2005 For Dummies
  0-7645-7755-7
- ✔Networking All-in-One Desk Reference
  For Dummies
  0-7645-9939-9
- ✔Preventing Identity Theft For Dummies
  0-7645-7336-5
- ✔Telecom For Dummies
  0-471-77085-X
- ✔Visual Studio 2005 All-in-One Desk
  Reference For Dummies
  0-7645-9775-2
- ✔XML For Dummies
  0-7645-8845-1